Springer-Verlag Berlin Heidelberg GmbH

Kazuhiro Arai

The Economics of Education

An Analysis of College-Going Behavior

With 18 Figures

Springer

Kazuhiro Arai
Professor of Economics
Hitotsubashi University
Kunitachi, Tokyo,
Japan

This English Translation is based on the Japanese original,
Kazuhiro, Arai; Kyoiku-no-Keizaigaku (The Economics of Education)
Published by Yuhikaku Publishing Company Ltd.

ISBN 978-4-431-66907-4 ISBN 978-4-431-66905-0 (eBook)
DOI 10.1007/978-4-431-66905-0

Printed on acid-free paper

Originally published by Springer-Verlag Tokyo Berlin Heidelberg New York in 1998

Typesetting: Best-set Typesetter Ltd., Hong Kong

SPIN: 10670328

To Lisa, Hiro, and Mayumi

Preface

Why do some go to college while others do not? Why have the percentages of various types of students going to college changed so dramatically throughout the world over the last few decades? The purpose of this book is to consider questions of this kind from an economics viewpoint. These are by no means simple questions and require accurate theoretical investigations and extensive empirical analyses to throw light on them.

The questions to be considered in this book are the main focus of a field of study called "the economics of education." Although this subdiscipline of economics is not well known, it is one of the most popular research fields in the world today.

Almost 40 years have passed since education became an object of serious research by economists, and in this period Theodore W. Schultz and Gary S. Becker received a Nobel prize for their research related to the economics of education. Kenneth J. Arrow, who likewise received a Nobel prize, also made an important contribution to the economics of education. Further, such prominent economists as Jacob Mincer, Michael Spence, and Joseph E. Stiglitz significantly advanced analyses in this field. Many other economists have also contributed to advances in this area, so that the economics of education is now one of the fields where the most interesting arguments are under way. In addition, because education can potentially determine the rise and fall of a state or nation, understanding it more fully surely serves a greater purpose than that of merely satisfying a thirst for knowledge.

Although the author has sought to make original contributions to this field in almost every chapter, he has tried to give this book two fundamental characteristics. First, elucidation is provided so that the reader can gain a multi-dimensional and comprehensive understanding of major issues related to college-going behavior. By emphasizing both theoretical and empirical analyses, this book discusses a variety of views and analytical results. The author has tried to systematize and synthesize these research results as much as possible.

One of the features of this book is that most chapters give serious consideration to cases of capital market imperfection, or present arguments with this imperfection in mind. Because capital markets are imperfect in most real economies, using the assumption of capital market perfection often leads to arguments which do not offer a good explanation of reality. This book has tried to overcome this problem as much as possible.

The second characteristic is that clarification is given so that even those who have little knowledge of economics or econometrics can understand this book, although its content is quite up-to-date. Hence, even specialists of pedagogy, sociology, and other social sciences can also easily understand it. Appendices on economics and econometrics are included for readers who have insufficient knowledge of these disciplines.

Further, since all economics terms used in this book are defined when they first appear or in attached notes, technical terms need not prevent readers from understanding the content. The subject index might also be useful for understanding definitions. Three sections (3.5, 3.6 and 4.2) have asterisks in their headings to indicate that the contents are technical in nature and can be skipped without reducing overall understanding.

The prerequisite for understanding this book is only elementary high-school mathematics. Even those without such knowledge will probably have little difficulty understanding most parts. Only Sect. 3.6 uses college-level mathematics, but it is one of the above three sections with an asterisk.

Although this book cites articles mainly from international journals as well as books, some cited studies and the empirical studies undertaken by the author himself are on Japan. Thus, readers will be able to gain some knowledge of Japanese higher education, facts about which have not been very well known internationally. In this sense, this book may be able to introduce aspects of Japanese education to the world.

This book will enable many readers, especially those whose majors are not economics, to understand first of all how economics explains college-going behavior. Those whose majors are economics can use it as a book on applied microeconomics or to examine empirical analyses that have been undertaken so far in this field. Many readers may realize that higher education and college-going behavior contain very interesting economic problems. They might also notice that many problems are still unresolved. It would give the author great pleasure if this book inspired a deeper interest on the part of readers in the economics of education.

This book is based on a book by the same author published in Japanese in 1995. However, some revisions have been made mainly to facilitate understanding by those who are unfamiliar with Japanese education. In particular, one appendix has been added to provide readers with basic knowledge of the Japanese education system.

In the process of writing this English version, the author was assisted by Hisami Anzai, Anne Heynes, and Harumi Seto, to whom he would like to extend his thanks. He would also like to acknowledge a grant-in-aid for publication of scientific research results provided by the Ministry of Education, Science, Sport, and Culture of Japan.

Kazuhiro Arai

Contents

Chapter 1
Basic Facts and the Purposes of This Book

The fundamental purpose of this book is to analyze college-going behavior both theoretically and empirically. For this purpose, it is useful to understand some basic facts which can be observed in education data from Japan. In this chapter, we first observe in Sect. 1.1 the percentage of Japanese students who went to college in the past several decades. Then we undertake some international comparisons in Sect. 1.2. By doing so, we can confirm how the percentage has varied in Japan and whether it is high in comparison with other major advanced countries. Sect. 3.3 explains the basic questions of this book and shows how they will be answered by giving a summary of each chapter.[1]

1.1 Variations in the Percentage of Students Going to College

The percentage of Japanese students going to college has changed dramatically in the past several decades. This can be seen in Fig. 1.1. which shows the variations in the percentage, classified in terms of college or junior college and men or women, over about forty years up to 1993. The percentage of students going to college (junior college) in a particular year is usually defined as the number of students admitted to college (junior college) in that year divided by the number of graduates from junior high school three years previous. Later we will also use the terms "enrollment rate" and "rate of enrollment" interchangeably with the "percentage of students going to college". The same definition is used here. The annual data (or time-series data) of the numbers of those admitted to college (junior college) and those who graduated from junior high school was obtained from the Ministry of Education, *Basic School Survey*.

This figure shows first that the percentage of men going to college increased rapidly during the 1960s and the first half of the 1970s. After this period, the percentage slightly decreased or stagnated, but it seems that it began to increase again in the 1990s.

On the other hand, the percentage of women going to college was quite low as compared with men over the whole period of observation. In the latter half of the 1950s in particular, the percentage was only about one sixth that of men. It began to increase in the 1960s and continued to increase until the middle of the 1970s as did the percentage for men. In the subsequent ten years, it rarely decreased. From the middle of the 1980s, it increased at a relatively high rate. In 1993, the percentage of women who went to college was about half that of men.

There are a small number of men who chose to go to junior college. During the period shown in the figure, only one or two percent of men went to junior college, and thus the percentage did not vary so much.

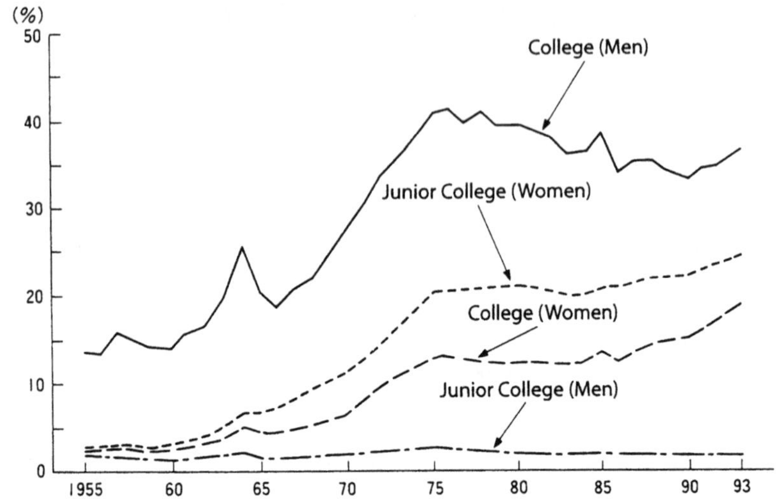

Fig. 1.1. Percentage of Students Enrolled in Higher Education

In contrast, the percentage of women going to junior college was very high. It was higher than the percentage of women going to college in each observation year. This means that more than a half of the women who received higher education did so in junior college. (However, in the middle of the 1950s, about a half went to college and the other half to junior college.) The pattern of variation of the percentage of women going to junior college is similar to that of the percentage of women going to college, but there are slight differences. First, the rate of increase in the 1960s was higher in the case of junior college. On the other hand, the rate of increase after 1986 was higher in the case of college, suggesting that the percentage going to college is very likely to exceed that going to junior college in the near future.

Since 1989, the percentage of women going either to college or to junior college has been higher than that of men. In other words, if junior college education is included, more women receive higher education than men these days.

Table 1.1 shows the numbers of men and women admitted to college (university) or junior college over the same period as in Fig. 1.1. It reveals that the scale of Japanese higher education greatly expanded in the past forty years or so.

Let us first look at college education. The number of men and women admitted to college quadrupled in the period from 1955 to 1993. The number for men more than tripled, while that for women became nine times as large. In 1993, precisely one third of those admitted to college were women. The Table also reveals that just like the percentage going to college, the absolute number itself of those admitted to college was decreasing or stagnant in the ten years after the mid-1970s.

Next let us consider junior college education. In this forty-year period, the number of those admitted to junior college increased about 6.8 times. This increase was larger than that for college education. Because the number of men admitted to junior colleges did not change greatly, this large increase was mostly due to the increase in the number of female students. In 1955 there was not a large difference between the numbers of men and women admitted to junior college, but the difference has wid-

Table 1.1. Number of students enrolled in institutions of higher education.

Year	College			Junior college			Combined total
	Men	Women	Total	Men	Women	Total	
1955	116,221	20,246	136,467	16,146	21,398	37,544	174,011
1956	119,802	19,789	139,591	13,895	22,390	36,285	175,876
1957	121,700	19,381	141,081	12,645	21,488	34,133	175,214
1958	126,281	20,096	146,377	12,170	22,718	34,888	181,265
1959	133,862	21,824	155,686	12,011	25,878	37,889	193,575
1960	142,253	24,508	166,761	12,693	29,625	42,318	209,079
1961	151,614	28,008	179,622	14,308	32,970	47,278	226,900
1962	168,616	32,509	201,125	15,870	39,743	55,613	256,738
1963	177,950	33,731	211,681	16,799	44,618	61,417	273,098
1964	182,287	35,476	217,763	16,342	44,728	61,070	278,833
1965	205,685	44,232	249,917	16,800	63,763	80,563	330,480
1966	237,921	55,037	292,958	19,521	88,531	108,052	401,010
1967	254,248	58,499	312,747	20,320	100,943	121,263	434,010
1968	265,113	60,519	325,632	20,928	106,437	127,365	452,997
1969	268,789	60,585	329,374	20,738	107,386	128,124	457,498
1970	270,944	62,093	333,037	19,707	106,952	126,659	459,696
1971	285,819	72,002	357,821	20,374	116,018	136,392	494,213
1972	296,984	79,163	376,147	19,357	122,274	141,631	517,778
1973	303,325	86,235	389,560	20,743	134,028	154,771	544,331
1974	315,514	92,014	407,528	20,069	144,008	164,077	571,605
1975	326,831	97,111	423,942	20,820	154,110	174,930	598,872
1976	322,349	98,267	420,616	18,812	155,871	174,683	595,299
1977	328,203	100,209	428,412	18,797	164,427	183,224	611,636
1978	329,282	96,436	425,718	18,847	162,334	181,181	606,899
1979	314,241	93,394	407,635	17,129	159,850	176,979	584,614
1980	317,358	95,079	412,437	16,255	161,960	178,215	590,652
1981	317,314	95,922	413,236	15,878	163,193	179,071	592,307
1982	317,264	97,272	414,536	15,913	163,688	179,601	594,137
1983	317,578	102,880	420,458	15,865	168,006	183,871	604,329
1984	312,232	103,770	416,002	15,971	165,252	181,223	597,225
1985	307,960	104,033	411,993	15,677	157,826	173,503	585,496
1986	323,777	113,119	436,896	16,600	189,483	206,083	642,979
1987	340,989	124,514	465,503	17,498	197,590	215,088	680,591
1988	340,957	132,008	472,965	17,672	200,364	218,036	691,001
1989	338,064	138,722	476,786	17,014	208,350	225,364	702,150
1990	343,694	148,646	492,340	17,721	217,474	235,195	727,535
1991	361,234	160,665	521,899	18,791	230,761	249,552	771,451
1992	368,996	172,608	541,604	19,160	235,516	254,676	796,280
1993	371,451	183,522	554,973	19,142	235,811	254,953	809,926

Source: Ministry of Education, *Basic School Survey*.

ened since the 1960s. As a matter of fact, the proportion of women among those admitted to junior college was 57% in 1955, but it increased to 92% in 1993.

1.2 International Comparisons

How does the percentage of students receiving higher education in Japan compare with other countries? This is an interesting question because the level of education in Japan in the Edo period (1603–1867) was comparable to that in advanced countries in Europe for the same period.[2] Exact international comparison is not easy, however, since there are institutional differences in higher education among countries, and the proportions of dropouts and exchange students vary greatly among them. Still, rough comparisons are possible. Tables 1.2a and 1.2b compare the percentages of students receiving higher education in Japan, the United States, the United Kingdom, West

Table 1.2a. International comparisons of students going to college or junior college: Japan.

(%)

Year	Men college	Men junior college	Women college	Women junior college	Men college & junior college	Women college & junior college	Men & women college	Men & women junior college	Men & women college & junior college
1982	37.9	1.9	12.2	20.5	39.8	32.7	25.3	11.0	36.3
1983	36.1	1.8	12.2	19.9	37.9	32.2	24.4	10.7	35.1
1984	36.4	1.9	12.7	20.1	38.3	32.8	24.8	10.8	35.6
1985	38.6	2.0	13.7	20.8	40.6	34.5	26.5	11.1	37.6
1986	34.2	1.8	12.5	21.0	35.9	33.5	23.6	11.1	34.7
1987	35.3	1.8	13.6	21.5	37.1	35.1	24.7	11.4	36.1
1988	35.3	1.8	14.4	21.8	37.2	36.2	25.1	11.6	36.7
1989	34.1	1.7	14.7	22.1	35.8	36.8	24.7	11.7	36.3

Source: Ministry of Education, *Basic School Survey*.

Table 1.2b. International comparisons of students going to college or junior college: US, UK, West Germany, and France.

(%)

Year	US			UK			West Germany			France
	Men college & junior college	Women college & junior college	Men & women college & junior	Men college	Women college	Men & women college	Men college & gymnasium	Women college & gymnasium	Men & women college & gymnasium	Men & women college
1982	39.1	41.5	40.3	23.4	18.7	21.1	24.5	17.4	21.0	
1983	40.3	43.3	41.8	23.0	18.7	20.9	25.8	16.6	21.3	
1984	41.4	45.0	43.2	24.3	20.0	22.2	24.4	16.3	20.4	
1985	42.0	46.3	44.1	24.8	20.8	22.9	23.0	16.2	19.7	
1986	42.4	46.9	44.6	25.7	21.9	23.9	24.1	16.9	20.6	
1987	42.2	47.5	44.8	26.3	23.3	24.9	26.7	18.8	22.9	29.4
1988	42.6	48.9	45.7	27.7	25.3	26.5	31.0	21.6	26.4	
1989	41.2	47.1	44.1	29.8	28.4	29.2	35.4	24.2	29.9	34.2

Source: Ministry of Education, *International Comparisons of Education Indicators*.

Germany, and France in the period from 1982 to 1989.[3] Because only limited data are available in Japan for the last four countries, Table 1.2a shows some Japanese data which can be compared with these as directly as possible.

The US data are for full-time students and include junior college education. The combined percentage of American male and female students receiving higher education is higher than for Japanese men and women (the average difference being about 7.5 percentage points). The difference is smaller if only men are compared. In contrast, there is a difference of more than ten percentage points between women. Considering the high dropout rate in the US, however, the proportion of those who graduate from higher education in the population under consideration might be higher in Japan than in the US.[4] A characteristic of US higher education is that as far as the period shown in the table is concerned, more women went to college or junior college than men. Though the percentage of women going to college or junior college exceeded that of men only in 1989 in Japan, in the US the former was already higher in the early 1980s. Table 1.2b shows that in the US the rate of increase in the percentage of women going to college or junior college was already quite high in the early 1980s.

A comparison with the UK (whose data are for full time students) reveals first that the percentage of Japanese men going to college was much higher. However, in this period, when the percentage in Japan was decreasing or stagnant, the percentage in the UK was increasing and thus the difference narrowed. As for women, the percentage in the UK was higher each year, though the percentage of Japanese women going to either college or junior college was higher than that for British women going to college. It can be seen that in the UK the percentage for women was increasing quite rapidly, so that by the end of the 1980s it had become quite high. It seems that because of this increase the difference in the percentage between men and women has almost disappeared in the UK.

The percentage of those going to college or gymnasium in West Germany looks similar to that of those going to college in the UK. However, in West Germany there is still a difference of about ten points in the percentage between men and women, because uniform increases occurred for both sexes in the late 1980s.

Table 1.2b has French data for only two years, which shows that the percentage was higher than for the UK and West Germany. In addition, French data for 1990 indicates that the percentage had risen to as high as 38.0%. This is higher than the percentage (36.3%) of Japanese men and women who were admitted to either college or junior college in the same year. Even from these three years of French data, we can see that the percentage was increasing very rapidly over those years.

These observations show that the percentage of students receiving higher education in Japan was by no means lower than those in other advanced countries. (It should be emphasized, however, that a high percentage does not always mean a favorable situation.) Yet, in recent years the percentage in Japan stagnated, whereas in other advanced countries it increased rapidly and some exceeded the percentage in Japan. One point especially noteworthy is that the percentage of women going to college in the US and UK increased dramatically. (French data are not available.) The percentage in Japan also increased. Therefore, the increase in the demand by women for higher education is a global tendency.[5]

1.3 The Questions to be Answered and a Summary of Each Chapter

Why did all these increases or changes arise? First of all, why do people go to college? What makes some decide to go and others not? The basic purpose of this book is to answer these questions both theoretically and empirically from the standpoint of economics. The analyses of this book can be classified into two parts: the theoretical analyses in Chaps. 2 and 3 on the one hand, and empirical analyses from Chap. 4 through Chap. 7 on the other.

Chaps. 2 and 3 will examine basic economic theories useful in explaining college-going behavior. (These theories were developed not merely to analyze higher education but also most types of education.) Economic theories provide bases for analyzing economic phenomena. It is fundamentally important to have an understanding of these theories because they increase the explanatory power of economic phenomena. However, each economic theory is only an abstraction of a part of the real economy, so even the collection of all existing theories cannot explain every aspect of the real world. Yet, even when facing a phenomenon that contradicts economic theories, knowledge of them will often enable us to infer reasons and obtain clues.

Chaps. 4 through 7 will consider specific questions concerning college-going behavior. In particular, Chaps. 4 through 6 emphasize empirical studies using Japanese data. These Chapters will also refer to a number of empirical studies undertaken in other countries to obtain a multidimensional understanding of major problems in college-going behavior.

The purpose of Chapter 2, College-Going Behavior as Investment in Human Capital, is to examine human capital theory, which is best-known as a theory of college-going behavior. This theory regards higher education as an object of investment which enhances one's productivity. Thus, in this theory individuals invest in education with the aim of earning increased remuneration in the future due to increased productivity.

This chapter first identifies the costs and benefits (returns) of investment in education. It then models the investment decision of an individual who faces a particular pattern of costs and benefits of education. We will consider two decision making models, i.e., the present-value method and the internal-rate-of-return method. The most important concept here is the internal rate of return which is computed from both the costs and benefits, and becomes a measure of how beneficial the education is.

These investment models are not necessarily sufficiently realistic, since they assume capital market perfection. Hence, we will also consider investment decisions under capital market imperfection.

It is quite common throughout the world to analyze education investment using the internal-rate-of-return method. Accordingly, this chapter will discuss in detail how to measure internal rates of return. It is very interesting to compute internal rates of return using real data, but they tend to have biases because it is difficult to measure correctly all the costs and benefits (including non-pecuniary ones) of higher education investment. This chapter will examine in detail a variety of biases that tend to arise when computing internal rates of return.

Rates of return to education are sometimes approximately measured using the so-called Mincer's earnings function. We will examine this method and actually use it to compute rates of return for Japan. Then we will compare these with the rates of return measured by the internal-rate-of-return method. This will reveal the shortcomings of the method based on Mincer's earnings function. Finally, this section will look at rates of return to education investment throughout the world, and discuss patterns that emerge.

Chap. 3, College-Going Behavior as Signaling, will investigate a theory quite different from human capital theory. Signaling theory considers that college education plays the role not of enhancing individuals' productivity but instead of conveying information to society about productivity already possessed before being admitted to college.

In the Spence model, which we consider first, those who are initially more productive and thus can obtain a degree easily (or at low costs) go to college, because the firm believes that those who have degrees are more productive than those who do not. This function of education is called the signaling function. This chapter will also consider the Arrow-Burdett filtering model and the Riley model which combines the signaling and human capital models.

All these models assume capital market perfection as do the present-value and internal-rate-of-return methods discussed in Chap. 2. Thus they are not very persuasive in view of the real world where capital markets are mostly imperfect. In the Spence model, for example, those who go to college are initially productive and those who do not are initially unproductive. This conclusion is not always consistent with the prevailing fact that the percentage of people going to college is very high among those from wealthy families. In order to overcome this shortcoming this chapter will develop a signaling model which can explain this prevailing fact. It will be shown in this new model that education investment has a similar property to the potlatch, an important research subject in anthropology, and also to conspicuous consumption, which is well-known in economics.

The purpose of Chap. 4, An Application of the Internal-Rate-of-Return Method: Rates of Return to Medical and Dental Education, is to compute the internal rates of return to medical and dental education using Japanese data and then consider problems related to these two kinds of education. As the internal-rate-of-return method is used quite commonly this chapter will also aim to explain how to actually apply this method.

Some interesting analyses will become possible by applying the internal-rate-of-return method to medical and dental education, which are special but important kinds of education. First, this will enable us to quantify how attractive these kinds of education investment are. We know that they are the most popular formal education today in Japan partly because the incomes of medical doctors and dentists are very high. The analysis will confirm that medical and dental education is a very beneficial investment opportunity, even though a student at a private medical or dental school has to bear extremely high education costs.

The problem of the socially optimal levels of investment in medical and dental education or the socially optimal numbers of medical and dental doctors is very important in view of the overall welfare of a country and is an issue in which many have expressed an interest. The internal-rate-of-return method will also shed some light on this issue. In other words, by actually measuring the internal rates of return, we will be able to judge whether or not we have too few doctors or dentists. We will argue that in contrast with this internal-rate-of-return method, the one which has been actually used in policy making lacks a concept of optimality.

Analyses in this chapter have scarcity values, because there are not many measurement examples of the rates of return to medical and dental education in the world (none in Japan), though there are countless measurements of the rates of return to higher education in general.

The purpose of Chap. 5, Causes of Changes in the Enrollment Rate, is to analyze what brought about these changes we observed in Sect. 1.1. Chap. 5 will consider only the case of men going to college, since the case of women is not easily analyzed partly due to a lack of available data.

We will first examine whether the internal-rate-of-return method is useful in explaining these changes. It will be demonstrated that the actually measured internal rate of return does not correlate well with the percentage of those going to college, suggesting weak explanatory power of the simplest internal-rate-of-return method. One reason is that this method assumes capital market perfection. It will be seen, however, that a regression model that has not only a variable for the internal rate of return but also a variable for the availability of funds for investment (such as a variable for family income) explains the variations of the percentage of those going to college quite consistently with the human capital theory.

Yet, we will realize that the real world is not so simple: a statistically better result will be obtained if the amount of tuition (and fees), which is merely a component of the internal rate of return, is used in the above regression model instead of the internal rate of return itself.

Because of this fact, we will estimate regression models which include variables not only for tuition and family income but also for forgone earnings, the wage difference between college and (senior) high-school graduates, the promotion probability difference between them, the wage growth rate, and so on. We will then see that these models can better explain college-going behavior. At the same time, some interesting results will emerge. Furthermore, we will be able to understand why the models based on internal rates of return have low explanatory power.

In all the models we have considered so far the dependent variable is the percentage of those going to college. Some Japanese researchers suggest that if the demand for higher education is to be analyzed, the dependent variable should be the application rate.[6] At the end of this chapter, the differences will be clarified between the models with the percentage of students going to college as the dependent variable and those with the application rate as the dependent variable. We will argue that the former are theoretically clearer empirical models.

Chap. 6, Individual Attributes and College-Going Behavior, will analyze what types of individuals tend to go to college. It will first analyze using Japanese data how family income, academic background of parents, father' occupation, mother's labor market participation, and proximity of institutions affect men's behavior of going to college, women's behavior of going to college, and women's behavior of going to junior college. Some of these factors affect the three different types of behavior differently. For example, the academic background of parents significantly influences the college-going behavior of men and women, but does not influence women's behavior of going to junior college.

Next, we focus attention on two very interesting questions and consider them by referring to empirical analyses undertaken abroad: the first is the effect of parents' academic background on college-going behavior and the second is the difference in college-going behavior between men and women.

What is noteworthy concerning the effect of parents' academic background is that in general the mother's is much stronger than the father's. We will investigate why such a phenomenon arises. At the same time, Chap. 6 will propose a hypothesis that the effect of the mother's academic background relative to the father's and the effect of both parents' academic background weaken as the economy develops.

What was prominent in college-going behavior is that as seen in the previous section, the percentage of women going to college had long been lower than that of men in almost every country. We will point out several factors giving rise to this phenomenon and examine them in detail. We will also explore causative influences for the fact that the percentage of women going to college has been increasing throughout the world, as noted in the previous section.

Chap. 7, The Purpose and Function of Higher Education, will discuss the relative plausibility in the real world of the human capital theory examined in Section 2 and the signaling theory examined in Section 3. As noted before, these two theories of college-going behavior assume perfectly opposing purposes or functions of higher education. Namely, the human capital model claims that higher education enhances students' productivity, while the signaling models claim that it merely conveys information to society about the students' initial productivity. It is difficult to obtain a decisive conclusion as to their relative plausibility, because each theory has empirical studies which support it. Nevertheless, it is possible to infer to which level and field of education each theory is more applicable.

The analyses up to this point constitute the primary aim of this book. However, as large scale reforms in higher education are in process in Japan today, a few relevant notes and opinions by the author will be added. Specifically, I would like to discuss changes in the information content of educational signals, academic abilities of students today, and the problem of training for leadership.

The first two appendices are written for readers who find they require more knowledge of economics or econometrics. Appendix A explains how the wage (rate) is determined in a competitive labor market. This appendix will be useful to those who would like more knowledge of economics, because this book will frequently deal with wage differences due to education. Appendix B explains the essentials of regression analysis. Most empirical studies cited in this book are based on regression analyses and Chaps. 5 and 6 will actually use them. Therefore, some basic knowledge of regression analysis will be necessary, though details are unnecessary. The level of knowledge provided in this appendix will be essentially sufficient to understand the empirical studies in this book. Explanations will aim to give the reader an intuitive understanding of regression analyses. Appendix C outlines the Japanese education system for those who are not familiar with it.

Notes

1. When this book uses the term "college" in the case of Japan, it refers either to four-year institutions (university) only or to both four-year institutions and junior colleges, which are two-year institutions. (Of course, it sometimes clearly distinguishes the two types of institutions.) This is because it is cumbersome to repeatedly use the term "college and junior college". The author tries to use the term "college" so that the reader can understand from the context what is meant by it. The term "college" is also used for "university" in other countries.
2. See Dore (1965), Passin (1965), Rubinger (1982), Arai (1990a), and so on for the education in the Edo Period and in the initial stage of modern economic growth in Japan.
3. See Ministry of Education, *International Comparisons of Education Indicators.* It has also definitions of the terms used.
4. Dropouts are rare in Japanese higher education.
5. If not limited to higher education, the increase in the level of women's education (relative to that of men's) is a world-wide tendency this century (Schultz, 1993).
6. Not all applicants are admitted to college or junior college in Japan. Each institution requires the applicants to take an entrance examination and admits only a portion of them. Every year there are some students who apply but are not admitted to any institution. The application rate is defined as the number of students who applied for at least one institution divided by the number of graduates from junior high school three years previous.

Chapter 2
College-Going Behavior as Investment in Human Capital

One of the theories dealing with an individual's college-going decision making is the theory of human capital. It assumes that higher education is an object of investment, which enhances the individual's productivity. This theory was formed in earnest around 1960 with the growing interest in economic growth and income distribution, and was gradually refined from that time. Together with this theoretical refinement, a large number of empirical studies have been undertaken in related areas. Today, the theory of human capital is one of the most fundamental concepts in labor economics.

This chapter will analyze college-going decisions on the basis of the theory of human capital. First, in Sect. 2.1 we will clarify the costs and benefits of education investment. Then we will examine in Sect. 2.2 two models of investment decision for an individual facing these costs and benefits. The most important concept in this argument is the internal rate of return. This rate is considered to play a crucial role in the investment decision. Sect. 2.3 will discuss several problems which arise when applying these models to real world situations. Sect. 2.4 will examine a simple method of calculating rates of return to education investment on the basis of Mincer's earnings function. Finally, Sect. 2.5 will discuss some general properties and tendencies of rates of return that have been actually measured all over the world.[1]

2.1 The Concept of Human Capital

2.1.1 Investment in Human Capital

To see the economic effects of higher education, let us first compare the average annual earnings of college and senior high-school graduates. Table 2.1 shows the difference in average annual earnings in 1992 among male workers in Japan for each age group of these graduates. The data is from the Ministry of Labor, *Basic Survey of Wage Structures*. Here, annual earnings are defined as the monthly earnings[2] times twelve plus annual bonuses. For example, the average college graduate aged between 50 and 54 received annual earnings of 10,338,700 yen, while the average senior high-school graduate in the same age group received annual earnings of 6,843,700 yen, the difference being 3,495,000 yen. It is clear from the table that the earnings difference continues to widen up to about age 60, though the average college graduate earns slightly less than the average senior high-school graduate of the same age when the former first starts working.

The fundamental idea of human capital theory is that this earnings difference is mainly due to the productivity-enhancing effect of higher education, or more

Table 2.1. Earnings differences between college and senior high-school graduates (males).

(ten thousand yen, 1992)

Age class	Annual earnings of college graduates (1)	Annual earnings of senior high-school graduates (2)	Earnings difference (1)–(2)
18~19	—	2,354.4	—
20~24	3,211.5	3,235.9	−24.4
25~29	4,471.8	3,987.8	484.0
30~34	5,624.6	4,654.4	970.2
35~39	6,652.9	5,362.1	1,290.8
40~44	8,088.8	6,013.9	2,074.9
45~49	9,236.9	6,701.4	2,535.5
50~54	10,338.7	6,843.7	3,495.0
55~59	9,692.2	5,984.3	3,707.9
60~64	7,236.1	4,159.8	3,076.3
65~	7,245.6	3,382.4	3,863.2

precisely, of the knowledge and skills obtained in higher education. In short, human capital theory considers that higher education enhances an individual's productive ability. It should be added that what is meant here by "knowledge and skills" is not only those obtained in the formal curriculum of higher education but also those obtained in extra-curricular activities such as in sports or hobby clubs and societies.[3] Some of the knowledge and skills acquired in higher education will be immediately and directly useful after graduation such as in engineering and medicine. (Almost all major fields in higher education must provide such knowledge and skills to some extent.)

The purpose of higher education, however, is not merely to provide knowledge or skills which will be immediately and directly useful after graduation, but to develop students' abilities to apply, analyze, think, judge, and so on. Of course, development of such abilities must also be a purpose of an education in engineering and medicine. If students acquire such abilities, they will be able to collect and interpret new information and respond to it easily, adapt themselves flexibly and promptly to technological or economic changes, and undertake innovation themselves. Therefore, the productivity-enhancing effect of higher education is particularly large when there are rapid technological or economic changes or in cases where high-level decision making is required.[4]

Higher education also provides students with the attitudes and discipline suitable for the jobs which are occupied mainly by college graduates (Bowles and Gintis, 1972). For example, managers need to have attitudes and discipline different from those of general workers. These attitudes and discipline are fostered in higher education, which makes much of freedom and independence on the part of students. In contrast, it is more important for students in school education below higher education to follow school rules and teachers' directions. Higher education can additionally affect students' values, tastes, motivations, communication abilities (abilities to express one's ideas persuasively), leadership, abilities to make plans, and so forth.[5]

Higher education, which lasts four years (two years in the case of junior college education) for each individual in Japan, entails a variety of costs, but the productivity-enhancing effect will generate benefits or returns for a long period of time after graduation. Put differently, individuals bear the expenditure for higher education in expectation of the long-lasting benefits. This can be regarded as an investment activity just as a firm bears the expenditure for machines or facilities in expectation of future returns. Because the investment considered in this chapter is in human beings, it is called human capital investment and the knowledge and skills accumulated by this investment are called human capital.

It is worthwhile to mention other forms of human capital investment. Training on the job, medical care, and labor mobility (the act of changing firms or work places) are also examples of human capital investment, because these are undertaken in expectation of the long-lasting benefits which will be generated by the initial expenditure. In the case of training on the job, for example, the firm and/or worker first bear the costs to improve his/her knowledge or skills, and the effect, which will last for a long period, will be realized later as an increase in his/her productivity.

In order to discuss investment in higher education, we need to clarify the costs and benefits of this investment which we will discuss in detail in the following.

2.1.2
The Costs of Higher Education Investment

There are two different approaches when considering the costs of higher education investment or human capital investment. One is the approach of the individual as a potential investor, and the other is that of society as a whole including the individual under consideration. In passing, the term "individual" here means not only the person who may go to college but also his/her family, especially parents, because the investment decision is usually made by all of these people. It is obvious, however, that the person receiving higher education is the main beneficiary of the investment. When this book refers to an individual who makes a college-going decision, it will sometimes include his/her family, so the reader should interpret this according to the context.

The costs seen from the standpoint of an individual are called private costs and are defined as the direct costs he/she has to bear additionally in order to receive higher education. By "direct costs" we mean that the costs do not include what the individual pays through tax. On the other hand, "additionally" implies "more than when the individual does not receive higher education".

The private costs include tuition and fees, costs of extra-curricular activities, costs of books and stationery, and commuting costs. It should be added that Japanese colleges require entrance fees, which are not small amounts. In addition to all of these costs, economics considers another form of costs called forgone earnings, the amount of which is larger than the total of all other costs.

Forgone earnings[6] is an example of what economics calls the opportunity cost.[7] This means the after-tax earnings one could obtain in four years (two years in the case of junior college education) if one did not go to college. If one works without going to college after graduation from (senior) high school, one can earn wages for four years (or two years) as a high-school graduate worker. These earnings become costs of higher education, because one has to forgo these earnings if one chooses to go to college. If a college student works part-time, his/her net forgone earnings should equal the above gross forgone earnings minus his/her part-time earnings.

While an individual is a college student, he/she is also obliged to bear a significant amount of costs in room and board. However, economics does not consider these to be costs of higher education, because they arise even if the individual does not go to college. In other words, the costs of room and board are not additional costs of higher education. (Strictly speaking, however, part of such costs could be costs of higher education, if they arise additionally.)

The costs of an individual's higher education seen from the standpoint of society as a whole are called social costs and cover costs to society including those the investor himself or herself has to bear. Social costs can be measured easily by slightly adjusting private costs. The first adjustment is to include the public subsidy in the costs. The second is to use before-tax earnings as forgone earnings. This is because the value of output that society forgoes when the individual receives higher education equals the before-tax earnings he/she would obtain.[8]

2.1.3
The Benefits of Higher Education Investment

Let us next identify the benefits or returns of higher education. We again consider both kinds of benefit, private and social. Private benefits are those that will accrue to the individual himself or herself additionally due to investing in higher education, while social benefits are those that will accrue similarly to society as a whole including that individual.

As part of the private benefits, we can first point out the after-tax wage difference between college and senior high-school graduates. The wage differences shown in Table 2.1 are based on before-tax cross-sectional data. Similar after-tax wage differences can be anticipated in the future. These are the pecuniary benefits that will arise additionally by receiving higher education. Of course, these benefits involve some uncertainty. In general, investments, including those undertaken by firms, usually entail uncertainty. Even if uncertainty is involved, investment will be made when sufficiently high returns are expected. Since the wage differentials from academic careers have been relatively stable in Japan, an investment in college education may be less risky than firms' investments in machines or facilities.

Some private benefits are non-pecuniary. For instance, college graduates are more likely to be engaged in jobs with better fringe benefits and/or working conditions than non-college graduates. Since these benefits are not included in the wage differences, they are called non-pecuniary benefits. (This matter will be discussed in more detail in Sect. 2.3.2.) Moreover, college graduates are more likely to become section chiefs and department heads than non-college graduates (see Chap. 5). If these positions bring about not only high monetary rewards but also psychological satisfaction, then investment in higher education will generate psychological benefits as well which are also non-pecuniary benefits.

It is likely that some of the private benefits arise outside the labor market. If (higher) education enhances an individual's productivity by improving his/her ability to communicate, collect information, make decisions, and so on, then these abilities are likely to yield benefits in capital markets and consumption good markets as well (Michael, 1982). This is because human capital is embedded in human beings and can be used outside the labor market.

More concretely, one will benefit if one acquires an ability to choose better financial assets or consumer durables by receiving higher education. There may also be benefits of "productivity" increases in the education of children within the family, health management of the family, and so on. Further, college graduates are likely to have favorable results when choosing a spouse, when choosing clubs, or when building human relations in general. (These points will be discussed in more detail in Sect. 2.3.2.)

It should be added that higher education also yields benefits which can be called future consumption benefits. These are the consumption benefits or enjoyment that college graduates will have through knowledge gained in college. One example is that knowledge of a foreign language enables one to read foreign novels and generates satisfaction. Similar benefits include being able to enjoy traveling abroad easily.

Let us briefly mention social benefits. Most of the benefits discussed above are included in the social benefits. In order to derive pecuniary social benefits, which are emphasized in the theory of human capital, we need to use before-tax wage data when computing the wage difference between college and (senior) high-school graduates. This is because the value of the product society obtains additionally from generating a college graduate is considered to appear in the before-tax wage difference. Strictly speaking, social benefits should include external economies, which will be discussed immediately below.

It should be pointed out that higher education has benefits which may be called present consumption benefits. These benefits arise while individuals are college students. An example is the benefit they have when participating in extra-curricular activities. The benefit that might arise from the life style of being a student itself is another example. Gullason (1989) shows in his empirical study that some American students enjoyed consumption benefits of higher education by evading conscription at the time of the Vietnam War. None of these are investment benefits because they arise when outlays for education are being made. When the benefits of present consumption are large, individuals have higher incentives to go to college even if the investment benefits (returns) are small. (This will be also discussed in Section 2.3.2.)

2.1.4 The External Economies of Higher Education

Economics considers the concepts of external economies and diseconomies. External economies mean the benefits an economic agent gives to another agent other than via a market (or without receiving any market remuneration). For example a fruit-grower gives external economies to a beekeeper, because the latter can increase the production of honey by the existence of the former. In this case, the beekeeper does not necessarily pay the fruit-grower. In contrast, external diseconomies mean the damage or costs an economic agent gives to another without paying compensation in the market. There are a large number of examples of external diseconomies. A typical one is the case of pollution. A firm which pollutes the air or water gives external diseconomies to other individuals.

Education does generate external economies. For example, if it teaches children desirable social norms or values, all economic agents will benefit. In addition, if a society has higher literacy and numeracy because of education, it will benefit through easier communication among its members.[9]

Does higher education generate external economies? One affirmative answer is concerned with the research undertaken in universities. Because the research results obtained in universities are available to society as a whole almost without charge, they are examples of external economies. However, students, especially undergraduate students, do not usually contribute much to the research undertaken in universities. Thus, the external economies generated at the undergraduate level of education seem to be small.

Another example of the external economies of higher education is the fact that education produces competent leaders who will have favorable effects on society for not necessarily high rewards. For example, if higher education produces competent statesmen and stateswomen, the society will greatly benefit because their abilities to negotiate and make decisions will enormously affect the welfare of the society. Nelson and Phelps (1966) give a slightly analogous example. They point out that when college graduate farmers introduce new kinds of production technology (which they are quick to do, as mentioned), other farmers can imitate them after observing the results. Thus higher education can generate external economies.

The fact that education generates external economies is a fundamental reason for its public subsidization. It does not seem, however, that today's higher education generally generates a large amount of external economies. If external economies are small, there is not a strong reason to concentrate public subsidies on national universities nor a strong reason for government subsidies themselves at least from the viewpoint of economics. Of course, those from low-income families will become able to go to college if tuition and fees are low because of government subsidies. However, there is not a convincing basis for setting a uniformly low level of tuition and fees as this will benefit those from high-income families as well. Those from low-income families will become able to go to college if a suitable system of financial aids is instituted. This latter situation is more desirable from an economic point of view.

2.1.5
A Summary of Private Costs and Benefits

It is the private costs and benefits that influence an individual's college-going decision, as far as he/she seeks for his/her own self-interest. It might be convenient, therefore, to briefly summarize here the basic costs and benefits of higher education investment from the standpoint of an individual.

Fig. 2.1 illustrates the point. The curve *HH* in the Figure shows after-tax annual earnings for the average senior high-school graduate at each age, while the curve *UU* shows that of the average college graduate. The pecuniary private benefits of higher education equal the vertical difference between *UU* and *HH* (area *A*) from the time of college graduation (age 22 in Japan) to the time of retirement. They are positive except

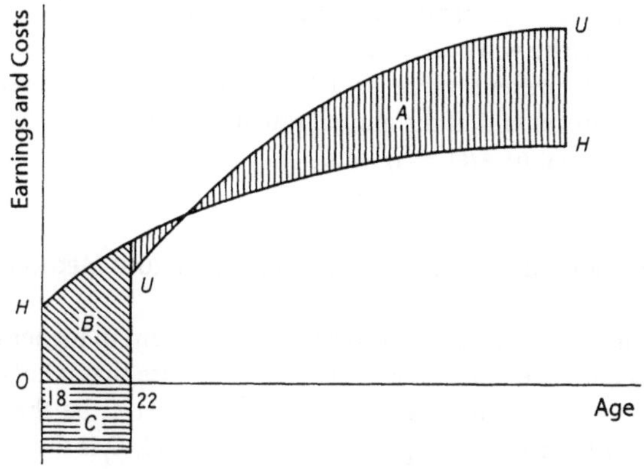

Fig. 2.1. Private Costs and Benefits of Higher Education Investment

for the short period immediately after graduation. The Figure does not show non-pecuniary benefits nor non-labor-market benefits, as these tend to vary greatly among individuals and also because they are hard to measure objectively. Area *B* corresponds to forgone earnings. If there is any income from part-time work, this amount should be subtracted from that area. Area *C* corresponds to the sum of the tuition and fees, costs of extra-curricular activities, costs of books and stationery, and commuting costs. (The benefits of present consumption are not shown in this Figure.) Hence, total private costs of higher education are the sum of Area *B* and Area *C*.

2.2 Basic Theories of College-Going Decision Making

2.2.1 The Rate of Interest and Present Value

So far we have examined the concepts of costs and benefits of investment in higher education. We can now consider theoretically the problem of college-going decision making. Before starting the discussion, however, we would like to summarize the economic concepts of the rate of interest and present value for the benefit of readers who are not familiar with these concepts.

Economic theory often assumes that only one rate of interest prevails in the capital market. In other words, it assumes that an individual can lend and borrow freely at one unique rate of interest. If the annual rate is five percent, for example, one will be able to obtain 1.05 million yen a year later if one lends a million yen today. To put it differently, the individual who borrows a million yen today must return 1.05 million yen a year later.

In this case, a million yen today and 1.05 million yen a year later can be considered to have the same value today, because they are exchanged. In this situation, we say that the present (discounted) value of 1.05 million yen a year later equals a million yen. In general, the present value of an amount of money a year later equals that amount divided by (1 + interest rate). Similarly, if an individual lends a million yen for two years, he/she will receive $1 \times (1 + 0.05)^2 = 1.1025$ million yen two years later. Therefore, the present value of 1.1025 million yen two years later equals $1.1025/(1 + 0.05)^2$. In general, if the annual rate of interest is i, the present value of A yen j years later is equal to $A/(1 + i)^j$ yen.

2.2.2 The Present-Value Method and the Internal-Rate-of-Return Method

Let us consider the decision making process of investment in higher education by an individual facing data like that shown in Fig. 2.1. Suppose that if he/she decides to go to college he/she will stay in college for four years. Let C_j be the private costs of investment in the j-th year in college. As discussed above, C_j is the sum of the tuition and fees, forgone earnings, costs of extra-curricular activities, costs of books and stationery, and commuting costs.

Suppose further that he/she will work until the T-th year, where the first year is the year when he/she might be a first-year student. Let R_k be the private investment benefits (returns) in the k-th year ($5 \leqq k \leqq T$). R_k includes the after-tax wage difference between college and high-school graduates and other private benefits.

From these definitions we obtain the following pattern or stream of investment costs and benefits:

$$\left(C_1, C_2, C_3, C_4, R_5, R_6, \cdots, R_T\right). \tag{2.1}$$

The components in (2.1) are of course what the decision maker expects, because they will be realized in the future (except C_1). What are the conditions regarding (2.1) that will induce the decision maker to invest in higher education? We will examine here two methods that can answer this question. One is called the present-value method and the other the internal-rate-of-return method.

First we will examine the present-value method. The idea of this method is quite simple. It says that one decides to go to college if the sum of the present values of the stream of returns exceed that of the present values of the stream of costs. Let i denote the rate of interest and the first year of investment be the present. Then the present value of (2.1) is expressed by the following stream:

$$\left(C_1, \frac{C_2}{1+i}, \frac{C_3}{(1+i)^2}, \frac{C_4}{(1+i)^3}, \frac{R_5}{(1+i)^4}, \frac{R_6}{(1+i)^5}, \cdots, \frac{R_T}{(1+i)^{T-1}}\right). \tag{2.2}$$

Since the first four components of (2.2) are costs and the others are returns, the net returns or the net present value $V(i)$ of this investment can be obtained by subtracting the sum of the former from the sum of the latter, i.e.,

$$V(i) = -C_1 - \frac{C_2}{1+i} - \frac{C_3}{(1+i)^2} - \frac{C_4}{(1+i)^3} + \frac{R_5}{(1+i)^4} + \frac{R_6}{(1+i)^5} + \cdots + \frac{R_T}{(1+i)^{T-1}}. \tag{2.3}$$

The net present value depends on the rate of interest, so $V(i)$ is a function of i.

What the present-value method says is "Invest in higher education if $V(i) \geqq 0$. Otherwise, do not invest." (Strictly speaking, the decision maker should be indifferent between investing and not doing so when $V(i) = 0$.) This decision rule is quite appealing to intuition. The present-value method transforms the stream of costs and benefits into comparable present values, and makes the decision by comparing the relative magnitude of the two.

Next let us examine the internal-rate-of-return method. It first computes what is called the internal rate of return. Suppose that each component in (2.1) is discounted by the discount rate r and that the sum of the stream of discounted costs happens to equal that of the stream of discounted benefits. It is this discount rate that is called the internal rate of return. The internal rate of return is the real solution to the following mathematically simple equation:

$$C_1 + \frac{C_2}{1+r} + \frac{C_3}{(1+r)^2} + \frac{C_4}{(1+r)^3}$$

$$= \frac{R_5}{(1+r)^4} + \frac{R_6}{(1+r)^5} + \cdots + \frac{R_T}{(1+r)^{T-1}}. \tag{2.4}$$

As a simple example, consider a project in which the investment of C_1' in the first year will generate a return of R_2' in the second year. According to the above definition, the internal rate of return of this investment project is the value of r that satisfies the following equation:

$$C_1' = \frac{R_2'}{1+r}. \tag{2.5}$$

Because this equation can be rewritten as $C_1'(1 + r) = R_2'$ or as $r = R_2'/C_1' - 1$, it can be easily realized that the solution of r is a suitable concept for the rate of return.

Let r^* be the real solution to Eq. 2.4. What the internal-rate-of-return method says is "Invest in higher education if r^* is no lower than the market rate of interest i. Otherwise, do not invest." (Strictly speaking again, the decision maker must be indifferent between investing and not doing so when $r^* = i$.)

Here the market rate of interest can be regarded as the opportunity cost of the investment. This is because the decision maker would be able to earn returns corresponding to the market rate of interest if he/she invested in the capital market rather than in higher education. Obviously it is unprofitable to invest in higher education when the internal rate of return to this investment is less than the market rate of interest. In contrast, when the internal rate of return is higher than the market rate of interest, investment in higher education will be profitable even if the decision maker has to borrow in the capital market, because the returns to the investment in college education will be larger than the sum of the principal and interest this decision maker has to repay.

We will now reexamine the present-value method and the internal-rate-of-return method using a graph (see Fig. 2.2). First note that $V(i)$ in Eq. 2.3 is a decreasing function of i: For a large value of i, the investment returns R_k in the distant future are more heavily discounted than the investment costs in the near future. As shown in Fig. 2.2, $V(i)$ decreases as the market interest rate increases, and becomes negative when i is sufficiently high.

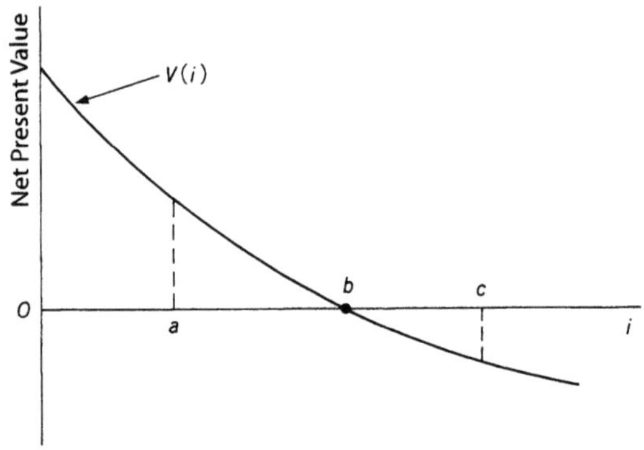

Fig. 2.2. The Net Present Value and the Internal Rate of Return

Let b denote the rate of market interest at which $V(i)$ intersects the horizontal axis. First choose an arbitrary rate of market interest a that is lower than b. Since $V(a) > 0$ in Fig. 2.2, the present-value method tells the decision maker to invest in higher education. A similar result holds for each rate of market interest lower than b. Next choose an arbitrary rate of market interest c that is higher than b. Since $V(c) < 0$ in the graph, the present-value method tells the decision maker not to invest in higher education. A similar result holds for each rate of market interest higher than b. For the market rate of interest equal to b, the decision maker is indifferent between investing and not investing in higher education, because the net present value of the investment equals zero.

The internal rate of return r^* obtained by the internal-rate-of-return method satisfies Eq. 2.4. Hence, if we substitute it into Eq. 2.3, we have $V(r^*) = 0$. This result implies the following: The internal rate of return is given by the value b at which V exactly intersects the horizontal axis ($r^* = b$). In other words, the internal rate of return is nothing but the discount rate that makes the net present value (net returns) of investment equal zero. This would be an alternative definition of the internal rate of return.

When the market rate of interest is equal to a, the internal rate of return b is higher than a, which implies that the investment decision based on the internal-rate-of-return method is to invest in higher education. On the other hand, when the market rate of interest is equal to c, the decision based on the same method is not to invest. When it is equal to b, the decision maker is indifferent. Therefore, (in a situation like this where the first several years are the investment period and the subsequent years generate returns) the internal-rate-of-return method and the present-value method produce the same solution to the investment problem (Arrow and Levhari, 1969). In other words, an individual will come to the same decision, whether he/she uses the present-value method or the internal-rate-of-return method.

Nevertheless, the economics of education makes use of only the internal-rate-of-return method in almost all cases where the advantageousness of investment is at issue. There are two main reasons for this. First, this method is more convenient for international comparisons, intertemporal comparisons, and so on. International or intertemporal comparisons based on the present-value method would face problems of differences in the market rate of interest, levels of general prices, and/or exchange rate problems, whereas internal rates of return are free of these problems. Secondly, the real economy usually has a variety of market rates of interest which are easily accommodated by the internal-rate-of-return method, since it does not require the additional complex computations of the present-value method.

To summarize this discussion, there are four basic factors affecting an individual's decision to invest in higher education. The first is the stream of costs and the second is the stream of benefits (returns). The smaller the value of the former and the larger the value of the latter, the more likely it is that the individual will decide to invest in higher education.

The third factor is the number of years in which the individual expects to acquire benefits. This may be called the harvest period. The older the age of retirement and/or the longer the expected longevity, the longer the harvest period and thus the more likely it is that the investment will be undertaken. Eq. 2.3 and Fig. 2.2 imply that the smaller the costs, the larger the benefits, and/or the longer the harvest period, the higher the position of V in Fig. 2.2. This means that the investment is more likely to be undertaken according to the above two methods of investment decision.

The fourth factor is the market rate of interest, where the lower the rate, the more likely it is that the individual will go to college.[10]

Even if each individual makes an investment decision in accordance with either of the two methods discussed above, that decision is not necessarily optimal from the standpoint of society as a whole.[11] There are three reasons for this. First, because investors do not bear all the costs of higher education (some of which are publicly borne), private costs do not coincide with social costs. Secondly, because private benefits are computed on the basis of after-tax wages, they do not correctly reflect the difference in the marginal value product between college and senior high-school graduates. Thirdly, if higher education generates external economies, social benefits exceed private benefits. Basic economic theory implies that if private costs coincide with social costs and private benefits with social benefits, an investment decision which is individually optimal will also be socially optimal.

It is theoretically possible to devise a way to achieve socially optimal levels of investment by individuals. By considering the stream of social costs and benefits of investment in higher education as in (2.1), we can compute the net social present value of investment or the social internal rate of return on investment in higher education. (In contrast, the above internal rate of return which is computed from the individual's standpoint is called the private internal rate of return.) The investment decision rule should be, then, to invest only if the social internal rate of return exceeds the (highest) alternative rate of return on investment. This rule will lead to investments in higher education that are most desirable to society as a whole.

The government can induce individuals to achieve a socially optimal level of investment. If the social internal rate of return is sufficiently high but the private rate of return is not so high, the government should induce more individuals to invest in higher education, because the goal of the government is to consider the welfare of society as a whole. There are two main ways to achieve this. The first is to increase subsidies to higher education, which lowers tuition and fees. The second is to adjust the tax system in favor of college graduates. Both will increase the private internal rate of return, and investment in higher education will be more attractive. If the social internal rate of return is low but the private rate of return is high, the government should employ the opposite policy by lowering the latter to discourage investment.

2.2.3 Capital Market Imperfection

The market rate of interest played a crucial role in the investment decision rules discussed above. Namely, investments are made if the net present value of investment computed using the market rate of interest is positive or if the internal rate of return exceeds the market rate of interest. In these rules it is immaterial whether or not a decision maker has his/her own funds for investment. An individual who does not have such funds is implicitly assumed to be able to borrow freely in the capital market at a constant interest rate which is equal to the lending interest rate. On the other hand, even if an individual has a sufficient amount of his/her own funds, he/she will not invest in higher education but will invest in the capital market when the former investment has a low internal rate of return. The capital market is called perfect if borrowing and lending are undertaken freely and the borrowing and lending interest rates are the same. The present-value method and the internal-rate-of-return method both assume capital market perfection.

Is the capital market in the real economy perfect? It has not been common in Japan to borrow in the capital market for investment in education, though it is becoming easier for average people to borrow from banks. If the capital market were perfect, students who want to go to college could borrow in the capital market in accordance with their needs and return the debt gradually after graduation. However, it has been impossible and is still almost impossible to do so in reality. (The financial aid system of the Japan Scholarship Society for higher education has not been very generous, but has existed mainly for a quite limited number of students who are of high academic standard but face financial difficulties. Financial aids could be incorporated into the discussion below.) The reason often given in the economics of education for this kind of capital market imperfection is that the student returning the debt would be so young that he/she has not yet established credit in the capital market. This may have been a fundamental reason in the past, but the situation is now changing in Japan. The following is an overview of the current situation.

When the average family income was low in Japan, banks were unwilling to loan money for individuals' investment in higher education. To put it differently, Japanese firms had such a strong demand for funds for investment that all the private financial institutions could do was simply meet this demand, leaving no money to spare for consumers. For this reason, very few current workers graduated from college using loans from private financial institutions.

In recent years, however, as the demand for loans by private firms declined, Japanese banks have become more willing to offer consumers credit. In other words, it has become much easier for individuals to use bank loans to purchase higher education on condition that they return the debt from future income.[12]

Even now, the "education loan" of most banks is limited to a maximum of three million yen (five million yen for some banks).[13] Moreover, in most cases the loan can be applied only to tuition and fees. (Some banks also supply loans for rent.) The interest rate of these loans is several percentage points higher than that of bank term deposits for consumer saving, implying that the borrowing and lending interest rates are significantly different. In addition, the term of repayment is as short as five to ten years, so it is likely that those who actually repay are the parents rather than the students. The "education loan", therefore, targets mainly those parents who temporarily have difficulty financing tuition and fees but will be able to repay in the near future.[14]

As shown above, the capital market has been extremely imperfect for investment in higher education at least in Japan, though borrowing is becoming easier to some extent. Hence, it has been impossible for students to borrow freely for higher education investment and repay gradually from the investment returns. In other words, the real economy could not achieve the basic pattern of investment that exists in economic theory. In the past, for this reason whether one could go to college depended greatly on how wealthy one's parents were. This situation has not yet disappeared. This implies that there have been individuals who could not or cannot invest in higher education even if it was or is an advantageous investment object in terms of the present-value method or the internal-rate-of-return method.

It is possible to build a model of education investment that takes this capital market imperfection into account. In accordance with Becker and Chiswick (1966), we would like to consider here how an individual's total investment in education is determined.

The model is shown in Fig. 2.3. The horizontal axis in the graph shows an individual's total amount of investment in school education. Since primary school and junior high-school education is compulsory in Japan, we may interpret the zero level of investment as corresponding to junior high-school graduation. The decreasing marginal private rate-of-return curve *DEF* shows the private internal rate of return to an additional amount of investment (or to an additional year of education). In the above, we considered the internal rate of return to higher education as a unit. Here however, we assume that investment in education can be divided into pieces and consider the internal rate of return for each piece.[15] The marginal private rate-of-

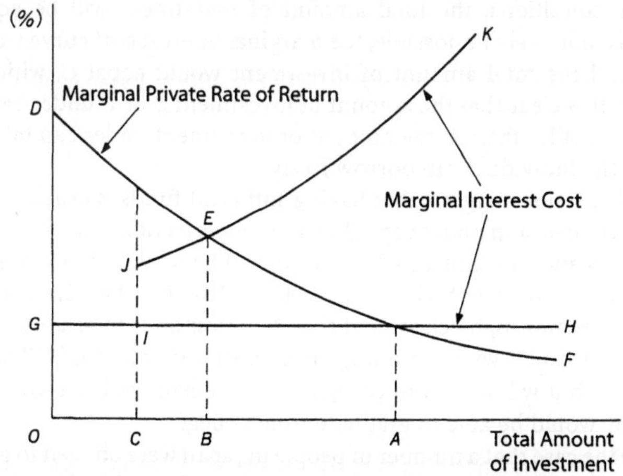

Fig. 2.3. Determination of the Total Amount of Investment in School Education

return curve is decreasing, because the productivity enhancing effect of additional education is usually considered to decrease with the total amount of education, a very common assumption in economics.

First assume that an individual can borrow or lend freely at the market rate of interest equal to *OG*. This is an assumption of capital market perfection. The marginal interest cost curve which the individual faces under this assumption is shown by the horizontal line *GH*, since the opportunity cost of additional investment, which equals the market rate of interest, is constant irrespective of the total amount of investment.

In these conditions, the individual chooses the level of total investment at *A*, where the marginal private rate-of-return curve intersects the marginal interest cost curve. For a level of investment lower than *A*, additional investment will generate net benefit even if the investment is financed by borrowing. In contrast, for a level of investment higher than *A*, some reduction in the total amount of education investment will be advantageous, even if the individual has sufficient funds of his/her own, because he/she can lend the reduced amount in the capital market at a rate higher than the marginal internal rate of return to education investment.

Next, we will consider how the total amount of education investment is determined when borrowing is not unlimited or the capital market is imperfect. This case corresponds to the marginal interest cost curve *GIJEK* in Fig. 2.3. This individual has his/her own funds for investment equal to *OC*. The marginal interest cost of investing this amount in school education equals the (lending) interest rate, which is the opportunity cost of investment.

Investment beyond *OC* requires him/her to borrow. But borrowing is not easy because of capital market imperfections. In other words, in order to borrow he/she has to pay a rate of interest higher than *OG*. In addition, the more he/she borrows, the fewer the opportunities in which he/she can borrow at low rates of interest. Therefore, the marginal interest cost curve slopes upwards. (*J* might be located below *I* if financial aids with low rates of interest are available. However, the amount of financial aids is normally small, so the marginal interest cost curve will eventually rise.)

Under these conditions, the total amount of investment will be equal to *B*. If borrowing was completely impossible, the marginal interest cost curve would become vertical at *C* and the total amount of investment would equal *C*, which would be smaller than *B*. It is clear that the amount of investment *B* or *C* under capital market imperfection is smaller than *A*, the amount of investment under capital market perfection, where the individual can borrow freely.

The above discussion suggests that having sufficient funds is crucial in one's education investment decision under capital market imperfection. An individual who has insufficient funds and has difficulty borrowing will be unable to invest in education even if the rate of return is high. Suppose here that *B* in Fig. 2.3 corresponds to graduation from senior high-school and that *A* corresponds to graduation from college. Then an individual with the marginal interest cost curve *GIJEK* will graduate from high school but will not go to college. If he/she had his/her own funds greater than *OA*, he/she would be able to graduate from college.

It used to be the case that a number of people in Japan were obliged to give up going to college because of insufficient funds. We can infer from the above consideration that increases in personal incomes and/or an enrichment in the financial aid system, which either shifts *C* to the right or shifts *JEK* downwards, will contribute much toward increasing the percentage of those going to college. It should be added that a proper financial aid system tends to achieve economic equality without sacrificing economic efficiency (Taubman, 1981).

We can also infer from the above consideration that not only the amount of one's own funds or personal income but also the number of one's siblings affects one's decision to invest in education under capital market imperfection. It is well-known that *ceteris paribus* the per capita amount of investment in school education is generally small in a household with large sibship size (Duncan, 1974; Parsons, 1975; Mare, 1980; Behrman, Hrubec, Taubman, and Wales, 1980; Micklewright, 1989; Steelman and Powell, 1991).

It should be added that not only the number of siblings but how their ages are dispersed is an important determinant of education investment. It is noteworthy that an individual with many siblings tends to have fewer years of school education, not only because of insufficient per capita funds but also because of less per capita time shared with parents and thus lower school performance (Hanushek, 1992). It may be said that some parents planned smaller families in order to increase the amount of education investment per child and thus the quality of each child (Becker and Lewis, 1973; Willis, 1973).[16]

2.3 How to Apply the Internal-Rate-of-Return Method

2.3.1 How to Measure Internal Rates of Return

Now we would like to examine how internal rates of return are usually computed. We will consider the case of private internal rates of return as an example. The private rate of return to higher education investment varies across individuals so that there is no common rate, because, as stated earlier, an individual's private rate of return should be computed from his/her expected costs and returns including those that are non-pecuniary.

If we use some simplifying assumptions, however, we can compute the average rate of return, which is objective to some extent.[17] The first simplifying assumption is to limit costs and benefits to those that are pecuniary. The second simplifying assumption concerns individuals' expectations. Although there may be a variety of assumptions that can be made, in most cases, either of the following two assumptions is made.

The first possible assumption about expectations is that individuals expect that the structure of average investment costs and average after-tax wages which is observable when they make their investment decision will be maintained in the future without change. According to this assumption, individuals expect that the structure of average investment costs for first-year through fourth-year students, which is easily observed when they make their decision, will be maintained in the future without change. They further expect that the structure of average after-tax wages for college and (senior) high-school graduates which is observable when they make their investment decision will also be maintained in the future without change. The plausibility of this assumption is especially high when the economy is expected to face little change in the future.

The second possible assumption about expectations is that individuals expect that average investment costs and average after-tax wages for college and high-school graduates which are observable when they make their investment decision will continue to grow at a constant rate. Thus individuals expect a simple form of economic growth under this assumption. This is in contrast with the previous assumption in which individuals expected no economic growth. It is unlikely that costs and benefits will continue to grow at a constant rate into the distant future, but it is likely that individuals have such expectations when they make their decision. The constant rate of growth in this assumption probably varies across individuals, because it is based on their expectations. An assumption which is frequently used in economics to obtain a single rate of growth is that individuals expect the average (economic) growth rate of the past few years to continue in the future.

If the first assumption about expectations is used to compute internal rates of return, the formula to apply for computation should be Eq. 2.4 with the values from tuition data, wage data, etc. observable at the time of the decision making being substituted into C_j and R_k.

On the other hand, if the second assumption about expectations is used, the same values as above must be substituted into C_j and R_k in the following formula, which is a modification of Eq. 2.4:

$$C_1 + \frac{C_2(1+g)}{1+r} + \frac{C_3(1+g)^2}{(1+r)^2} + \frac{C_4(1+g)^3}{(1+r)^3}$$
$$= \frac{R_5(1+g)^4}{(1+r)^4} + \frac{R_6(1+g)^5}{(1+r)^5} + \cdots + \frac{R_T(1+g)^{T-1}}{(1+r)^{T-1}}. \tag{2.6}$$

This equation is formulated under the assumption that costs and benefits grow at an annual rate of $100g$ percent. Thus, the farther into the future, the larger the costs and benefits become.

There is a simple relationship between the two rates of return computed under these two assumptions. To see it, we divide both the numerator and the denominator of each fraction in Eq. 2.6 by $(1 + g)^j$ and obtain the following equation:

$$C_1 + \frac{C_2}{\left(\frac{1+r}{1+g}\right)} + \frac{C_3}{\left(\frac{1+r}{1+g}\right)^2} + \frac{C_4}{\left(\frac{1+r}{1+g}\right)^3}$$
$$= \frac{R_5}{\left(\frac{1+r}{1+g}\right)^4} + \frac{R_6}{\left(\frac{1+r}{1+g}\right)^5} + \cdots + \frac{R_T}{\left(\frac{1+r}{1+g}\right)^{T-1}}. \tag{2.7}$$

Note that the numerators in Eq. 2.7 are the same as those in Eq. 2.4 and that the part which equals $(1 + r)/(1 + g)$ in Eq. 2.7 corresponds to the part which equals $(1 + r)$ in Eq. 2.4.

Therefore, it must hold that $1 + r^* = (1 + r^{**})/(1 + g)$, where r^* is the real solution to Eq. 2.4 and r^{**} is that to Eq. 2.7. This equality implies the following:

$$r^{**} = r^* + g + r^*g. \tag{2.8}$$

This is the relationship that has been sought. In most cases, r^*g is quite small. For example, if the growth rate g equals 3% and the internal rate of return r^* computed from Eq. 2.4 equals 10%, r^*g equals only 0.3%. For this reason, the internal rate of return computed from Eq. 2.7 by assuming economic growth is approximately equal to the sum of the internal rate of return computed from Eq. 2.4 on the assumption of no economic growth and the rate of growth, i.e., $r^{**} \doteqdot r^* + g$. Incidentally, the real solution to Eq. 2.4 can be computed easily using a computer.

2.3.2 Biases in Measuring Internal Rates of Return

2.3.2.1 *Downward Biases*

The above simplified methods of measuring internal rates of return obviously have several unsatisfactory aspects. In other words, they are likely to generate biases in comparison with true internal rates of return, since simplifying assumptions are used for computation. Factors generating biases can be classified into two groups: the downward bias factors, which cause underestimation of the true internal rate of return, and the upward bias factors, which cause over-estimation. We will examine several such major factors.

Starting with downward bias factors, as stated before, the above measurement methods do not consider any non-pecuniary benefits of investment. The real benefits of higher education, however, should include the psychological satisfaction which can be gained from jobs college graduates take. Suppose an individual gains great psychological satisfaction from teaching high-school students. This cannot be gained without going to college and obtaining the necessary qualifications. Thus, this satisfaction is unambiguously the benefit of higher education, but it is not measured in the above methods. This kind of benefit may be called future consumption benefit. It derives from the interest, challenge, and/or pleasant human relations the individual has in a job which is available only to college graduates.[18]

There are benefits of future consumption which are independent of jobs. To repeat an example used before, college education provides graduates with the benefit of being able to read foreign novels and magazines.

These benefits are all omitted from measurements of internal rates of return, first because they differ greatly among individuals and fields of major, and secondly because they are hard to quantify. The benefit mentioned before that higher education enhances "productivity" outside labor markets is also omitted. All these factors cause underestimation of true internal rates of return.

Non-pecuniary benefits also include differences in fringe benefits and working conditions between college and senior high-school graduates. Higher education tends to generate benefits in terms of fringe benefits, if college graduates are more likely than high-school graduates to take jobs or positions with large fringe benefits. These investment benefits are not grasped in the above two methods because they do not appear in wage data. Similarly, underestimation of true internal rates of return can result if the fact that college graduates tend to engage themselves in occupations with better working conditions than high-school graduates is not considered.

Duncan (1976) provides a systematic analysis of the relationship in the United States between years of education and levels of fringe benefits and working conditions. According to his study, an increase in the years of education of an individual improves almost all kinds of fringe benefits and working conditions for which data are available.

He considers fringe benefits to include vacation days with full pay, full-pay sick days, medical insurance for off-the-job illness, life insurance for off-the-job death, retirement programs, training programs to improve skills, profit sharing, free or discounted meals, and free or discounted merchandise. Working conditions in this case include healthy and safe work, overtime hours control (whether the worker can refuse overtime work without penalty), and employment stability (whether the job is seasonal or has frequent layoffs). The results of his study show that workers with longer years of education tend to enjoy better fringe benefits and working conditions.[19] He estimates that the benefits of education increase by 10 to 25% if this effect is taken into consideration.

Lucas (1977a) points out similarly that internal rates of return measured without considering working conditions would underestimate the effects of education. He suggests that the proportion of non-pecuniary benefits in the total benefits of education is likely to increase with years of education. The empirical study by Mathios (1989) confirms this point.

In relation to working conditions, it is worth mentioning that education also has negative non-pecuniary benefits, in other words, non-pecuniary costs. College graduates are likely to take jobs which generate high levels of stress. Rates of return measured without consideration of these future costs would overestimate true rates of return.

There are several further downward bias factors. Many empirical studies show that those with longer years of education may enjoy other benefits including increases in the quality (health and intelligence) of their children, choice as to family size, increased efficiency in consumption, choice of suitable spouses in the marriage market, improved health for themselves and their spouse, and low rates of participation in crime. It is found in addition that a highly educated wife can provide her husband with useful information and advice, and thus increases her husband's earnings. Benham (1974) shows that given the level of husband's education and his years of work experience, his earnings increase between 3.0 and 4.1% for each year of his wife's education.[20] Because usual rate-of-return analyses measure few of these benefits, the measured rates of return have downward biases to that extent.[21]

It is obvious that the aggregate wage data used to compute internal rates of return is compiled from (average) wages paid to those who actually worked. There are, however, unemployed workers, who are not considered in such wage data. Thus, measuring internal rates of return without taking account of unemployment will generate biases. These biases are probably very small in Japan, where the unemployment rate has been low for the last several decades. In most other industrialized countries these biases are unlikely to be negligible due to very high rates of unemployment.

If rates of unemployment were the same for college and high-school graduates, internal rates of return to higher education computed without taking account of unemployment would overestimate the true rate. This is because the true rate should be computed after reducing the average wages of both college and high-school graduates by the amounts corresponding to the unemployment rate.

However, there are in fact differences in unemployment rates between college and high-school graduates, with the rate for college graduates usually being lower. According to the study by Bloch and Smith (1977) based on US data for 1977, an increase of one year in the education of whites leads to an increase of 6% in the probability of being employed. (See also Nickell (1979) and Ashenfelter and Ham (1979).) If this is the case, an expected wage difference between college and high-school graduates which takes account of unemployment may be larger than one which does not. Thus, not taking account of unemployment will underestimate the true internal rate of return to higher education.

A bias is also generated by the fact that the wages used to compute internal rates of return are average wages. In Japan, the dispersion of wages of college graduates is smaller than that of (senior) high-school graduates (Yano, 1991).[22] A large dispersion in the wages of workers with a certain level of education means that the risks they face are large. This is because they are obliged to receive very low wages when unfortunate, though they may receive quite high wages when fortunate. Strictly speaking, wages with large risks should be averaged by deducting a large premium (risk premium) from the arithmetic average. If there is a difference in the wage dispersion as above, the wage difference between college and high-school graduates computed by this method may be larger than the difference between the simple arithmetic averages. Therefore, an internal rate of return ignoring the risk difference is likely to underestimate the true rate.[23]

Biases may also be generated in the measurement of costs of higher education. It was pointed out previously that higher education has benefits of present consumption. These are the psychological benefits a college student enjoys by acquiring new knowledge, participating in extracurricular activities, and so on. The simple methods of measuring internal rates of return underestimate the true rates, because they do not separate the costs for these consumption benefits from the investment costs.

The study by Lazear (1977a), however, shows that education tends to bring "negative utility" to students. Namely, the disutility associated with school attendance tends to lower the satisfaction of the students. In other words, education is "bad", though whether this is true seems to depend on individuals and kinds of education. If education has this property, individuals stop short of acquiring the wealth-maximizing level of education. (It may be insisted from this fact that education should provide some enjoyment.)

However, we should not consider the "absolute level of disutility" of higher education when discussing a rate of return. Rates of return should be computed exclusively from additional benefits and additional costs of higher education. Therefore, taking a rigorous approach, we should consider the difference in disutility between studying in college for four years and working for four years as a high-school graduate. If the former has smaller disutility, higher education does have benefits of present consumption. Most people in Japan consider that this condition is satisfied.

2.3.2.2
Upward Biases

Next we would like to consider upward biases. If college graduates generally have higher intelligence which is either innate or acquired at home, then part of the wage difference between college and (senior) high-school graduates is not due to higher education but due to this intelligence difference. If this is the case, the internal rate of return computed on the basis of the two simple methods we discussed before overestimates the true rate. How large would this bias be? There are several empirical studies which answer this question and most report that the bias is quite small.

A useful approach to this question is to examine the income augmenting effect of higher education among those who have equal pre-education intelligence. Becker (1993, Chap. 5) notices that the average intelligence quotient (IQ) of college dropouts is almost the same as that of high-school graduates who do not go to college. (The academic records in high school are also almost the same.) If there is an income difference between these two groups, it can be regarded as due to the part of higher education college dropouts received. Becker actually estimated using data for 1939 the rate of return to the partial higher education received by college dropouts. The estimated rate of return is 9.5% and equals about two thirds of 14.5%, the rate of return to higher education of college graduates. This result implies that higher education itself has a strong income augmenting effect.

A recent study by Ashenfelter and Krueger (1994) on identical twins also shows that rates of return computed without taking account of intelligence differences will barely overestimate the true rates. Identical twins of the same parents have identical genetically determined ability, because they have exactly the same biological traits. Furthermore, the ability they acquired at home can be considered to be almost the same, as the same parents raised them in almost the same way.[24]

We can point out an upward bias factor which is virtually unique to Japan (and some Asian countries). This is associated with the students' costs of preparing for entrance examinations given by colleges. As parts of this preparation, students purchase lecture and information services supplied by *juku* (cram schools) and preparatory schools as well as a variety of materials including books and educational CDs. These purchases are undertaken prior to admission to colleges, but the costs should be regarded essentially as investment costs of higher education rather than as costs of high-school education. However, they are usually ignored in the above simple methods of measuring rates of return, as suitable data are not easily obtainable. Thus, rates of return obtained using these two methods are biased upward in comparison with rates which consider these costs.

To the above biases we should add what are called selection biases. An individual may go to college because his/her ability for jobs occupied mainly by high-school graduates is low. On the other hand, another individual may not go to college because his/her ability for jobs occupied mainly by college graduates is low. In these cases, the internal rate of return to higher education computed by the above simple methods has a downward bias towards those whose abilities are more suitable to jobs for college graduates. It has an upward bias, however, towards those whose abilities are more suitable to jobs for high-school graduates.[25]

Finally, we would like to mention the problem of prediction difficulty, though this is not related to measurement biases. The above two simple methods use cross-section data to compute internal rates of return. Hence, they measure something like instantaneous wind velocity. When the rate of return in some field of major, say engineering, is high, the total amount of investment in that field will increase, i.e. a large number of individuals will choose to major in that field. This is likely to cause the rate of return to decrease substantially several years later because of the increase in the number of workers in that field. This may cause a decrease in the total amount of investment in that field so that the rate of return will increase several years after that, setting up a cycle that is repeated.

This kind of economic phenomenon is known as the cobweb cycle. It occurs because investment in higher education takes time and instantaneous adjustment is impossible. In Japan, the wage structure for different academic backgrounds has been quite stable and this kind of cycle has not appeared at least in terms of higher education as a whole.

2.3.3
Problems with Human Capital Theory

The above biases arise because it is difficult to measure correct internal rates of return. In addition, the internal-rate-of-return method and the human capital theory themselves have some serious problems. We would like to discuss some of the major problems here.

It can be pointed out first of all that there are very few people in the real economy who make college going decisions after taking the trouble to compute the internal rate of return to higher education on the basis of the internal-rate-of-return method. What human capital theory claims, however, is not necessarily that individuals make investment decisions by computing internal rates of return. What it really claims is that individuals make investment decisions by comparing the investment costs and benefits sufficiently carefully and that the internal-rate-of-return method is a close approximation to real decision making.

Yet, this method is not always a close approximation, as will be shown in Chap. 5. For example, real decision makers may place more weight on investment costs than on benefits when comparing them. They may also put more weight on costs of tuition and fees than on forgone earnings.

Next we would like to mention some important problems of human capital theory. Some criticisms of this theory are offered by Thurow (1972, 1975), who points out the following four facts in the United States that human capital theory cannot explain.

First, the distributions of education and IQ are more equal than the distribution of income. Moreover, the shapes of the distributions are markedly different. Second, while the distribution of education has moved in the direction of greater equality over the post-war period, the distribution of income has not. Third, the college-educated labor force was growing at a rate of 3% in the early 1950s and at a 6% rate in the late 1960s, but there does not seem to be any evidence that the rate of growth of productivity in the economy as a whole has accelerated correspondingly. Fourth, not only is there considerable variance in wages for different individuals with the same skills;

there is also little tendency for the existence of unemployment to lower wages. For these reasons Thurow is skeptical about the productivity enhancing effect of education and suggests that equal education does not generate equal income.

The fundamental idea of human capital theory is that higher education enhances individuals' productive ability (productivity) and thus investments in higher education increase their wages. This idea is not without problems in the sense that it does not necessarily have empirical support as can be seen in Thurow's argument (see also Maglen (1990)). In order to explain the causal relationship of the form "higher education → an increase in wage", human capital theory has introduced or assumed the intermediary term of "an increase in productivity" and hypothesized the causal relationship of the form "higher education → an increase in productivity → an increase in wage".

However, it is difficult in many cases to measure the productivity of an individual and thus to prove that the above hypothesis according to human capital theory is true.[26] It is certain that there are few cases where higher education does not enhance productivity at all, especially in the fields of natural sciences. But there is little evidence to show that most of the wage increase due to higher education investment derives from the related productivity increase. As we will see later, there are several economic issues that human capital theory should be able to address but cannot, besides many others that it only partially explains. In this sense, human capital theory is not yet complete and may need to be merged with other theories to increase its explanatory power.

2.4 Mincer's Earnings Function and Rates of Return

2.4.1 Basic Theory

Rates of return to (higher) education are sometimes estimated by a different method which is based on Mincer (1974). Mincer mainly aimed to estimate the traits of an individual that determine his/her earnings, in other words to estimate the earnings function, and not necessarily to make a rigorous estimation of the rate of return to education. One of the two traits he attached most importance to is the individual's academic background. In the process of estimating the effect of this trait on earnings, an approximate value of the rate of return to education is obtained.

The other trait he attached most importance to is the number of years of labor market experience (the number of years the individual has worked after graduation from school). He regards this as a proxy variable for the amount of human capital accumulated on the job after graduation from school. It is assumed that the longer the experience, the larger the amount of human capital accumulated on the job.

In general, training (and education) undertaken within firms is classified into the following four types: on-the-job training, which is undertaken during work; off-the-job training, which is undertaken in a classroom; learning by doing, in which a worker accumulates knowledge and skills by his/her own device or imitation; and other informal forms of acquiring knowledge or skills. As in the case of school education, these types of training within firms are supposed to enhance the worker's productivity. (Incidentally, an important function of school education is to amplify the effect of training within firms, or in short, to increase the trainability of trainees.)

Mincer's earnings function is very well-known and is frequently used in analyzing wage determination problems. In this section, we will examine how it estimates the rate of return to higher education investment.

As a first step (but the main step for the purpose of this section), we examine how an individual's earnings are expressed when no training is undertaken within firms. It is assumed for simplicity that there is no economic growth. When firms do not undertake training, an individual worker will not accumulate human capital after graduation from school. Thus, his/her productivity or wage is determined solely on the basis of the human capital he/she has accumulated by the time he/she graduates from school. In the following, we mainly consider an individual who goes to college.

Let E_1 denote the earnings potential of an individual at the time he/she is in the first year of higher education. The earnings potential means the earnings that would be obtained if this individual worked full time during this period of time. Because college students do not usually work full time though some work part time, this earnings potential is normally not fully realized.

E_1 equals the marginal value product which would realize in the labor market of human capital accumulated by the time this individual graduated from senior high school. Let C_1 be the total cost of investment in higher education in the first year. Then the earnings potential E_2 in the second year of higher education is expressed by

$$E_2 = E_1 + \varrho C_1, \tag{2.9}$$

where ϱ is the rate of return to this investment. This holds because this first-year investment increases the earnings potential per year by ϱC_1.

It is assumed here that the rate of return is the same across each year's investment in the four years of higher education. Then, the same logic as above shows that the t-th year's earnings potential after staying in college for $t - 1$ years is expressed by

$$E_t = E_{t-1} + \varrho C_{t-1}. \tag{2.10}$$

Let k_t denote the ratio between the cost of investment C_t and the earnings potential E_t in the t-th year in college, i.e., $k_t = C_t/E_t$. Then, using this definition, Eq. 2.10 can be rewritten as

$$E_t = E_{t-1}\left(1 + \varrho k_{t-1}\right). \tag{2.11}$$

By letting $t = 2, 3$, etc., we have

$$E_t = E_1\left(1 + \varrho k_1\right)\left(1 + \varrho k_2\right)\cdots\left(1 + \varrho k_{t-1}\right). \tag{2.12}$$

Taking the natural logarithm of both sides of Eq. 2.12 generates

$$\ln E_t = \ln E_1 + \sum_{i=1}^{t-1} \ln\left(1 + \varrho k_i\right). \tag{2.13}$$

In Eq. 2.13, $(1 + \varrho k_i)$ is quite close to 1 since k_i is close to 1 and the rates of return in advanced countries are close to 10%. Thus, the following approximation holds: $\ln(1 + \varrho k_i) \fallingdotseq \varrho k_i$. In general, since the function $y = \ln z$ takes on the value of zero at

$z = 1$ and the slope $(1/z)$ of the tangent line to this function equals 1 there, the values of this function around $z = 1$ can be approximated by those of the function $y = z - 1$. A use of this approximation transforms Eq. 2.13 into:

$$\ln E_t = \ln E_1 + \varrho \sum_{i=1}^{t-1} k_i. \tag{2.14}$$

Let us consider k_i $(=C_i/E_i)$ in Eq. 2.14. The largest cost item in investment in higher education is forgone earnings and the second largest is tuition and fees. All the other costs are quite minor. Hence, C_i can be roughly regarded as the sum of forgone earnings and tuition and fees. If an individual does not have an income from part time work when studying in college, his/her forgone earnings equal E_i. If he/she has, his/her (net) forgone earnings become less than E_i. In Japan, k_i is usually greater than 1 because tuition and fees are normally larger than the income from part time work. Financial aids reduce real tuition and fees and thus lower k_i, but this effect is small on average.

The important assumption that Mincer used in this situation is that the sum of financial aid and income from part time work of the individual is just equal to the amount of tuition and fees. In short, he assumed that $k_i = 1$. Of course, this assumption was used to simplify the earnings function. Thus its plausibility will differ across countries. Mincer's earnings function will be derived in the following under this assumption.

It is assumed further that an individual who goes to college will stay there for s years ($s = 4$ in Japan) and then start working full time. Let Y_t denote the earnings a college graduate will obtain by working full time in the t-th year from the first year in college ($t \geqq s + 1$). (It should be noted that while E_t denotes potential earnings, Y_t denotes actual earnings.) Then, $Y_t = E_t = E_{s+1}$ for $t \geqq s + 1$. If these equalities are used together with $k_i = 1$ in Eq. 2.14, an earnings function of the form

$$\ln Y_t = \ln E_1 + \varrho s \quad \left(t \geqq s + 1\right) \tag{2.15}$$

is obtained, which does not depend on t for $t \geqq s + 1$. This is because first the amount of human capital is constant after graduation from college due to the assumption of no training on the job and secondly because the assumption of no economic growth makes the productivity or wage after graduation constant. From Eq. 2.15, the rate of return to higher education can be computed as the following:

$$\varrho = \frac{\ln Y_t - \ln E_1}{s} = \frac{1}{s}\ln\left(\frac{Y_t}{E_1}\right). \tag{2.16}$$

Next, we will discuss the earnings function in the case where training is undertaken on the job. Mincer obtained it by transforming Eq. 2.15. He first depicted the graphs which show the relationships between years of experience in the labor market and the logarithm of average earnings ($\ln Y_t$) for different kinds of academic career. (These graphs are examples of what are called wage profiles.)

Fig. 2.4 illustrates such graphs for which the horizontal axis is years of experience in the labor market and the vertical axis is $\ln Y_t$. Mincer noticed that the graph shifts almost vertically in accordance with the kind of academic career to be considered. In order to express this property in the earnings function, we have only to add to the right-hand side of Eq. 2.15 a function which shows the effect of labor market experi-

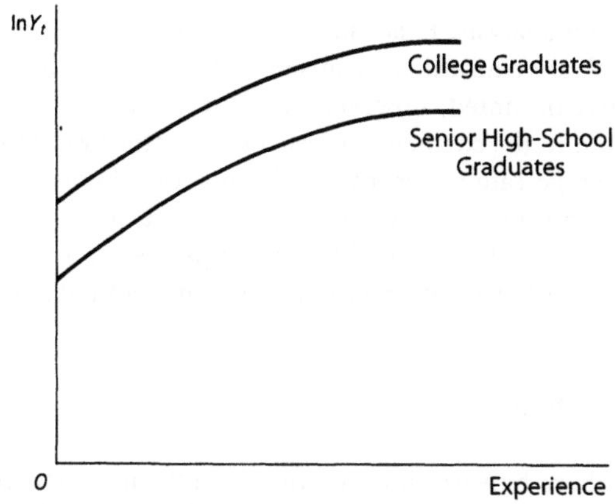

Fig. 2.4. Relationship between Experience/Education and Earnings

ence. If this is done, the new function $\ln Y_t$ surely shifts vertically in accordance with the presence or absence of the term of ϱs.

Mincer further noticed that the slope of the graph of $\ln Y_t$ is large ($\ln Y_t$ grows rapidly) when labor market experience is short and that the slope gradually decreases as experience increases. This means that the graph of $\ln Y_t$ is approximately a concave function as shown in Fig. 2.4. For this reason, he specified the effect of labor market experience by a quadratic function.[27]

The reason the slope of the graph of $\ln Y_t$ is decreasing in labor market experience is that while much training is undertaken when experience is short, the amount of investment in training decreases as the age of retirement approaches because the harvest period of the investment becomes shorter. In the stage where labor market experience is short and investment in training is large, the marginal value product (or wage) is low, because much time is invested in training. On the other hand, in the stage where labor market experience is long and investment in training is small, the marginal value product is large, because more time is spent for production and also because the returns to the past investments realize.

Specifying these effects of training on the job, Eq. 2.15 can be transformed into the following:

$$\ln Y_t = \left(\ln E_1 + \alpha\right) + \varrho s + \beta x + \gamma x^2, \tag{2.17}$$

where $x = t - s$ is the number of years of labor market experience, α is a constant, β is a positive coefficient, and γ is a negative coefficient.

In the above discussion, E_1 was interpreted as the earnings potential at the time of graduation from senior high school. In general, however, it can be considered as the earnings potential at any particular education stage, and this stage can be chosen freely in accordance with the purpose of the research.

Eq. 2.17 was originally derived to show the determinants of earnings by regression analysis (see Appendix B for the basic theory of regression analysis). In some studies, the right-hand side of Eq. 2.17 has other variables, e.g., variables for IQ, race, sex, residential area, to test the effects of these variables.

In such a regression analysis, E_1 is usually interpreted as potential earnings at the beginning of compulsory education, because s is the total number of years of school education. (It should be noted, however, that the research interest is not in this earnings potential but in the coefficient of each explanatory variable.) In such a case, ϱ stands for the average rate of return to all kinds of school education, since it is estimated on the assumption that all kinds of school education have the same rate of return. Of course, the rates of return to different kinds of school education are actually different. Therefore, the specification in Eq. 2.17 is only an approximation.

2.4.2 Measuring Rates of Return

What difference is there between internal rates of return computed on the basis of Eq. 2.4 and rates of return computed from Mincer's earnings function? To answer this question, we would like to compare them by actually computing each.

First we should make sure whether it is possible to measure the rate of return to higher education by directly applying Eq. 2.16. This equation was derived by assuming that no human capital accumulation is undertaken after graduation from school. Consequently, both the wage of the senior high-school graduate and that of the college graduate are constant at any time or age in this formula. Actual wage data reveal, however, that the wage differs across ages mainly because the wage changes in accordance with labor market experience. Thus we face the question of which wages we should use to compute the rate of return.

For this reason, we will devise a different method of computing the rate of return by slightly transforming Eq. 2.17. In order to compute the rate of return to higher education, we first divide the whole period of school education into two parts: the first s' years up to the time of graduation from senior high school and the remaining s years of higher education. Then, Eq. 2.17 can be transformed into the following:

$$\ln Y_t^U = (\ln E_1 + \alpha) + \varrho' s' + \varrho s + \beta x + \gamma x^2, \tag{2.18}$$

where ϱ' is the average rate of return to school education up to the time of graduation from senior high school, ϱ is the rate of return to higher education, and the labor market experience x is given by $x = t - s' - s$ since $t = 1$ is the year when school education starts. In Eq. 2.18 we have used the superscript U to denote the earnings Y_t^U of the college graduate in the t-th year. The earnings of the senior high-school graduate in the t-th year are denoted by Y_t^H. Because the high-school graduate worker did not receive higher education, his/her earnings function becomes the following:

$$\ln Y_t^H = (\ln E_1 + \alpha) + \varrho' s' + \beta x + \gamma x^2, \tag{2.19}$$

where $x = t - s'$.

In each of Eqs. 2.18 and 2.19, t implies the number of years that have passed since the start of compulsory education. Thus t corresponds to a particular age. If we choose ages such that $t = \tau$ for the college graduate and $t = \tau - s$ for the senior high-school graduate, the college and senior high-school graduates at these ages have the same number of years x of labor market experience. Hence, Eqs. 2.18 and 2.19 generate

$$\ln Y_\tau^U - \ln Y_{\tau-s}^H = \varrho s, \tag{2.20}$$

which in turn results in

$$\varrho = \frac{\ln Y_\tau^U - \ln Y_{\tau-s}^H}{s}$$
$$= \frac{1}{s}\ln\left(\frac{Y_\tau^U}{Y_{\tau-s}^H}\right). \tag{2.21}$$

This is the formula for measuring the rate of return to higher education on the basis of Mincer's earnings function.

This formula looks similar to Eq. 2.16, but differs from the latter in that it specifies the relationship between the ages at which wages are measured, though the value of τ is not specified. Put differently, the rate of return to higher education can be measured from the wage of the college graduate at a particular age and the wage of the senior high-school graduate four years younger, since $s = 4$ in Japan.

We would like to compare the approximate rate of return computed by this method with the internal rate of return computed on the basis of Eq. 2.4. Here we undertake this comparison using data for Japanese male workers. The computation procedure based on Eq. 2.4 will be discussed in more detail in Chap. 5, but two notes are relevant here. One is that investment costs include forgone earnings and tuition and fees and that all other minor costs are ignored. The other is that workers are assumed to work until 59 years old and to retire at this age.

In order to compute the approximate rate of return using Eq. 2.21, we need only have wage data classified by age and academic career. Such data are available from *Basic Survey of Wage Structures*, Ministry of Labor. This data gives average wages for each age group in five year groups above twenty years old from 1973. This facilitates computation of rates of return beyond what was previously possible. For comparison we use cross-sectional data for 1974, 1979, 1984, and 1989.

To apply Eq. 2.21, we need to know both the average annual earnings Y_τ^U of college graduates of a particular age group and the average annual earnings $Y_{\tau-4}^H$ of (senior) high-school graduates four years younger. Here, average annual earnings are computed by multiplying the average monthly earnings by twelve and adding average annual bonuses. Because the data give average wages for five-year age groupings, we cannot obtain directly both Y_τ^U and $Y_{\tau-4}^H$, but we can directly obtain Y_τ^U, Y_τ^H, and $Y_{\tau-5}^H$. Thus, we estimate $Y_{\tau-4}^H$ using the following formula: $Y_{\tau-4}^H = Y_{\tau-5}^H + (Y_\tau^H - Y_{\tau-5}^H)/5$. We should note that the method based on Eq. 2.21 cannot specify the value of τ, so we consider several alternative age groups for τ.

Table 2.2 shows rates of return computed in this way for six age groups of college graduates. The corresponding age groups of high-school graduates are four years younger than those in the Table. More precisely, the "Rate of return" in the Table is computed by the formula $[\ln(Y_\tau^U/Y_{\tau-4}^H)]/4$ on the basis of Eq. 2.21. On the other hand, the "Reference" shows what the rate of return would be if the wage data at the same age were used for college and high-school graduates, or if the following formula were used: $[\ln(Y_\tau^U/Y_\tau^H)]/4$, which may be an interpretation of Eq. 2.16. The internal rates of return computed on the basis of Eq. 2.4 are shown on the right of the calendar years as r^*.

Table 2.2. Estimation of rates of return to higher education by Mincer's earnings function (males).

(%)

Age group	1974 $r^* = 7.24$		1979 $r^* = 6.88$		1984 $r^* = 6.44$		1989 $r^* = 6.61$	
	Rate of return	Reference	Rate of return	Reference	Rate of return	Reference	Rate of return	Reference
25~29	6.05	1.74	6.13	0.84	6.03	1.38	7.06	2.86
30~34	8.12	3.72	7.19	3.51	7.36	3.26	7.83	4.33
35~39	8.84	6.64	8.62	5.42	8.20	5.50	8.69	5.54
40~44	9.52	8.13	9.76	8.42	9.63	6.82	9.40	7.20
45~49	11.76	11.02	11.31	10.48	10.55	9.94	10.88	8.73
50~54	11.85	10.61	12.75	12.94	11.40	11.44	11.07	11.38

Notes: r^* is computed from Eq. 2.4.
"Rate of return" is computed from $[\ln(Y_\tau^U/Y_{\tau-4}^H)]/4$.
"Reference" is computed from $[\ln(Y_\tau^U/Y_\tau^H)]/4$.

This Table shows that the rate of return computed approximately on the basis of Eq. 2.21 increases with the age used for computation. The difference between the lowest and highest rates of return amounts to four to seven percentage points in the Table. Therefore, this rate of return would be quite different depending on which age group's wage data is used for computation.

Let us now compare the results based on Eq. 2.4 with those based on Eq. 2.21. We find that the latter are likely to be close to the former when we use for computation the wages of college graduates of about thirty years of age (thus the wages of senior high-school graduates of about twenty-six years of age), though this latter equation still generates too high a rate of return in the case of 1989. It should be noted that this fact emerged empirically after computing rates of return on the basis of the two methods and comparing them, having not been previously known from theory. These observations demonstrate that rates of return computed on the basis of Mincer's earnings function are likely to be rather inaccurate.

The highest and lowest computation results shown in the columns of "Reference" differ by about ten percentage points. These are larger than the previous dispersions based on Eq. 2.21. Therefore, the results in the "Reference" columns are worse than those based on Eq. 2.21 not only from the principle of Mincer's earnings function but also from these empirical results.

It is obvious why rates of return measured on the basis of Mincer's earnings function become inaccurate. First, this method does not correctly measure investment costs, especially tuition and fees. (Hence, it cannot analyze how tuition and fees affect the rate of return.) In addition, this method uses wage data only at a particular age for each of the college and high-school graduates. This implies that it does not make use of much wage information though this is available. Moreover, this method lacks a theory which specifies the age for measuring the wage. (Of course, this problem of age specification will not arise when estimating Eq. 2.17 by regression on the assumption that s stands for the total number of years of school education. The rate of return ϱ estimated in this way is nothing but the average rate of return to all kinds of school education.)

In spite of these shortcomings, the approximation method based on Mincer's earnings function is extremely simple and has an advantage of not requiring many data or computer computation. Thus this approximation method may be useful when we know by experience which wage data to use.[28]

2.5 General Properties of Rates of Return

2.5.1 Development Stages and Rates of Return

The rates of return to (higher) education have been measured in many countries in the world. Psacharopoulos (1985) has a collection of measurement results for primary, secondary, and higher education in over sixty countries. From this we can find some general properties or tendencies the rates of return have.

We should, however, be cautious in attaching importance to one or two percentage point differences in returns across countries and points of time. This is because there may be differences in the methodology used to make the estimates (especially what adjustments have been made on the benefits side), and because many authors of the original studies do not always state explicitly the nature of the sample used (for example, urban, rural, national).

Table 2.3 shows the arithmetic means of the rates of return in the 1970s or 1980s to the three different types of education in different regions and development stages. It should be noted that rates of return to primary education cannot be measured in advanced countries because it is compulsory there (forgone earnings do not exist). For this reason, the corresponding cells in the table have NAs.

We can find the following global properties or tendencies in the Table. First of all, both social and private rates of return are quite high. In particular, those to primary and secondary education are high (see also Behrman and Birdsall (1987)). There are probably few cases in which such high rates of return realize to investments in physical capital such as factories, facilities, inventories, and infrastructures.

Secondly, rates of return tend to be lower for higher levels of education. This tendency is especially clear in the case of social rates of return. As for private rates of return, those to higher education tend to be higher than those to secondary education in developing countries, though all private rates of return to primary education are higher than those to secondary and higher education. The high rates of return

Table 2.3. Average returns to education by country type and level.

(%)

Region Country type	Social			Private		
	Primary	Secondary	Higher	Primary	Secondary	Higher
Africa	26	17	13	45	26	32
Asia	27	15	13	31	15	18
Latin America	26	18	16	32	23	23
Intermediate	13	10	8	17	13	13
Advanced	NA	11	9	NA	12	12

Note: NA = not available.
Source: Psacharopoulos (1985).

to primary education are due to the fact that the education costs are lower for primary than for secondary and higher education and literacy greatly increases productivity.

Thirdly, the rate of return to a particular level of education tends to be lower in developed countries than in developing countries. One of the factors generating this tendency is that as the economy develops, the average number of years of education increases and thus the scarcity of highly educated workers decreases. Jain (1991) notes, however, that the dispersion in the rates of return is large among developing countries. The rates of return in some developing countries are in fact similar to those in developed countries. Therefore, there are several factors influencing the levels of rates of return, and the relationship between the level of economic development and the levels of rates of return is not necessarily so simple.

Fourthly, private rates of return are higher than social rates of return. This is because large public subsidies are provided to school education. The discrepancy between private and social rates of return tends to be larger for less developed countries and for higher levels of education. Though the social rates of return decrease with the level of education in developing countries, the private rates of return to higher education are generally higher than those to secondary education because of large public subsidies to the former.

2.5.2 Changes in Rates of Return Over Time

There are also global tendencies in the changes over time in the rates of return. Table 2.4 shows these changes in social rates of return to the complete school education in nine countries, as collected by Psacharopoulos (1989). All the rates of return in the Table are estimated using Mincer's earnings function. This Table reveals that rates of return decline in most countries as their average years of schooling increase. It should be noted, however, that the effects of special factors in a particular year may have generated distortions, because the rates of return are estimated only in two points of time in all countries but the United States.

As we will see in Table 5.1 in Chap. 5, the internal rate of return to higher education in Japan also declined over time since the mid-1960s (see *B* in that Table). Therefore, the fifth global tendency in the rate of return is that it is likely to decline over time.

The declines, however, are moderate. The decline in the internal rate of return shown in Table 5.1 is also quite moderate in spite of a rapid increase in the percentage of students going to college. This economic phenomenon can be explained in the following way (Welch, 1970; Griliches, 1970).

Two factors are operating here, that is, the demand for and supply of college graduate workers. If more people go to college, the supply of workers with college education increases. (In Fig. A.1 in Appendix A, the labor supply curve *SS* or *S′S′* shifts to the right.) If the demand for workers with college education was fixed, this increase in supply would lower the wage for college educated workers.

In actuality, however, the demand for college educated workers, who have a high level of knowledge and skills, increases. (In Fig. A.1, the labor demand curve *DD* shifts to the right.) This increase in demand derives from changes in product composition and technological progress due to economic growth.

Table 2.4. Returns to investment in education over time.

Country	Year	Rate of return	Average years of schooling completed
Developing Countries			
Brazil	1970	16.5	3.9
	1980	14.5	5.7
Chile	1974	8.3	5.9
	1980	9.6	8.1
Colombia	1965	17.3	2.8
	1974	12.8	5.0
Venezuela	1975	13.7	4.6
	1984	11.2	6.6
Cyprus	1975	12.5	8.4
	1984	11.0	9.5
Industrial Countries			
Canada	1972	16.0	10.0
	1980	11.6	11.8
France	1962	16.3	9.4
	1977	15.4	11.4
United Kingdom	1972	9.7	10.5
	1975	8.0	10.5
United States	1950	7.1	9.7
	1960	10.5	10.6
	1970	8.4	12.1
	1980	6.4	12.5

Source: Psacharopoulos (1989).

To put it more precisely, as income increases, the composition of the products consumed tends to change, and those products whose shares increase are likely to be produced in industries which use college graduates relatively intensively. In addition, it is likely for some particular reasons that technological progress uses more high-skilled workers (college graduates) or that these workers are complementary to the new physical capital (machines, equipment, etc.) installed in response to technological progress. Moreover, the productivity of college graduates may increase over time as the quality of higher education improves. In other words, present college graduates may have higher ability (knowledge and skills) than those of the past. (This is especially true in engineering.)

Because of these factors, the wage for college graduates does not decline so much in comparison with the wage for less educated workers (because both supply and demand curves shift to the right in Fig. A.1, the new equilibrium wage is not much lower or even becomes higher in some cases), and thus the rate of return to higher education does not decline so rapidly. According to the result shown in Table 2.4 and Becker's (1964) estimate, rates of return to higher education and high-school education increased in the 1950s in the United States in spite of an increase in the number of highly educated workers.

The benefits of higher education did in fact begin to decline in the United States at the beginning of the 1970s, and the employment of professionals and managers did not increase much relative to the increase in the number of college graduates. Freeman (1975, 1976, 1977, 1980) points out that the incomes of college graduates decreased much since the beginning of the 1970s and that this tendency was especially prominent among young males.

More precisely, the real income of male college graduates decreased in 1974–75 in comparison with 1969, particularly among new college graduates. In contrast, the real income of high-school graduates of the same age increased.[29] Furthermore, it became increasingly difficult for college graduates to become professionals such as accountants and school teachers. The wage of female college graduates did not decrease much, but it became more difficult for them to become professionals as in the case of male college graduates.

It should be added that these empirical studies by Freeman ignore the difference in rates of unemployment between college and high-school graduates. In fact, as far as the unemployment rates of workers younger than twenty-four are concerned, the unemployment rate for college graduates was 6.4% in 1975 as compared with 16.1% for high-school graduates. Moreover, the income of new college graduates is not compared with that of new high-school graduates in those empirical studies (Levin, 1977).

Using 1969 and 1976 data, Rumberger (1980) estimated the benefits of college education by applying an earnings function similar to Mincer's to male workers with labor market experience of less than five years. According to his study, the economic position of male college graduates as measured by relative earnings did not deteriorate appreciably in this period, though the absolute occupational position of college graduates did worsen when occupational position is measured by the degree of utilization of educational skills.

Variations in the internal rate of return in the 1970s in the United States can be seen in Mattila (1982), as will be discussed in Chap. 5 (see Table 5.2). He shows that the internal rate of return in 1977 was just above 80% of that of 1969.[30]

Notes

1. The basic literature (or survey literature) which discusses various aspects of education investment from the viewpoint of the theory of human capital (as one of the viewpoints) includes Schultz (1963, 1971), Becker (1964, 1993), Mincer (1970, 1974), Blaug (1966, 1968, 1970, 1976), Cohn (1972), Psacharopoulos (1973), Rosen (1977), McMahon and Geske (1982), Freeman (1986), and Schultz (1988).
2. The monthly earnings include tax and various allowances such as commuting allowances, family allowances, and overtime allowances. This data is collected every June.
3. Amano (1995) points out that education has both "a visible curriculum" of classroom activities and "an invisible curriculum" of extracurricular activities which is important for personality development. He suggests that the age has come when we need to understand consciously these two curricula as important parts of education.
4. Welch (1970) indicates the following two effects of education. One is to increase the total output from given resources such as materials, time, and so on. The other is to enable the individual to devise an efficient combination or allocation of production inputs. He says that the latter effect is important to American farmers, because they have a high degree of discretion in the combination or allocation of inputs and this decision must be made continually. Nelson and Phelps (1966) emphasize that education eases adaptation to technologi-

cal change. According to Wozniak's (1987) empirical study on American farmers, education reduces the adoption cost of new technology and uncertainty about the outcome. The empirical study by Bartel and Lichtenberg (1987) on US manufacturing industries shows that the demand for highly educated workers is large in industries characterized by high rates of innovation, because those workers have a comparative advantage with respect to the adjustment to and implementation of new technologies. Schultz (1975) emphasizes that the acquisition of "allocative abilities" is an important purpose of education. Those who have allocative abilities can perceive, interpret correctly, and undertake action that will appropriately reallocate their resources in response to changes in economic conditions. In his empirical study on American farmers, Huffman (1977) shows that education actually has such a function. See also Ram (1980).

5. A few interesting findings apply here. Wise (1975) and Jones and Jackson (1990) show in their empirical studies that not only the academic background of college education but also academic records in college have a positive effect on individual earnings. (In economics, a wage is considered to represent individual productivity. See Appendix A.) Hansen, Weisbrod, and Scanlon (1970) have undertaken an empirical study on those who were rejected for military service in the United States. They estimate the relationship between individual earnings and scores in the Armed Forces Qualification Test, which covers word knowledge, arithmetic, mechanical understanding, and ability to distinguish forms and patterns. This study does not directly relate to higher education, but is still informative to some extent in the present context. It shows that the AFQT score was a more important determinant of earnings than years of schooling, though there is a positive correlation between the test scores and the years of schooling. This result implies that the knowledge and skills one actually possesses are more important determinants of earnings than the mere fact of spending time in school.

6. While a wage rate stands for the price of labor service per hour, earnings stands for the reward paid in a certain period of time such as a month or a year, and includes various allowances such as overtime pay, family allowances, bonuses, etc. What is often called wages in Japan are mostly earnings (Nakamura, 1981). In such a case, wages and earnings are substitutes. However, we usually say forgone earnings rather than forgone wages. Economic theory mainly uses the terms of a wage rate and a wage, the latter of which equals the former times the number of hours worked. When the work hours per period is fixed, there is only a difference in measurement between a wage rate and a wage, and thus the two are essentially the same. An income is the sum of earnings and non-labor incomes such as dividend and interest incomes. In empirical studies, family incomes of workers are often represented by family earnings.

7. The opportunity cost is defined as the benefit one loses when one does not use or forgoes an economic opportunity. If one owns land but does not use it, an opportunity cost will arise, because making it a parking lot will generate incomes. If one keeps in one's safe some money not for immediate use, an opportunity cost will arise again, because lending it to a bank will generate interest.

8. A competitive market is often (implicitly) assumed in discussions in economics. In a competitive labor market, an individual's wage (rate) equals his/her marginal value product (see Appendix A). Thus, the wage paid to an individual represents how much value he/she produces in the economy.

9. See Weisbrod (1962) for external economies of education. It should be noted, however, that he includes what cannot be called external economies in the rigorous sense of economics.

10. Ben-Porath derives similar properties by introducing a production function of human capital into his work life model which takes into consideration not only investment in school education but also investment in training on the job. Here, the production function of human capital for a particular individual means a function that relates the amount (hours) of his/her human capital service and the amount of purchased input (materials, teachers' service, etc.) used for production of human capital to the amount of human capital produced.

11. A fundamental proposition of economics is that the allocation of resources in the market will be optimal if each individual (economic agent) acts according to his/her own self-interest. The optimality concept used in this proposition is called Pareto optimality. An allocation of resources is Pareto optimal if an individual cannot be made better off without making another individual worse off. It should be added that this proposition holds only when a number of conditions are satisfied, one relevant condition being that there is no government. Another is that there are no external economies nor diseconomies. It may be possible, however, that the allocation of resources becomes optimal with some of these conditions not satisfied, if the government applies suitable policies.

12. See Chap. 3 of Suzuki (1989).

13. The average annual amount of tuition and fees for private universities was 977,840 yen in 1994 (Ministry of Education, *Abstract of Education Statistics*). Information about the Japanese yen exchange rate is available in Appendix C.

14. Very recently, a bank began to offer secured loans of up to thirty million yen with a repayment term of thirty years. (As we see in Chap. 4, one needs very large funds to go to medical or dental school in Japan.) All these types of loans may be only temporary responses to the recent monetary ease, but may also continue to exist in the future.

15. In the United States, there are a large number of dropouts and divisibility of education is actually utilized. In fact, college dropouts earn more than high-school graduates. Additional investment here means an increase in investment in education, e.g., of 10,000 yen or by a week. The marginal private rate of return should theoretically be computed from this incremental cost and the corresponding benefit. Because this is a theoretical argument, each kind of school education is supposed to be minutely divisible.

16. Moreover, Behrman, Pollak, and Taubman (1989) show that there is an inverse relationship between sibship size and sib schooling and earnings similarities. This is because intelligent children with large sibship size have easier access to financial aids and face especially low education costs. This tendency becomes weak if generous financial aids are offered equally as in the case of World War II veterans, who were eligible for educational benefits through the GI Bill.

17. See also Hansen (1963), Blaug (1965, 1970), Hines, Tweeten, and Redfern (1970) for how to measure internal rates of return.

18. According to Bailey and Schotta (1972), the private rate of return to graduate school education in general is less than one percent. One reason why some go to graduate school even at this low rate of return is that this education generates benefits in the form of future consumption. However, Figa-Talamanca (1974) and Tomaske (1974) are critical of this study.

19. Using another data set, he further considers the following three working conditions: whether or not a worker has discretion in increasing his/her work hours, whether or not a worker has discretion in decreasing his/her work hours, and the stability of income. The results obtained are similar to those in the text.

20. This estimation uses Mincer's earnings function, which will be discussed below. See also Scully (1979).

21. Haveman and Wolfe (1984) classify benefits of education into twenty categories including that of enhancing productivity on the job. They also allow that more education tends to generate costs such as divorce and work stress.

22. Weiss (1972) compares the variation coefficient of incomes of scientists with Ph.D. degrees with that of incomes of those with B.A. degrees and finds that the former is smaller. The variation coefficient is defined as the standard deviation divided by the mean.

23. Economics usually assumes that workers are risk-averse. This means that given a choice of receiving a wage of 10 million yen with a probability of 50% and a wage of 6 million yen with a probability of 50% on one hand, or a definite wage of 8 million yen, the mean of the previous option on the other hand, a risk-averse individual prefers the latter. Moreover, he/she prefers the state in which he/she will obtain a wage of 8.5 million yen with a probability of 50% and a wage of 7.5 million yen with a probability of 50% to the first random wage

above, though the means are the same. This implies that the first random wage must be evaluated by deducting a larger premium (risk premium) from the mean wage of 8 million yen. See Olson, White, and Shefrin (1979) for rates of return to higher education which take account of risks. Even after considering risks, the rates of return remain quite high, though this result depends on the assumptions used.

24. Other studies which show that the effect of IQ on incomes is small relative to the effect of school education include Ashenfelter and Mooney (1968), Hansen, Weisbrod, and Scanlon (1970), Hause (1972, 1975), Griliches and Mason (1972), Taubman and Wales (1973), de Wolfe and van Slijpe (1973), Griliches (1977), and Cohn and Kiker (1986).

25. According to the estimate by Willis and Rosen (1979), while a typical college graduate's rate of return to higher education equals 9.9%, the rate of return that a typical non-college graduate could achieve by graduating from college would be 9.3%.

26. Making use of US Navy data of warships and their crews, Horowitz and Sherman (1980) provide a rare empirical analysis of the relationship between human capital and realized productivity. It shows that those crews with high-school education and higher entry test scores tend to keep a ship in better operational condition. This tendency is especially prominent where technologically complex equipment is involved. (The level of maintenance of equipment will influence the "productivity" of the warship.)

27. This specification is used very frequently in empirical studies, but there are some criticisms. The empirical study by Murphy and Welch (1990) indicates that the specification by a quadratic function does not approximate well the relationship between experience and earnings.

28. There are many works that have examined Mincer's earnings function. Heckman and Polachek (1974) support Mincer's earnings function to some extent as the simplest functional form. Blinder (1976) clarifies the assumptions used to derive the earnings function which includes the effect of training on the job, and also considers alternative functional forms. Leibowitz's (1974b) empirical study based on US data indicates that the assumption of $k_i = 1$ will generate a bias. Lucas (1977b) points out that Mincer's earnings function is derived only by operating identities and that it has little to do with the market process. Light and Ureta (1995) emphasize that the conventional earnings function yields downward biased estimates of early-career wage growth, and propose a different earnings function with an array of variables that measure the fraction of time worked during each year of the career. Other works include Wallace and Ihnen (1975), Willis (1986), Lillard, Smith, and Welch (1986).

29. Freeman uses the active job market hypothesis to explain the fact that the influence of economic changes is especially prominent in the wages and employment of young workers. According to this hypothesis, older workers in the United States tend to be protected from the direct influence of economic changes by job security, customs, etc. (In other words, they are said to have jobs in internal labor markets.) Because of this, the influence of economic changes (an increase in the number of college graduates, for instance) concentrates among young workers.

30. In the United States, the rate of return to higher education increased again in the 1980s. Katz and Revenga (1989) insist that this results from the interplay of an increase in the demand for college graduates due to the changes in technology and product demand, a decline in the growth rate of the number of college graduates, macroeconomic factors (increased openness, trade deficits, and labor market slack), changes in institutional structures (the decline in unionization), and so on. See also Blackburn, Bloom, and Freeman (1990).

Chapter 3
College-Going Behavior as Signaling

There is a theory of college-going decision making which is quite different from human capital theory. This alternative theory is based on the idea that the role of a college degree is not to certify the knowledge and skills acquired in college, but simply to convey information to society about the degree holder's productivity. This productivity may be innate, or may have been acquired (at home) by the time of the start of college education. According to this theory, those who have high productive capabilities go to college so that firms can identify degree holders (or highly educated people) as more productive and pay them more. Here, college education does not enhance the productivity of the students, but only plays a role of judging how productive each individual originally is. This role of education has been called signaling, screening, filtering, or sorting, by different authors (in slightly different problem settings). This "signaling" theory is very powerful and competes with human capital theory to explain college-going behavior.

In Sects. 3.1 and 3.2, we will examine in detail the well-known signaling model by Spence which was one of the most important theories generated in the 1970s. Its influence can still be seen today in game theory. We will also examine in Sect. 3.5 the filtering model by Arrow and Burdett and in Sect. 3.6 the Riley model which combines the signaling and human capital theories.

As in the present value and internal-rate-of-return methods discussed in the previous chapter, it is immaterial in the signaling or filtering models whether or not an individual has his/her own funds for investment in college education. In other words, these models all assume capital market perfection. As stated in the previous chapter, however, capital markets are imperfect in most real economies and thus whether or not the individual has his/her own funds is a very important factor in college-going decision making. For this reason, we will develop in Sect. 3.3 signaling models which consider capital market imperfections. Sect. 3.4 will discuss statistical discrimination which is closely related to signaling.

3.1
Preliminary Considerations

3.1.1
Basic Questions

It is not difficult to understand the basis of the idea that higher education does not enhance the students' productivity but conveys information to society about their productivity. We can therefore begin with intuitive considerations.

Many people probably believe that college graduates work more productively in firms than non-college graduates. This difference in productivity, however, may not be due to their college education as they may in fact have been more productive before they were admitted to college. Nevertheless, people in society may believe that college graduates are more productive because they actually graduated from college. Put differently, an individual who is as productive as college graduates but does not have a college degree may not be regarded by society as equally productive. For this reason, those who are more productive may decide to go to college in order to inform society of their high productivity. This is the essence of the signaling model by Spence (1973), which will be discussed first.

To discuss Spence's model more specifically, consider the case where a firm is planning to hire new workers. Suppose that job applicants are not identical in the sense of economics and thus that their productive abilities are dispersed. It is assumed that each applicant knows his/her own ability but the firm does not know it. It is assumed further that even after hiring, it takes a long time for individuals' real capabilities to become apparent or that it is too costly to identify their real capabilities in a short period of time. When there is this kind of difference in the amount of information possessed by labor suppliers (workers) and demanders (firms), we say that there is information asymmetry.

When there is information asymmetry and the firm has difficulty identifying the ability of each job applicant, the firm may estimate it on the basis of the applicants' personal characteristics which are directly observable and are considered to provide indirect but relevant information. Such characteristics include education levels, job history, race, sex, and age. As explained above, the firm is likely to regard the productivity of a college graduate as higher than that of a high-school graduate. The productivity of an individual of a particular ethnic group may be considered to be generally high. In this sense, some observable characteristics can be considered to contain information about the job applicant's productivity.

Spence (1973) classifies such characteristics into two categories. The first category includes education levels and job history, which are alterable and thus are under individual control. The second category includes race, sex, and age, which are not alterable. He called the first category of characteristics signals and the second indexes. Of course, there may be personal characteristics which are difficult to classify into either of these two categories.

In the following, we will first examine the basic signaling model by Spence (1973, 1974a) and consider how the education signal conveys information to the firm about the job applicant's productive capability. This consideration will show how an individual makes a decision to invest in higher education to signal his/her ability. The reason we discuss the Spence model first is that it is quite simple as an economic theory and at the same time it is best known as a signaling model.

3.1.2 Assumptions

We consider here an economy which has only one firm and many job applicants with varying productive capabilities. It is assumed that there is information asymmetry in this economy. Thus the firm will know the productivity of each of its workers only after a sufficiently long period of time has passed after hiring. It is essentially difficult to identify an individual's productive capability in a short period of time. In addition, it takes time for an individual to become used to a job or to undergo specific training before he/she can handle certain kinds of jobs.

In order to simplify discussion, it is assumed that the lifetime wage of each worker is determined at the time of hiring. This is a rather extreme assumption, but it is likely in the real economy (especially in Japan) that firms offer at the time of hiring predetermined wages which apply for the initial several years. (In order to make analysis simple and clear, economics often introduces extreme assumptions which enable us to focus on the essence of the problem under consideration.) The firm pays each of its workers a wage in proportion to his/her expected productivity. Namely, if worker A is considered to be twice as productive as worker B, the former will be paid twice as much as the latter.

The firm is assumed to believe that a college graduate is more productive than a non-college graduate. In this case, job applicants who can graduate from college at low cost may decide to go to college. (The costs of higher education here include not only pecuniary costs but also mental and time costs of study.) This is because they will be able to receive higher wages by going to college and informing the firm of their high productivity. This can be considered a signaling activity, in which individuals signal their productivity using academic careers. It should be noted that those who decide to go to college are not necessarily aware that they are signaling their productivity. They may go to college simply because they can earn high wages in comparison with their costs of college education.

The fundamental difference between the theory of signaling and that of human capital is that in the former individuals have incentives to go to college even if college education does not enhance their productivity (knowledge or skills) at all, while in the latter college education is assumed to have a productivity-enhancing effect as we saw in the previous chapter.[1] In the following Spence model, higher education is assumed not to enhance productivity at all.

The costs of college education can be called signaling costs, since they are the costs of signaling. As stated above, signaling theory emphasizes mental and time costs in addition to pecuniary costs of education.[2] This is because it is crucial in the Spence model that education costs differ across individuals, as explained in detail below.

There is usually very little difference in tuition and fees of higher education among individuals (going to the same institution), but there are actually large differences in mental and time costs. Some may be able to graduate at low mental cost, whereas others may have to spend much more time studying to obtain necessary credits. The very high costs of preparing for college entrance examinations borne by Japanese high-school students are not actually costs of high-school education but can be regarded as costs of higher education. Within these costs, the portion of time and especially mental costs is quite large and so these costs would vary greatly among individuals.

Concerning this difference in the costs of higher education among individuals, the Spence signaling model introduces the following critical assumption; that an individual's costs of higher education or signaling are negatively correlated with his/her productive capability. This means that those who have high capabilities can obtain necessary credits and graduate from college at low cost, whereas those who have low capabilities can graduate only at high cost.

Implicit in this assumption is the idea that there is a similarity between studying in college (or for college entrance examinations) and engaging in production in a firm. In other words, the Spence model incorporates the idea that studying in college to obtain necessary credits is similar to working in a firm to produce as much output as possible. Those who can obtain a college degree at lower cost are considered to produce more output in a firm in a given period of time. If there was no difference in the costs of higher education among individuals even though there is a difference in their productive capabilities, higher education would not be able to distinguish those with high capabilities from those with low capabilities, and thus signaling using higher education would not function.

As stated before, the firm has subjective beliefs about the relationship between a job applicant's academic career and his/her productivity, namely, that a college graduate has a higher level of productivity than a non-college graduate. We may assume for simplicity that each of these levels can be measured without uncertainty. But we may assume as well that there is a dispersion in the productive capabilities among those of the same academic background and that each of the above levels of productivity indicates the respective mean of the dispersion.[3]

In accordance with the above beliefs, the firm promises to pay a college graduate a high wage and a non-college graduate a low wage. Each of these wages equals the (expected) marginal value product of each type of worker. Each job applicant knows this wage scheme and makes a decision about signaling or investment in higher education by comparing his/her own signaling costs with these wages.

To rephrase, the firm distinguishes job applicants on the basis of their education signals and pays them differently. Over a sufficiently long period of time, the firm will learn about the actual productive capabilities of the workers it has hired. If the productivity of the workers corresponding to each level of education is as anticipated, the firm will not alter its beliefs. If not, the initial beliefs will be altered into new beliefs. If the initial beliefs are not altered, the labor market under consideration can be considered to be in an equilibrium. This is called a signaling equilibrium.

3.2 The Spence Model

3.2.1 Derivation of the Signaling Equilibrium

The model can be illustrated using elementary mathematics. All job applicants work for the above firm and are assumed to be classified into either of two groups, GI and GII. The productivity of each member of GI is assumed to equal 1 and that of each member of GII to equal 2.[4] Let q denote the proportion of GI members among the job applicants ($0 < q < 1$). Then, the proportion of GII members equals $1 - q$.

All job applicants are assumed to be able to signal their productive capabilities by investing in higher education. The amount of investment in higher education is measured by a composite index of years and performance, denoted by y ($y \geqq 0$).

Table 3.1. Data of the signaling problem.

Group	Marginal product	Proportion of population	Cost of education level y
GI	1	q	y
GII	2	$1 - q$	$y/2$

A high level of y corresponds to many years of higher education and/or much knowledge acquired in college.

As emphasized above, education costs include not only pecuniary but also mental and time costs. It is assumed that the costs of an education level y for a GI individual are exactly y, while the costs of y for a GII individual are $y/2$. For instance, the costs of y years of higher education for a GI member are y million yen, whereas those for a GII member are $y/2$ million yen. By the critical assumption discussed above, investment costs for each of the more productive individuals are lower and here are exactly half the costs for each of the less productive individuals. (It is assumed in this model that the costs of higher education, productivity, and the wages which will be discussed below are all discounted to present values at the time of college-going decision making so that they can all be directly compared.) These numerical assumptions are summarized in Table 3.1.

As to the firm's beliefs, the following assumption is used: there is an education level $y^* > 0$ such that the firm believes that if $y < y^*$, then productivity is 1 with probability one, and that if $y \geqq y^*$, then productivity is 2 with probability one. An interpretation of y^* is that it is a particular number of years of higher education. Another is that it is a particular number of credits to be taken in college. Under these beliefs, the wage schedule the firm offers looks like *ABDE* in Fig. 3.1. More precisely, the firm pays each worker with a level of education $0 \leqq y < y^*$ a wage equal to 1, because it believes that his/her productivity equals 1. On the other hand, it pays each worker with a level of education $y \geqq y^*$ a wage equal to 2.[5]

Being aware of the wage schedule in Fig. 3.1, each job applicant decides how much to invest in higher education. If an individual chooses a level of y that satisfies the condition $0 \leqq y < y^*$, then he/she must choose $y = 0$ (or not to go to college), because education is costly and the wage for $0 \leqq y < y^*$ is the same as that for $y = 0$. Similarly, an individual who chooses a level of y that satisfies the condition $y \geqq y^*$ must choose $y = y^*$. Therefore, each individual chooses either $y = 0$ or $y = y^*$. In other words, each job applicant chooses either not go to college or to go to college and graduate at the minimum cost.

In order for the above beliefs of the firm to be confirmed later, all GI members must choose $y = 0$ and all GII members $y = y^*$. This is because the productivity of each member of GI is 1 and that of each member of GII is 2. Is there some level of y^* that gives rise to a signaling equilibrium? In other words, what level of y^* will induce GI and GII members to choose voluntarily $y = 0$ and $y = y^*$, respectively? We will explore this problem below.

Fig. 3.1 also depicts the cost schedules facing GI and GII. C_1 is the cost schedule for each member of GI and its slope equals 1 as assumed in Table 3.1 and elsewhere. On

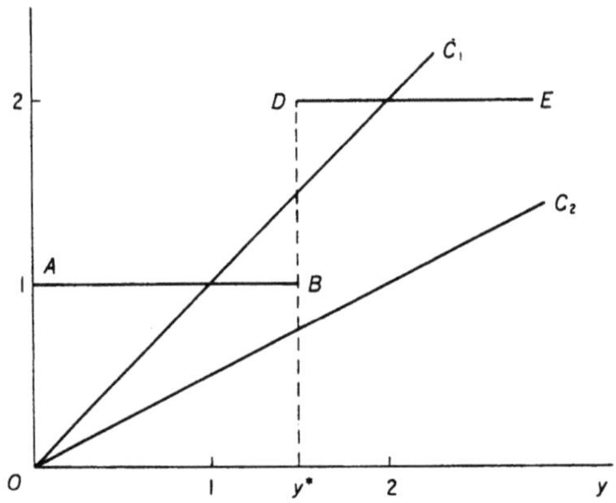

Fig. 3.1. Signaling Equilibrium

the other hand, C_2 is the cost schedule for each member of GII and its slope equals 1/2. Here, each individual chooses the level of y that maximizes the difference between wage and education cost. In other words, each chooses the level of y that maximizes the vertical distance between the wage and cost schedules in Fig. 3.1. This decision making is exactly the same as that in human capital theory in the sense that both are based on a comparison of the costs and benefits of education. The difference exists only in the role of higher education. In human capital theory the role of higher education is to enhance productivity of students, whereas in the signaling theory it is to inform society of students' productive capabilities which are innate or acquired prior to college admission.

If y^* is located as in Fig. 3.1, every member of GI chooses $y = 0$ whereas every member of GII chooses $y = y^*$. That is, those with low productive capabilities do not go to college and those with high productive capabilities do go to college. This is because the distance between the wage and cost schedules is maximized at $y = 0$ for GI members and at $y = y^*$ for GII members. Therefore, if y^* is located as in Fig. 3.1, the firm will confirm its beliefs and a signaling equilibrium will result.

Strictly speaking, what is the condition for y^* that gives rise to a signaling equilibrium? The condition for each GI member to choose $y = 0$ is given by

$$1 > 2 - y^*. \tag{3.1}$$

The left-hand side of this inequality equals the wage 1 minus the education cost 0 in the case where a GI member chooses $y = 0$, whereas the right-hand side equals the wage 2 minus the education cost y^* in the case where he/she chooses $y = y^*$. Since each individual chooses either $y = 0$ or $y = y^*$ as stated above, each GI member chooses $y = 0$ if the left-hand side is larger than the right-hand side of Eq. 3.1.

On the other hand, the condition for each GII member to choose $y = y^*$ is given by

$$2 - y^*/2 > 1. \tag{3.2}$$

The left-hand side of this inequality equals the wage 2 minus the education cost $y^*/2$ in the case where a GII member chooses $y = y^*$, whereas the right-hand side equals the wage 1 minus the education cost 0 in the case where he/she chooses $y = 0$. Each GII member chooses $y = y^*$ if the left-hand side is larger than the right-hand side.

Inequalities 3.1 and 3.2 together generate the following:

$$1 < y^* < 2. \tag{3.3}$$

If y^* is set to satisfy (3.3), then all GI members will choose $y = 0$ and all GII members $y = y^*$, and therefore the firm's initial beliefs will be confirmed. In other words, if y^* is between 1 and 2, a signaling equilibrium will arise. Because any level of y^* that satisfies (3.3) will give rise to a signaling equilibrium, there are an infinite number of signaling equilibria corresponding to different levels of y^*. In any of these equilibria, the firm can correctly predict a job applicant's (expected) productivity from his/her educational background.

3.2.2 Properties of the Signaling Equilibrium

We will use the term "payoff" for the value of the wage minus the education cost. Then, in the signaling equilibrium, the payoff of each GI member equals 1 and that of each GII member equals $2 - y^*/2$. We see from this that the payoff for each GII member, which is a function of y^*, will differ for different equilibria corresponding to different levels of y^*. That is, the payoff for each GII member will decrease if the level of y^* increases, though the payoff for each GI member will remain the same. A comparison of these different equilibria shows that the closer to 1 the level of y^* (> 1), the higher the welfare of the economy. This is because although a higher level of y^* requires larger costs of college education on the part of GII (or in society as a whole), college education itself does not enhance the productivity of GII members (or of society) at all.

Let us consider here how the existence of the signal of higher education affects the payoff for each group. If there was no higher education in this economy, the firm would not be able to distinguish the job applicants' productive capabilities and thus would pay each the same wage which would equal the average productivity, i.e.,

$$1 \times q + 2 \times (1 - q) = 2 - q. \tag{3.4}$$

Since q is between 0 and 1, $2 - q$ is larger than 1 or the payoff of each GI member. Therefore, if higher education does exist and distinguishes workers, GI workers will necessarily be disadvantaged. If there were no higher education in this economy the firm would not be able to tell which workers are more productive, and thus it would pay the same wage to each worker. This means that those with low productive capabilities would be subsidized by those with high capabilities.

It may seem that the existence of higher education enables GII members to be distinguished from GI members and brings benefits unconditionally to the former, but this is not true. Let $q \leqq 0.5$. Then, because $y^* > 1$ in any equilibrium, the payoff of $2 - y^*/2$ to each GII member is less than the average wage $2 - q$ in the case where higher education did not exist. As q stands for the proportion of GI workers among all workers, the condition that $q \leqq 0.5$ means that GII is the majority. When GII is the majority, the existence of higher education as a producer of signals disadvantages not only GI workers but also GII workers.

If $q > 0.5$, or if GII is the minority, a level of y^* exists which makes all GII members better off in a signaling equilibrium than in the case where there is no higher education. Such a level of y^* can be obtained from the condition $1 < y^* < 2q$, which derives from $2 - y^*/2 > 2 - q$ and condition (3.3).

So far we have discussed the basic signaling model by Spence. We will now clarify important properties of the signaling equilibrium. First, as mentioned before, neither job applicants nor the firm may be aware that higher education plays the role of signaling, although some may be aware of it. GII members may invest in higher education simply because the net benefit is large. The firm, on the other hand, may believe that college graduates are more productive simply because college education enhances productivity, as in human capital theory.

Secondly, the content of higher education is almost immaterial in the signaling model. To the extent that costs of higher education are negatively correlated with the individual's productive capability, the signaling role can be played by any field of education such as management, mathematics, or ancient Greek.

Thirdly, higher education has no social returns in the signaling model. Since education is assumed not to enhance productivity, the total output of the GI and GII members is constant whether all choose $y = 0$ or some choose $y > 0$. From the standpoint of society as a whole, investment in higher education is nothing but a waste of resources. Therefore, the signaling equilibrium in which some choose $y > 0$ is not Pareto optimal. According to this signaling model, higher education merely distinguishes workers and determines how the pie is distributed among them. This property has profound meaning.

The real economy may have other types of signals revealing worker productive capabilities. Examples can be found in the intensity of training and that of work within firms. Some workers may participate in hard training to signal their higher capabilities. Others may join a team that works intensively for the same purpose. Such workers are likely to exert excessive (above optimal) effort in order to reveal differences. These are examples of the rat race as analyzed by Akerlof (1976).

As a theory of investment in college education, the signaling model is quite different from the human capital model. Hence, one may naturally ask which is correct or which is better. A natural answer is that both models are correct and higher education has both signaling and productivity-enhancing functions. As a matter of fact, even among those who develop signaling models there are few who believe that higher education does not enhance the productive capabilities of students at all. Similarly, even those who analyze education investments from the viewpoint of human capital theory may not completely ignore the signaling function of higher education.

It is in fact possible to combine these two competing theories and build a unified model, as will be shown in Sect. 3.6 of this chapter. However, many may ask which theory is relatively more applicable to reality. In other words, they may wonder which is more predominant in higher education, the signaling function or the productivity-enhancing function. This is a question to be answered by empirical studies. We will examine several empirical results in Chap. 7.

3.3 Signaling Equilibria under Capital Market Imperfection

3.3.1 Parents' Wealth and Signaling Costs

According to the above Spence model, those who hold degrees are initially more productive than those who do not, and have invested in higher education to signal their high productivity. Most people, especially those in developing countries, will not agree with this conclusion because they know that there are many who are sufficiently intelligent but cannot go to college while there are others who are not so intelligent but still go to college.

The basic reason the Spence model cannot convince these people is that it assumes those with the same productive capabilities or intelligence face the same signaling costs. There are, however, many cases in which this assumption does not hold. For instance, those who live near a college face lower signaling costs. Similarly, those who have highly educated parents can easily obtain useful advice about study and reduce their signaling costs as well.

Because of capital market imperfections, moreover, parents' wealth or income decisively affects the signaling costs of their children. Those with poor parents face comparatively higher signaling costs. As they cannot borrow in the capital market to invest in education, they would have to find part-time work to pay for their education. This makes their signaling costs very high. (The earnings from part-time work are generally not enough to pay education costs in full.) Even if borrowing is possible, signaling costs will still be high as the borrowing interest rate is high owing to capital market imperfections, as we saw in Chap. 2. Thus, productive or intelligent individuals with poor parents have difficulty signaling their productivity.

In contrast, those with rich parents face comparatively low signaling costs as they do not have to rely on the capital market to pay their investment costs. (The opportunity cost of their investment in higher education is the lending interest rate, which is lower than the borrowing interest rate.) In the current situation in Japan, those with wealthy parents can purchase efficient preparation services for entrance examinations from private schools and cram schools (*juku*), thus lowering their signaling costs.[6]

If the capital market is perfect, the affluence of parents will not affect signaling costs: Productive or intelligent individuals will be able to signal this either by using their parents' funds or by borrowing in the capital market. They will all be able to go to college at the same opportunity cost of capital. Therefore, the Spence model implicitly assumes perfection of the capital market: that is, it assumes that all individuals can raise investment funds for education under the same conditions. It further assumes that there are no essential differences among individuals in their location and in their parents' stock of knowledge.

This section derives signaling equilibria in simple models assuming capital market imperfection. This assumption is more realistic especially in developing countries. What this section emphasizes is that the meanings of the signaling equilibria are very different from those of the Spence model, in other words education signals have quite different meanings in different situations. Specifically, it will be argued that a college

Table 3.2. Data for the job applicants.

Group	Productivity	Proportion	Signaling costs
G11	1	q_{11}	$(m_1 + p_1)\, y = y$
G12	1	q_{12}	$(m_1 + p_2)\, y = y/c$
G21	2	q_{21}	$(m_2 + p_1)\, y = y/c'$
G22	2	q_{22}	$(m_2 + p_2)\, y = y/2$

degree is used to signal the affluence of a job applicant's family and worker traits related to affluence. In fact, it plays a role similar to that of the potlatch in anthropology or conspicuous consumption described by Veblen.[7]

We now specify the contents of signaling costs under capital market imperfection. Suppose the signaling costs of an individual have two parts. The first is the mental (psychological) and time cost or cost of forgone leisure, which depends on the intelligence or productivity of an individual. It is lower for an intelligent individual in that he/she can obtain required credits with less effort or time. This assumption is the samè as that in the basic Spence model.

The second part is pecuniary cost (tuition, fees, and forgone earnings) and depends on an individual's social background. It is lower for a person from a rich family because he/she can use his/her parents' wealth to cover this cost. In contrast, a person from a poor family would have to cover this cost mostly by part-time work or borrowing at a high interest rate because of capital market imperfection.

We consider here four groups of job applicants: G11, G12, G21, and G22. It is assumed that the members of G21 and G22 are intelligent or productive and those of G11 and G12 are not. Therefore, we assign to each member of G21 and G22 the level of productivity 2, and to each member of G11 and G12 the level of productivity 1. The members of G12 and G22 are from rich families and those of G11 and G21 are from poor families. Thus, i in Gij is for intelligence or productivity and j is for social background. The proportion of the members of Gij among all job applicants is denoted by $q_{ij} > 0$, where $i, j = 1, 2$ and $q_{11} + q_{12} + q_{21} + q_{22} = 1$.

Let y denote a level of higher education and let $(m_i + p_j)y$ be the signaling costs for a Gij member to acquire y, where $m_i y$ is the mental and time cost and $p_j y$ is the pecuniary cost. By the above assumption $m_1 > m_2$ and $p_1 > p_2$. For simplicity, let $m_1 + p_1 = 1$, $m_1 + p_2 = 1/c$, $m_2 + p_1 = 1/c'$, and $m_2 + p_2 = 1/2$, where c and c' are real numbers between 1 and 2. These data are shown in Table 3.2.

If the mental and time cost dominates the pecuniary cost in the sense that

$$m_1 - m_2 > p_1 - p_2, \tag{3.5}$$

the signaling costs for a G12 member are higher than those for a G21 member, since $m_1 + p_2 > m_2 + p_1$ or $c < c'$. In this case, all intelligent job applicants face lower signaling costs and therefore a signaling equilibrium similar to that we discussed in the previous section may arise. In such an equilibrium, all G21 and G22 members obtain degrees while no member of G11 and G12 does.

In contrast, if the pecuniary cost dominates so that

$$m_1 - m_2 < p_1 - p_2, \tag{3.6}$$

the signaling costs for a G21 member are higher than those for a G12 member ($c > c'$), though the productivity of the former is higher. It is in this case that a signaling equilibrium different from that in the previous section may arise. In the following we will consider this second case, in which all G21 members are regarded as unproductive because they do not have degrees, although they are actually productive. By comparison, all G12 members are regarded as productive because they have degrees, although they are, in fact, unproductive.

3.3.2 Signaling Wealthiness

When $c > c'$, it is possible that no individual with poor parents will go to college and all individuals with rich parents will. Then the firm may regard all members of G11 and G21 as unproductive and pay them low wages. On the other hand, all members of G12 and G22 may be regarded as productive and paid high wages.

In order to understand this, we first calculate the average productivity of individuals from poor families. As the proportion of the members of G11 in the class of G11 and G21 equals $q_{11}/(q_{11} + q_{21})$ and that of the members G21 equals $q_{21}/(q_{11} + q_{21})$, the average productivity of the poor is equal to:

$$1 \times \frac{q_{11}}{q_{11} + q_{21}} + 2 \times \frac{q_{21}}{q_{11} + q_{21}} = 1 + Q_{21}, \tag{3.7}$$

where $Q_{21} = q_{21}/(q_{11} + q_{21})$. Next, the average productivity of the rich can be calculated similarly as follows:

$$1 \times \frac{q_{12}}{q_{12} + q_{22}} + 2 \times \frac{q_{22}}{q_{12} + q_{22}} = 1 + Q_{22}, \tag{3.8}$$

where $Q_{22} = q_{22}/(q_{12} + q_{22})$.

The condition that all the rich go to college and all the poor will not requires the firm to regard the average productivity of the former as greater than that of the latter, i.e.,

$$Q_{21} < Q_{22}. \tag{3.9}$$

This inequality implies that the proportion of productive individuals among the rich is comparatively larger than among the poor. We assume here that Eq. 3.9 actually holds. The meaning of this assumption in the real world will be discussed later.

Suppose a job applicant with a level of education $y \geqq y^{**}$ has a degree. As in the model in the previous section, the firm believes that the productivity of an applicant with a degree is $1 + Q_{22}$ and that of an applicant without a degree is $1 + Q_{21}$. Each individual will be paid a wage according to these beliefs. In order for these beliefs to be confirmed, the poor must choose $y = 0$ and the rich $y = y^{**}$.

Because the signaling costs for G11 are higher than those for G21, each member of G11 chooses $y = 0$ if each of G21 does the same. Thus, the condition for each poor individual to choose $y = 0$ is that

$$1 + Q_{21} > 1 + Q_{22} - y^{**}/c', \tag{3.10}$$

where the left-hand side equals the wage paid to a G21 member when he/she has chosen $y = 0$, while the right-hand side equals the wage minus the signaling cost when he/she has chosen $y = y^{**}$. The following inequality can be derived from (3.10):

$$c'(Q_{22} - Q_{21}) < y^{**}. \tag{3.11}$$

Because the signaling costs for G22 are lower than those for G12, each member of G22 chooses $y = y^{**}$ if each of G12 does so. Thus, the condition for each rich individual to choose $y = y^{**}$ is expressed as

$$1 + Q_{22} - y^{**}/c > 1 + Q_{21}, \tag{3.12}$$

where the left- and right-hand sides can be understood as being similar to (3.10). From (3.12) the following inequality can be obtained:

$$y^{**} < c(Q_{22} - Q_{21}). \tag{3.13}$$

Eqs. 3.11 and 3.13 together imply that the firm's initial beliefs are confirmed if y^{**} satisfies the following:

$$c'(Q_{22} - Q_{21}) < y^{**} < c(Q_{22} - Q_{21}). \tag{3.14}$$

This is the condition for the existence of a signaling equilibrium in this model. In this equilibrium, no poor individual will go to college and all rich individuals will obtain degrees.

Hence, the class of job applicants who do not have degrees contains productive people (G21). These productive people do not have degrees because they face high signaling costs owing to capital market imperfection. Their wage, which equals $1 + Q_{21}$, is lower than their productivity, which equals 2. They are thus subsidizing the G11 members, each of whom receives $1 + Q_{21}$ as a wage though their productivity equals 1. This arises because the firm cannot distinguish members of G21 from those of G11. On the other hand, the class of applicants who have degrees contains unproductive people (G12), who face low signaling costs as their parents are wealthy. Each of these unproductive people is subsidized by G22 members.[8]

In this signaling equilibrium, the firm does not believe that a job applicant has (does not have) a degree because his/her productivity is high (low). In fact, it knows that one goes (does not go) to college regardless of one's level of productivity if one's parents are (are not) wealthy. It is true that those who have degrees are more productive on average than those who do not have degrees in this model. Low productivity, however, does not inhibit one from going to college whereas poverty does. In other words, one will (will not) go to college with certainty if one's parents are wealthy (poor). As a matter of fact, in this model the difference in productivity does not give rise to significant difference in signaling costs. Even if intelligent or productive, a poor individual will not be able to obtain a degree by studying with less effort, because the pecuniary cost is too high.

In contrast, Spence's (1974a, Chap. 6) modified model considers three different groups of individuals: the productive and rich, the productive and poor, and the unproductive. It assumes that only those in the first group face low signaling costs and that all others face equally high signaling costs. In this equilibrium, only the former obtain degrees and the latter do not. (Thus, the productivity of those who obtain degrees is again larger than the average productivity of those who do not). Because low productivity and poverty affect signaling decisions exactly equally or symmetrically, this model specification does not clearly reveal the role of affluence of parents in college-going behavior. This might be a partial reason for Spence (1974a) allowing that the basic pattern of the signaling equilibrium in the modified model is much like the one observed in the initial Spence (1973) model. Since the affluence of parents plays a more critical role in signaling decisions in the model we have discussed than in the modified model by Spence, the meaning of this role will become clearer below.

The inequality in (3.9) was crucial in the above derivation of the signaling equilibrium. It corresponds to Spence's (1973) basic assumption that productivity and signaling costs are negatively correlated. Under (3.9), the firm believes that those from rich families are on average more productive than those from poor families, and it uses the education signal to judge from which type of family a job applicant comes. These beliefs are easily formed in the real world. First, people are likely to interpret the affluence of a family as due to the ability of the head of that family. In addition, they tend to believe that its children inherit that ability biologically and/or sociologically. Second, there are countless sociological studies demonstrating that students from rich families are in fact likely to achieve higher academic performance (in compulsory education).

3.3.3 Signaling Worker Traits

The equilibrium obtained above showed that there are some productive individuals who cannot signal their high ability because of capital market imperfection. We consider here a different situation in which capital market imperfections will be used to distinguish the productive job applicant from the unproductive.

In some white-collar jobs, advanced knowledge learned in college is virtually useless. What is much more useful is a worker's desirable habits of good behavior and thinking, good manners, and genial or polished personality. Typical examples of these jobs have been found in the financial sector (of a developing country). These traits tend to be held mainly by those from rich families. Such traits lead to high productivity, firstly because managers also have these traits and organizational efficiency is high when workers have similar values and manners (Arai, 1997b), and secondly because business partners and customers want workers to have these traits.

It is usually hard to judge at the time of hiring whether a job applicant has the above desirable habits. Even his/her manners and personality cannot be assessed completely. In this situation, holding of a degree is used to determine whether he/she is from a rich family. Therefore, those from rich families invest in higher education to signal that they have the desirable traits. This investment mechanism is different from that above in that those from rich families are actually more productive in these jobs than those from poor families. In the previous model, those from rich families exhibited only on average the desirable trait of high productivity.

This mechanism can be easily modeled. It is assumed as before that the members of G21 and G22 are intelligent and those of G11 and G12 are not, in the sense that the former can obtain required credits with less effort or time than the latter. However, intelligence does not imply high productivity here. In contrast with the previous model, the members of G12 and G22 are assumed to be more productive than those of G11 and G21 because the former have the desirable worker traits. More specifically, the productivity of each individual of the former class is assumed to equal 2 and that of each of the latter class to equal 1. There are no other differences between this model and the previous one.

We consider here the signaling equilibrium which separates G12 and G22 from G11 and G21. The firm is assumed to believe that the productivity of those who have degrees equals 2 and that of the others equals 1, and to pay wages according to these beliefs. (We may assume that degree holders are assigned to different jobs from those who do not hold degrees.) As the signaling costs for G11 are higher than those for G21, the former group of individuals do not go to college if the latter do not. Similarly, as the signaling costs for G22 are lower than those for G12, the former group of individuals go to college if the latter do. In order for this equilibrium to arise, Eq. 3.6 (or $c' < c$) is again necessary.

The desired equilibrium can be easily obtained. Suppose that only those with $y \geqq y^{\#}$ have degrees. In order for each of G21 to choose $y = 0$, the following inequality must hold:

$$1 > 2 - (m_2 + p_1)y^{\#} = 2 - y^{\#}/c'. \tag{3.15}$$

On the other hand, each of G12 chooses $y = y^{\#}$ if

$$1 < 2 - (m_1 + p_2)y^{\#} = 2 - y^{\#}/c. \tag{3.16}$$

These inequalities imply that if $y^{\#}$ is set so that

$$c' < y^{\#} < c, \tag{3.17}$$

then the desired signaling equilibrium will arise.

In this equilibrium, individuals from rich families can signal their desirable traits by investing in college education, simply because the capital market is imperfect. This imperfection prevents intelligent but poor individuals from obtaining degrees and allows rich people to enjoy high wages. If G21 members obtained degrees, the wages for G12 and G22 would be lower because the latter would need to subsidize the former. Capital market imperfection enables complete screening here. Hence, the individuals of G12 and G22 have a strong incentive to oppose low tuition and generous financial aids in preference for a "competitive" education market which enables them to signal their traits more clearly.

3.3.4
The Education Signal and Potlatch

The above analyses show that the firm uses an applicant's possession of a degree to determine whether he/she is from a rich family or not. This information is used to guess their productivity because those from rich families are more productive either on average or with certainty. In principle, there are other ways to convey similar information, such as certificates of savings deposits and car ownership. However, these do not function well in the real world not only for ethical reasons but because a savings balance can be increased and a superior car can be held only temporarily. In contrast, higher education is almost always expensive. It is difficult in many cases, especially in developing countries, to obtain a college degree to bluff about one's family wealth. Thus, the holding of a degree becomes a good signal of family wealth and related worker traits.

This type of investment is similar to potlatching and conspicuous consumption. The former is an important research subject in cultural anthropology which was formerly observed by tribes of the Northwest Coast of America such as the Tlingit, Kwakiutl, and Haida. The latter concept was devised by Veblen (1899), who seems to have been influenced by potlatch studies. A potlatch is a congregation of people ceremoniously invited to witness a demonstration of family prerogative, and takes the form of a feast characterized by the host's display of wealth and lavish distribution of gifts. In an extreme case, the host destroyed or burnt his valuable property before the eyes of the participants (Benedict, 1970).

As Barnett (1938) insists, the primary purpose of the potlatch was to satisfy the prestige demands of the host. Potlatch presents were investments in prestige. Basically, being wealthy was prestigious. As wealthiness could be measured by the amount of surplus wealth, the host "signaled" this by feasting his guests and distributing gifts among them, and at times by destroying or burning his property. What was important about the potlatch was that all aspects of it were undertaken in full view of the participants so that they could all see the sum total of the property used up in the event.[9]

The potlatch, however, was not a simple custom or institution. It generally had multiple purposes (or interpretations). McClellan (1954), for instance, emphasizes that potlatching was a religious activity. All food eaten in the potlatch was in fact to honor the dead. Other food and goods like blankets which were put in the fire were also believed to reach the departed — the names of the dead who were to receive them were announced loudly so that the spirits of the other world might hear. Potlatching put the dead in the position of being ready to be born again. Only through feeding and giving gifts could the host benefit their own dead in the spirit world.

Barnett (1938) allows that this multiplicity of purposes has generated confusion in the minds of anthropologists. The orthodox anthropological opinion, however, seems to be that the basic purpose of the potlatch was to satisfy the prestige demands of the host. The present author would like to emphasize that the multiplicity itself eased the satisfaction of prestige demands. A direct or ostentatious display of wealth is likely to provoke antipathy in any ethnic group. Thus, in order to satisfy prestige demands and at the same time to repress antipathy or control it to a reasonable level, more subtle means (sublime ceremonies, their religious meanings, etc.) became necessary. It may also have reduced guilt and humbled the host who wasted resources to acquire prestige. In sum, indirectness is required to avoid the negative effects involved in displaying wealth, and a multiplicity of purposes offers a useful means of doing so.

Higher education similarly has multiple purposes in the real world. First, it distinguishes rich from poor as argued above. Second, it has the eminent purpose of teaching knowledge which is considered valuable in society. In the above signaling models, however, this knowledge is completely irrelevant to production: therefore the second purpose becomes nothing but a common illusion. This may also be the case in the real world, but this illusion plays the important role of repressing antipathy toward those who display wealth by going to college.

In the Spence model (1973) students need to study hard to obtain degrees, since if everybody could obtain a degree without studying hard, higher education could not distinguish the productive from the unproductive. In contrast, when higher education plays the role of signaling wealth, it need not require students to study hard since what is more important to them is the payment of pecuniary costs. Still, they may need to pretend to be learning advanced valuable knowledge in order to avoid antipathy toward them. Studying is also important to the extent that it prevents intelligent but poor students from working part-time to pay for tuition, fees, and costs of living.

It is easy in uncivilized societies to display wealth by potlatching. Conspicuous consumption is also an effective means of doing so at a stage of economic development where the mobility of people is low. However, as the economy develops and mobility increases, it will become increasingly difficult for people to display their wealth. An employer does not constantly observe job applicants' consumption at this stage of economic development. If fact, the former has generally not seen the latter before. The above models suggest that investment in higher education plays the role of using resources to demonstrate wealth in a way that lets others make accurate judgments concerning that wealth. In this way, higher education becomes a customary and culturally approved mode of signaling one's social background. It is noteworthy that the first equilibrium under capital market imperfection presents a kind of statistical discrimination in which the rich invest in college education so that the employer discriminates in favor of them and against the poor.

The degree to which parents' wealth affects their children's levels of education is particularly large before an economy reaches maturity. Until that stage, higher education tends to be costly in comparison with average family income or wealth. Inequalities in family income or wealth are also likely to be large, and the capital market is probably quite imperfect. These tendencies are likely to be found in most developing countries. Thus the models of this section seem to be most applicable to these countries, where those from rich families can easily go to college and obtain degrees. Even many advanced counties have not yet completely eliminated these tendencies, as illustrated by the fact that students enrolled in leading universities tend to be from rich families.[10]

As an economy approaches maturity, the above tendencies are reduced and family income and wealth will become less important in determining an individual's signaling costs. What becomes relatively more important is the mental and time cost of acquiring a certain amount of knowledge. The condition in (3.5) thus becomes more applicable. Correspondingly, college education will examine students' knowledge more strictly than before. Then, as the signaling costs of an intelligent individual become lower, the Spence (1973) model tends to become more applicable. (However, even in a nearly mature economy what is discussed in this section may still hold in some form. For instance, the white-collar jobs mentioned before may be filled by graduates from leading universities.) From these considerations we can propose a hypothesis that the applicability of different kinds of signaling models depends to a large extent on the development stage of the economy.

3.4 Statistical Discrimination

The concept of statistical discrimination mentioned in the previous section will also be used in Chap. 6, so we will describe the essence of its mechanism in this section. Statistical discrimination arises for some individuals of a group which is distinguished on the basis of race, sex, origin, and so on. These individuals are treated differently because of the statistical attributes of their group, even though they themselves are virtually identical with others in all respects but the group-forming characteristics.

In the first model of the previous section, for example, the members of G21 in the large class of individuals with poor parents were discriminated against and received low wages even though their productivity was the same as that of G22 members. This arose because of the low average productivity of the large class of individuals with poor parents (a statistical attribute) and because of the firm's inability to distinguish G21 members from G11 members.[11]

In general, statistical discrimination arises when employers have imperfect information about worker attributes such as productive capabilities. Under such imperfect information, employers determine hiring, job allocations, wages, promotions, etc., not on the basis of true individual attributes, which are difficult to observe, but on the basis of the statistical attributes (averages, variances, etc.) of the individual's group. Groups are classified here according to characteristics such as race, sex, and origin, which are difficult to alter. (These characteristics are close to Spence's indexes.) Typical examples of statistical discrimination are racial and sex discrimination. As Chap. 6 will deal with sex discrimination, we would like to summarize the basis of statistical discrimination by considering the example of sex discrimination.

Historically speaking, even women who wanted to work as equals to men tended to be obliged to accept lower wages or auxiliary jobs. One fundamental reason for this was the high average quit rate of female workers as a group due to marriage, childbearing, child care, and so on. Facing this high quit rate, employers did not train female workers seriously nor allocate them to important positions. Though there were some female workers whose quit rate was as low as male workers', employers could not tell sufficiently accurately which individuals had this low quit rate. In this situation, employers treated each female worker as an individual with the average quit rate of the group of all female workers. In this way, even those female workers who wanted to work as equals to men were treated as average female workers, thereby being discriminated against.

The difference in average attributes among different groups can be generated by common prejudices held by employers. To see this, suppose almost all employers believe that the members of a particular group lack ability for some attractive job. In this case, individuals of that group do not have incentives to accumulate knowledge and skills necessary for the job, because they are unlikely to be hired. (It is assumed here that the job requires not only knowledge and skills which can be observed through academic background but also such abilities as responsibility, leadership, desirable habits of behavior and thinking, etc. which cannot be easily observed.) As a result, even if a firm tentatively hires some members of that group for the job, it will simply find that they lack ability. In this way social prejudices sometimes become self-fulfilling. What should be noted here is that this vicious circle arises even though the members of the group are fairly good at acquiring such abilities as responsibility and leadership.

A similar phenomenon also arises when it is especially difficult for most employers to judge the productive capabilities of a particular group of workers. When firms determine the hiring, allocation, or promotion of workers, they usually test worker capabilities. This test includes not only paper and interview examinations but also observing workers by temporarily hiring them or allocating them to lower positions. If male superiors test female workers, for example, either test costs might become relatively high or judgment errors might become large. The vicious circle of statistical discrimination again arises in such a case. Let us examine this reason in detail in the following.

To see the effect of test costs, we consider a simple situation in which there are two types of jobs. The first type can be done only by competent workers, whereas the second can be done equally both by competent and ordinary workers. Each worker is assumed to be either competent or ordinary. The wage for the first type is higher. Allocation of workers to the first type of job requires testing worker capabilities beforehand, but test costs are higher in the case of female workers than in the case of male workers.

Because of this difference in test costs, most firms do not test female workers and allocate them to the second type of job. As all workers are paid equally there and thus competence is not rewarded, women do not try to acquire high capabilities. As a result, the proportion of women with high capabilities decreases. Then, even if a firm tentatively hires female workers for the first type of job, it will find most of them ordinary and merely face high test costs. Thus it will avoid testing female workers all the more. This vicious circle discourages women from improving their capabilities or accumulating human capital.

Almost the same thing happens when there are differences in errors in judging capability among worker groups. Using an extreme assumption to clarify the point, assume that most employers can judge men's capabilities perfectly but that they cannot judge women's so accurately. Assume further that the dispersion of productive capabilities is initially the same between men and women. Then, each firm in a competitive labor market pays each male worker differently in accordance with his productive capability. Because judgment of capabilities is accurate in the case of male workers, each is paid his marginal value product.

The situation for women, however, is quite different. First of all, they are all paid almost the same wages because the errors in judging capability are large and thus judgments are not emphasized. Further, though the productive capabilities of male workers are certain at the time of hiring, those of female workers are uncertain. If firms are risk-averse and try to avoid workers with uncertain capabilities, the demand for male workers increases relative to female workers and thus the wages for male workers increase. The average wage of female workers is lower than that of male workers by the amount of the risk premium. This low average wage for female workers, which does not reward women's effort, discourages them from improving their capabilities or accumulating human capital as above.

The theory of statistical discrimination is one of the theories of discrimination. Another well-known theory explains discrimination by tastes (Becker, 1957; Arrow, 1973b). This latter theory claims for example that wages for whites are higher than those for blacks with equal productive capabilities because white employers like white workers better than black workers and thus the demand for the former is larger. Firms employing white workers satisfy their tastes at the sacrifice of pecuniary gains as their production costs would be lower if they employed blacks. Theoretically, such firms are driven out of the market by firms employing black workers, because the former do not minimize production costs and are thus inefficient.

In contrast, firms which discriminate workers statistically are obviously behaving rationally. Since they maximize expected profits (minimize expected costs) in many cases, they are unlikely to be driven out by competition in the product market. Therefore, this type of discrimination is likely to persist. The main economic problem of statistical discrimination is that members of particular groups are discouraged from sufficiently accumulating human capital or exerting effort, and therefore economic inefficiency is generated.

3.5* The Arrow-Burdett Model

Arrow (1973a) also developed a theoretical model in which the academic background of job applicants conveys information about their productivity to firms. Higher education in this model admits a portion of high-school leavers and then graduates some of the admitted. Arrow called this the filtering function of higher education. As in the Spence (1973) model, higher education in the Arrow model is assumed not to enhance students' productivity at all. (However, Arrow himself states that he does not consider higher education to have no influence on students' productive capabilities.) Yet, the methods of information production in the two models are quite different.

As the essence of the Arrow model is clarified by Burdett's (1978) numerical examples, this section will make use of these. Burdett points out two functions of higher education. One is called the sorting function which implies that using known information higher education sorts students according to their capabilities. The other is called the testing function, and is fulfilled if higher education creates new information about students' capabilities.

Arrow considers a situation in which each high-school graduate is characterized by his/her pre-college record y and productivity z the latter of which becomes observable only after a sufficient amount of time has passed since hiring by a firm. The pre-college record is interpreted differently in accordance with methods used in various countries to determine whom to admit to higher education. It may mean each individual's high-school record, his/her result of a nationwide common examination, or his/her result of a college entrance examination.

Because higher education is assumed not to enhance students' productivity, the value of z for a particular individual will not change even if he/she goes to college. It is assumed that there is a statistical correlation between y and z. More specifically, the value of z is assumed to tend to increase with the value of y. Thus, though there are some dispersions, those who have high pre-college records will on average achieve high productivity after graduation from school (college).

The Arrow-Burdett model does not explicitly consider education costs and assumes that all high-school graduates want to go to college. But higher education in the model has only a limited number of places and thus cannot admit all applicants. The model assumes that admissions are determined on the basis of the probability with which an applicant can graduate from college.

For simplicity, the pre-college record y is expressed in terms of the probability with which the applicant will graduate from college. (For example, an applicant who has obtained 600 points out of 1,000 in an entrance examination may have a value of y equal to 0.6.) Then, the value of y is between 0 and 1. An individual admitted to college is assumed either to graduate or to fail to graduate. The college determines admissions so as to maximize the expected number of graduates subject to the number of places available. More specifically, the college selects a level of pre-college record y_0 and admits only high-school graduates with $y \geqq y_0$.

Arrow insists that higher education acts as a double-filter in this theoretical framework. It first selects entrants, and then decides whether to pass or fail students. The admission procedure specified above produces positive information if the expected (average) productivity of college entrants is greater than that of all high-school graduates (including college entrants). In other words, higher education provides firms with useful information about individuals' productive capabilities if this condition is satisfied. Similarly, the graduation policy of higher education produces positive information if the expected productivity of graduates is greater than that of all college entrants. The college is said to act as a filter if the admission and/or graduation policies produce positive information.

Let us examine the functions of higher education by a numerical example. We classify all high-school graduates into three equal sized groups according to the levels of their pre-college record y (see Table 3.3). The value of y for each member of Group 1 is 0.4. The level of productivity z for a member of this group equals 0.3 with a probability 1/2 and 0.5 with a probability 1/2. Hence, the expected productivity equals $0.3 \times (1/2) + 0.5 \times (1/2) = 0.4$. Similarly, Groups 2 and 3 are characterized as shown in Table 3.3. Suppose the college selects $y_0 = 0.5$.

Then the following expected (or average) values can be computed:

The expected productivity of all high-school graduates
$= 0.4 \times 1/3 + 0.5 \times 1/3 + 0.6 \times 1/3 = 0.500;$
The expected productivity of all college entrants
$= 0.5 \times 1/2 + 0.6 \times 1/2 = 0.550;$
The expected productivity of all college graduates
$= 0.5 \times 5/11 + 0.6 \times 6/11 = 0.556.$

Some explanations as to the derivation of the above second and third expressions may be necessary. First note that only Group 2 and Group 3 members are admitted to college. Because each member of Group 1 has a pre-college record lower than $y_0 = 0.5$, none of them are admitted to college. Because the expected productivity of Group 2 is 0.5 and that of Group 3 is 0.6, and because both groups are of equal size,

Table 3.3. Numerical example of the filtering function.

Group	Proportion	Pre-college record y	Productivity z	Probability	Expected productivity
1	1/3	0.4	0.3 0.5	1/2 1/2	0.4
2	1/3	0.5	0.4 0.6	1/2 1/2	0.5
3	1/3	0.6	0.5 0.7	1/2 1/2	0.6

the expected productivity of all college entrants is represented by the second expression.

As the pre-college record y implies the probability of graduation, five out of ten Group 2 members will graduate on average. Similarly, six out of ten Group 3 members will graduate. Then, among eleven (= 5 + 6) college graduates, on average five are from Group 2 and six are from Group 3. In other words, because of the difference in graduation probability between the two groups, 5/11 of all college graduates are from Group 2 and 6/11 are from Group 3. Since the expected productivity of each member of Group 2 equals 0.5 and that of Group 3 equals 0.6, the expected productivity of all college graduates is represented by the third expression.

According to the above computation, the expected productivity of all college entrants is larger than that of all high-school graduates. Thus, the college acts as a filter by its admission policy. Similarly, as the expected productivity of all college graduates is larger than that of all college entrants, it also acts as a filter by its graduation policy. It should be noted that higher education does not perform a testing function defined above in the determination of entrants because it does not create new information about individual capabilities. In other words, it performs only a sorting function by which it sorts high-school graduates using the existing information of the pre-college records.

More importantly, the college does not perform a testing function in its determination of graduates either. This is because the expected productivity of individuals with a pre-college record 0.6 (0.5) will remain 0.6 (0.5) even if they have obtained a college degree.[12] That is, the college does not produce any new information about individual productive capabilities in its determination of graduates. What it does here is to graduate 60% (50%) of all college entrants with a pre-college record 0.6 (0.5) as if they are selected at random from all individuals with a pre-college record 0.6 (0.5). In fact, if the college randomly selects 60% (50%) of high-school graduates with a pre-college record 0.6 (0.5) and admits them, the total number of college entrants and their expected productivity will become exactly the same as those of the above college graduates. Indeed, if a firm obtained information about the pre-college records of job applicants, it could do exactly the same thing as the college is doing here.

In contrast with the above Arrow model, Burdett considers how the college can perform a testing function by which it produces new information. He first assumes that the college uses the same admission policy as in the Arrow model, i.e., $y_0 = 0.5$. He then assumes that the college administers a test to all college entrants such that (1) all individuals with productivity at least as great as 0.6 can be certain of passing, (2) all individuals with productivity less than 0.5 are certain to fail, and (3) 20% of all individuals with productivity of 0.5 will pass the test, while all others with this productivity fail. Passing the test implies graduation and failure implies non-graduation.

Then, the following can be computed:

The expected productivity of all college graduates with y equal to 0.6
$= 0.7 \times 5/6 + 0.5 \times 1/6 = 0.667$.

This can be understood by the following logic: Table 3.3 shows that for individuals with $y = 0.6$, five out of ten have productivity of 0.7 on average, while the other five have productivity of 0.5. All the first five individuals will pass the above test according to condition (1). On the other hand, on average one out of the latter five individuals will pass it according to condition (3). Thus six out of ten individuals with $y = 0.6$ will graduate. Then, among the graduates with $y = 0.6$, 5/6 have productivity of 0.7 and 1/6 have productivity of 0.5 on average, and the above expression holds. Further, it is obvious from Table 3.3 that

The expected productivity of all high-school graduates with y equal to $0.6 = 0.6$.

Next, we consider individuals with $y = 0.5$. Because half of them have productivity of 0.6 and the other half have productivity of 0.4, the first half will graduate and the second half will fail. Hence,

The expected productivity of all college graduates with y equal to $0.5 = 0.6$.

Finally, it is obvious from Table 3.3 that

The expected productivity of all high-school graduates with y equal to $0.5 = 0.5$.

If the college implements the above test, it performs a testing function, because it produces new information about individual capability by deciding on the basis of the test result whether to confer a degree to an entrant. More specifically, the expected productivity of an individual with $y = 0.6$ becomes 0.667 rather than 0.6 if he/she holds a degree. Similarly, the expected productivity of an individual with $y = 0.5$ becomes 0.6 rather than 0.5 if he/she holds a degree. Incidentally, it can easily be confirmed that this graduation policy also acts as a filter.

3.6* Combining Signaling and Human Capital Models

All the above signaling (filtering) models assume that (higher) education does not improve students' talents. However, this was an assumption made mainly to simplify analyses, and it is actually possible to build a model in which (higher) education enhances individuals' productive capabilities and at the same time plays a role of signaling. This section examines such a model built by Riley (1976). (Riley uses the term "screening" rather than "signaling".)[13]

The education considered in his model can be interpreted as either higher education or all types of school education. It is assumed in the model that the innate unobservable characteristics or the pre-school productive capabilities of individuals are distributed continuously in the closed interval of $[n_l, n_h]$. That is, the lowest productive capability in this economy equals n_l and the highest n_h. As in the Spence (1973) model, only the individual himself/herself knows his/her capability.

Consider an individual whose pre-school productive capability equals n and who is going to attain a level of education z. The levels of z imply high-school graduation, college graduation, and so on, and can be observed by employers. This individual can attain z by staying in school for the first t years of his life, where t is a function of n and z, i.e.,

$$t = t(n, z),\quad t_n < 0,\quad t_z > 0. \tag{3.18}$$

The first inequality in (3.18) implies that an individual with higher capability can finish a given level of education z in fewer years. On the other hand, the second inequality suggests that a higher level of education requires an individual with a given level of capability n to spend more time.

We can interpret (3.18) as it is if there are significant differences among individuals in the number of years necessary to finish a particular level of education as in the United States. But we need to interpret it slightly differently if there is almost a one-to-one correspondence between particular levels of education and numbers of years necessary to achieve them as in Japan. An interpretation that is more suitable to the Japanese situation is the following: the mental and time cost to an individual with lower productive capability of attaining a particular level of education is larger than that to an individual with higher productive capability. The effect of this difference in mental and time cost (expressed in terms of monetary units) in the real economy is interpreted as the same as the effect of a delay in starting work in the Riley model.

An additional restriction that is imposed on (3.18) is $t_{nz} < 0$, that is, the time needed to achieve a marginal increase in education (that is t_z) is everywhere lower for those with higher values of n.

Now consider the marginal value product (or wage) of an individual who has attained a level of education z by spending t years obtaining it and who is going to start working. Let M denote his/her lifetime marginal value product discounted to the time of entry into the work force. M is assumed to depend on his/her unobservable characteristic n and upon his/her education z achieved prior to entering the labor market, i.e.,

$$M = M(n, z),\quad M_n \geqq 0,\quad M_z \geqq 0. \tag{3.19}$$

The condition $M_n \geqq 0$ implies that an individual with higher pre-school capability will achieve higher marginal productivity. On the other hand, the condition $M_z \geqq 0$ implies that an individual with a higher level of education will achieve higher marginal productivity. This latter condition signifies that this model incorporates the human capital effect of education.

We first consider the case in which marginal productivity is costlessly observed as in the traditional human capital model. Let the non-time costs (such as tuition and fees) of education be c' per year. Then an individual staying in school for t years has a present value of lifetime earnings (net of education costs) at the time of starting receiving education

$$\begin{aligned} P(n, z) &= e^{-rt}M(n, z) - \int_0^t e^{-r\tau}c'd\tau \\ &= e^{-rt}\{M(n, z) + c\} - c, \end{aligned} \tag{3.20}$$

where r is a discount (interest) rate and $c = c'/r$.[14]

The individual chooses a level of education z so as to maximize $P(n, z)$. Maximizing $P(n, z)$ with respect to z is equivalent to maximizing $\ln\{P(n, z) + c\}$ with respect to z, where ln stands for the natural logarithm, because c is a constant and ln is a monotonically increasing function. Hence, by letting $\ln\{M(n, z) + c\} = m(n, z)$, this maximization problem reduces to

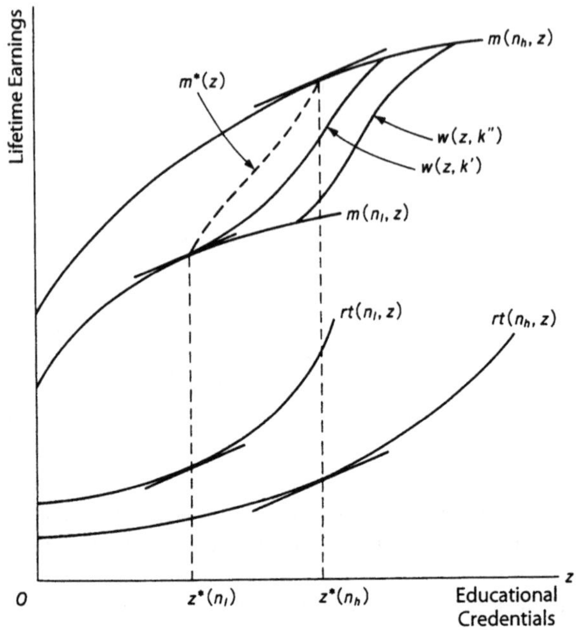

Fig. 3.2. Earnings Function

$$\underset{z}{\text{Max}}\left\{m(n,\, z) - rt(n,\, z)\right\}. \tag{3.21}$$

The solution to this maximization problem is shown in Fig. 3.2. This figure has curves named $m(n_l, z)$ and $rt(n_l, z)$ for individuals with pre-school capability n_l, and those of $m(n_h, z)$ and $rt(n_h, z)$ for individuals with pre-school capability n_h. Because of the difference in pre-school capability, $m(n_h, z)$ is located above $m(n_l, z)$ and $rt(n_h, z)$ is located below $rt(n_l, z)$. The optimal level of education $z^*(n_l)$ for individuals with pre-school capability n_l is determined where the slope of the tangent lines to $m(n_l, z)$ and $rt(n_l, z)$ coincide, since the distance between the two curves or $\{m(n_l, z) - rt(n_l, z)\}$ is maximized at that level of z. Similarly, the optimal level of education $z^*(n_h)$ for individuals with pre-school capability n_h is determined where the slope of the tangent lines to $m(n_h, z)$ and $rt(n_h, z)$ coincide. In this way, optimal levels of education for all values of n are determined. Such levels are shown as $m^*(z)$ in the Figure.

We next consider the case in which marginal productivity on the job is very costly to measure at least in the early years as in the signaling model. Suppose that an individual with a level of education z will be offered lifetime earnings $W(z)$, which are discounted to their value at the time he/she starts working. Then, an individual with pre-school productive capability n will choose z so as to maximize the expression that can be obtained by replacing $M(n, z)$ in Eq. 3.20 by $W(z)$. Writing $w(z) = \ln\{W(z) + c\}$, this maximization problem reduces to

$$\underset{z}{\text{Max}}\left\{w(z) - rt(n,\, z)\right\}. \tag{3.22}$$

The necessary conditions for this maximization are:

$$w'(z) - rt_z = 0, \quad z > 0, \tag{3.23}$$

$$w''(z) - rt_{zz} \leqq 0. \tag{3.24}$$

Differentiating Eq. 3.23 with respect to n yields

$$\left[w''(z) - rt_{zz}\right]\frac{dz^s}{dn} = rt_{nz}, \tag{3.25}$$

where the optimal level of education z^s in this signaling case has a superscript of s to be distinguished from that in the previous human capital case. (It is more accurate to use z^s for the arguments of w' and w'' as well.) Since we assumed $t_{nz} < 0$, Eqs. 3.24 and 3.25 imply that

$$\frac{dz^s}{dn} > 0 \tag{3.26}$$

or that those more favorably endowed with the unobservable n attain higher educational credentials.

Further, in order for employers' predictions about productivity levels to be eventually confirmed, the gross earnings of those choosing an educational level z must equal their marginal value product, i.e.,

$$w(z) = m(n, z). \tag{3.27}$$

In principle, Eqs. 3.23 and 3.27 together generate a whole family of earnings functions $w(z, k)$ offered by employers, where k is an undetermined constant of integration. This family of earnings functions satisfy the following Spencian equilibrium conditions: firstly, individuals choose that education level which maximizes discounted earnings; secondly, the earnings of individuals achieving a given level of education equals (the average of) their marginal value products.

Fig. 3.2 depicts two examples, $w(z, k')$ and $w(z, k'')$, of the above earnings functions. Under these earnings functions, or when there is information asymmetry, the level of education each individual chooses is in general higher than when marginal productivity is costlessly observable. In other words, $w(z, k)$ is located on the right of $m^*(z)$ in the Figure.

This fact can be formally proved as follows. Differentiating Eq. 3.27 with respect to n yields

$$\left[w'(z) - m_z(n, z)\right]\frac{dz^s}{dn} = m_n. \tag{3.28}$$

Since Eq. 3.19 implies $m_n \geqq 0$, Eqs. 3.28 and 3.26 together generate

$$w'(z) \geqq m_z(n, z). \tag{3.29}$$

Because the optimal level of education z^s in the case of information asymmetry is a function of pre-school productive capability n, let it be expressed as $z^s(n)$. Then inequality 3.29 implies that

$$\begin{aligned} &m_z(n, z^s(n)) - rt_z(n, z^s(n)) \\ &\leqq w'(z^s(n)) - rt_z(n, z^s(n)) = 0, \end{aligned} \tag{3.30}$$

where the equality is due to Eq. 3.23.

On the other hand, the optimal level of education in the case where there is no information asymmetry is also a function of n and thus can be expressed as $z^*(n)$. Then, the first order condition for (3.21) implies

$$m_z(n, z^*(n)) - rt_z(n, z^*(n)) = 0. \tag{3.31}$$

Now consider a function $\{m(n, z) - rt(n, z)\}$. Eq. 3.31 implies that $z^*(n)$ maximizes this function, whereas Eq. 3.30 implies that $z^s(n)$ is located (weakly) beyond the level of z that maximizes it. Therefore, it holds that $z^*(n) \leqq z^s(n)$. This argument has proved that the level of education each individual chooses is generally higher in the case where there is information asymmetry than in the case where marginal value productivity is costlessly observable.

In this way, an equilibrium similar to that in the Spence (1973) model can be derived under information asymmetry even if education enhances individual productive capability. Riley (1975) shows that only $w(z, k')$ in Fig. 3.2 will survive if employers can try several alternative earnings functions $w(z, k)$. Under this particular earnings function, the individuals with the lowest pre-school productive capability ($n = n_l$) will choose the same level of education and receive the same wage as those in the case where marginal productivity can be costlessly observed. This is due to the fact that they do not have to invest in education to signal their difference because no other individuals have lower pre-school productive capabilities.

In addition to the signaling models considered in this chapter, there are several other models that are game-theoretically more refined or that consider different situations. Interested readers should see Spence (1974b, 1981), Stiglitz (1975), Riley (1979b), Weiss (1983), Mailath (1987), Cho and Kreps (1987), and so on.

Notes

1. In fact most signaling models assume that education does not enhance the productivity of students at all. As we will see in Sect. 3.6, however, it is possible to build a model in which education plays a signaling role and at the same time enhances student productivity. On the other hand, even if education does not enhance individual productive capabilities, it may help enhance productivity because it reveals aptitude, and this information enables correct matching of individuals to firms or jobs. (The productivity of an individual tends to be low if he/she works in an environment which does not suit him/her.) This is the problem of matching, in which education helps allocate heterogeneous individuals to their most productive use. See Jovanobic (1979) and MacDonald (1980) for job matching.
2. Even in human capital theory, all additional costs of higher education, whether mental or time costs, are investment costs of higher education. As we have seen in Chap. 2, however, human capital theory tends to make light of unmeasurable costs.
3. When using the latter assumption, the firm is assumed to be risk-neutral. A risk-neutral firm is supposed to behave so as to maximize expected profits.
4. Each of these values should be interpreted as the total present value of the products that each type of individual can produce from the time of hiring to the time of mandatory retirement. Strictly speaking, those values should be called marginal value products, but they are called productivity in the following for simplicity, because it is implicitly assumed here that marginal productivity is constant regardless of the number of workers employed and because the price of the product can be assumed to be unity. This set of assumptions can be rephrased in accordance with Fig. A.1 in Appendix A: a special case is assumed here in which the demand curve (like D_1D_1 or DD) for each group of workers becomes horizontal if the two groups are

distinguishable. (Because only one firm exists in this economy, D_1D_1 is identical with DD.) Of course, the demand curve for GI is different from that for GII, the height of the former being 1 and that of the latter 2. If the two groups are not distinguishable, the demand curve for labor becomes a horizontal line with a height equal to the average productivity of the two groups.

5. Because workers are paid wages equal to their productivity, the firm's (expected) profits become zero, as far as its beliefs are correct. In other words, the firm behaves so as to maximize (expected) profits, but maximized profits are zero. It is possible to consider a case in which maximized profits are positive, but this causes the model to become complex.

6. According to Shigeno and Matsuura (1995), parents' income, wealth, and social status significantly affect their children's purchase of private school education and cram school education at the stage of compulsory education.

7. Spence (1974a, Chap. 6) mentions the case where some productive individuals cannot go to college because their parents are poor. He allows, however, that the basic pattern of the signaling equilibrium in this case is much like the one obtained in Spence (1973). This will be discussed in Sect. 3.3.2.

8. The signaling equilibrium in this model is obviously disadvantageous to G21 members. This disadvantage may be removed by introducing a financial aid system in which those from poor families can use loans at a low interest rate to receive higher education. Under such a system, the members of G21 may be able to go to college in the same way as those of G12 and G22. Then not only the welfare of G21 members but also that of G12 and G22 members will increase, because the average productivity of the whole group of college graduates will increase. (To simplify the story, we assume that receiving a financial aid does not become a signal.) In contrast, non-college graduates will be only G11 members and their wage will decrease to 1. However, such a large-scale financial aid system can exist only in very mature welfare states. Other countries cannot provide such generous financial aids. Moreover, if there is competition for admission as in Japan, those from poor families may not succeed in this competition and thus cannot obtain financial aids which are offered on condition that they are admitted to college.

9. The benefits of potlatching and conspicuous consumption are mainly psychological, whereas those of investment in higher education in the above models are pecuniary. However, the above models also provide insight into the case where individuals purchase higher education to obtain psychological benefits. Suppose that displaying wealth by consuming higher education brings about psychological benefits. Then, wealthy individuals, for whom education costs are low in comparison with psychological benefits, purchase higher education. These are benefits of present and future consumption according to the classification of the benefits of education in Chap. 2.

10. Higuchi (1992) shows in his empirical study that students enrolled in universities with keen competition for admission tend to be from high-income families and the graduates of those institutions tend to obtain jobs which offer high lifetime salaries.

11. See Phelps (1972), Akerlof (1976), Borjas and Goldberg (1978), Aiger and Cain (1977) for statistical discrimination.

12. Those whose pre-college record is 0.6 actually lose from the existence of filtering, because though their expected productivity is 0.6, the expected productivity of those who have a college degree is regarded as 0.556. This fact is contrary to Arrow's idea of filtering, but firms in his model are assumed not to know job applicants' pre-college records.

13. This section presupposes that the reader has elementary knowledge of partial differentiation.

14. When time changes continuously in an economic model, the rate of growth of a variable x which is a function of time t can be expressed as $(dx/dt)/x$. This is because when time changes by one unit, x grows by dx/dt and the rate of growth equals the ratio of dx/dt to x. If you lend 1 yen at an annual interest rate of r, it grows at the annual rate of r and will become e^{rt} yen in t years. This is because $(de^{rt}/dt)/e^{rt} = r$ and e^{rt} certainly grows at the rate of r. Since 1 yen at present and e^{rt} yen t years later have the same economic value, the present value of y yen t years later equals $e^{-rt}y$ yen.

Chapter 4
An Application of the Internal-Rate-of-Return Method: Rates of Return to Medical and Dental Education

The internal-rate-of-return method examined in Chap. 2 is an approach frequently used to analyze college-going behavior. In this chapter, we will compute internal rates of return using actual data and use the computation results to consider problems concerning college-going behavior.

We consider in this chapter medical and dental education as special cases of higher education which have some interesting features. Firstly, these are the two most popular types of higher education today in Japan. An important reason for this is probably that physicians and dentists earn extremely high incomes. If we apply the internal-rate-of-return method we can quantify attractiveness of investment in medical and dental education.

Secondly, investments in these types of education relate to the question of socially optimal numbers of physicians and dentists. This is very important when considering the welfare of a society, and interests many researchers. The internal-rate-of-return method can again provide useful information in answering this question.

Thirdly, computation of rates of return to medical and dental education has a scarcity value. As we saw in Chap. 2, the world has countless computation examples of rates of return to general higher education. In comparison, there are much fewer computation examples in the fields of medical and dental education.

With these points in mind, this chapter will compute internal rates of return to medical and dental education and consider economic problems related to these types of education. Sect. 4.1 will discuss the basic theory of supply of and demand for physicians and dentists, with special emphasis on the problem of regulation of their numbers. Sect. 4.2 will examine a view which is used in actual policy making but which differs markedly from that of this book and can be a good object for comparison. Costs and benefits of medical and dental education will be measured in Sects. 4.3 and 4.4 using data available for Japan. Sect. 4.5 will show the computed internal rates of return and evaluate them for policy implications.

It should be added that in this chapter "physicians" implies all kinds of medical doctors except dentists. Also, this section sometimes shortens "internal rates of return" simply into "rates of return". The author would like to report that computation of the rates of return shown in this chapter was possible because he could access data which were unpublished.[1]

4.1 The Supply of Physicians and Dentists

4.1.1 Why the Numbers of Physicians and Dentists are Regulated

The supply of ordinary workers working for private enterprises does not become an important economic issue. This can be seen in such examples as assembly line workers, computer operators, and sales people. The reason is that free competitive markets are considered to determine supply automatically. More precisely, when such workers are scarce, wages will go up, and in response supply will increase up to optimal levels. On the other hand, when they are abundant, wages will go down, and in response supply will decrease up to optimal levels.[2]

In contrast, the supply of physicians and dentists becomes a very important economic issue because it is determined by artificial means or policies rather than by the market mechanism. Even if the earnings of physicians and dentists are outstandingly high, one cannot freely become a physician or dentist.

There are two basic reasons to use policy to determine the supply of physicians and dentists. Training costs for physicians and dentists are extremely high, and also, medical and dental services may deal with issues of life and death. If training costs are high, medical and dental education need to rely partially on public subsidies, which suggests that the numbers of physicians and dentists will be policy determined. The necessity of maintaining the quality of medical and dental services tends also to invite determination of the supply of physicians and dentists by policies. A similar example can be found in the legal profession, where it can be said that the number of successful candidates in a judicial examination is determined artificially to maintain the quality of judges and lawyers.

It should be noted, however, that from a purely theoretical viewpoint, high training costs and maintenance of the quality of medical and dental services could not be the absolute reasons for policy determination of the numbers of physicians and dentists. Optimal numbers could be determined automatically by supply and demand in free competitive markets provided that the following two conditions are satisfied: that the capital market is perfect and thus individuals can borrow freely to invest in education, and that there is an institution which accurately evaluates the quality of physicians and dentists and which makes this information freely available.

This chapter assumes that this kind of free market determination of optimal numbers of physicians and dentists does not occur, and argues considerations that should be taken into account when policy determination is used. The internal-rate-of-return method discussed in Chap. 2 will be very useful in such an argument. It should be added, however, that the main purpose of this chapter is not to undertake rigorous computation of the specific numbers of physicians and dentists necessary today. To do so would require a large volume of data and detailed estimation but would not interest many readers. Rather, the main purpose of this chapter is to discuss the basis of how to determine optimal numbers of physicians and dentists using the internal-rate-of-return method. If we make some simplifying assumptions, this discussion will enable us to examine whether or not the real economy has insufficient physicians and dentists.

4.1.2
Marginal Valuation of a Physician

Physicians (and dentists) are workers who provide services in the medical industry. In order to judge whether or not the number of workers in an industry is optimal (whether or not it is excessive), economics uses the concept of marginal valuation of (the good or service produced by) workers. Marginal valuation means the evaluated value of the good or service produced by an additional worker in the industry under consideration in a certain time unit such as a day or a year. (Here, "additional" means "added to the market".)

When marginal valuation is relatively high, all workers in the industry can be regarded as rendering useful services to the market or society, and thus an increase in the number of workers in this industry will enhance social welfare. In other words, the number of workers is judged to be too small. In contrast, when marginal valuation is relatively low, some of the workers in the industry can be considered not to be rendering very useful services to society, and thus a reduction in the number of workers will enhance social welfare (by avoiding wasteful usage of human resources). In other words, the number of workers there is judged to be too large.

The medical industry can actually be finely classified into many industries. Physicians and dentists belong to completely different industries which supply different kinds of services. Physicians can be classified further into physicians in the narrow sense, ophthalmologists, brain surgeons, and so on, each group of which can be considered to belong to a different industry. In order to argue the optimal numbers of physicians and dentists for policy making, we may need to consider these finely classified industries. In addition, we may need to pay attention to the optimal numbers of physicians and dentists in each geographic region, because those who are in a different region belong to a different market. However, because the main purpose of this chapter is to discuss the basis of how to determine optimal numbers, we draw here a distinction only between physicians and dentists, and make no further classifications nor consider regional markets.

Let us examine the concept of marginal valuation in a very simple model. As an example we consider the case of physicians. It is assumed here that all physicians belong to the same industry or market. Marginal valuation in this industry means the value of the services provided in a unit of time by a physician who is added to this industry. This value shows how consumers evaluate the services of this additional physician. In the following, we choose one year for the time unit and measure value in yen. Then, marginal valuation can be defined as the maximal amount of money in terms of yen that the market of medical services or society as a whole is willing to pay for the services supplied by an additional physician in a year.

Fig. 4.1 depicts a marginal valuation curve, which relates the number of physicians to the corresponding marginal valuation. In general, as the number of physicians increases, the marginal valuation decreases. For instance, marginal valuation equals w_1 when the number of physicians equals N_1, but it decreases to w_2 when the number of physicians increases to N_2.

The reason for this is that when the number of physicians in the market is small, the medical services provided by an additional physician are so precious that they will be

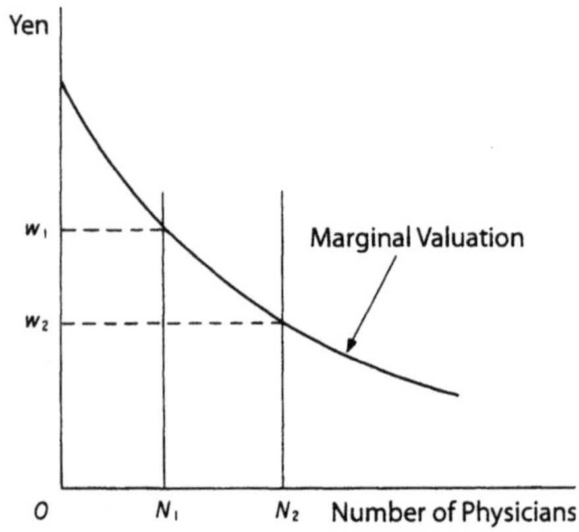

Fig. 4.1 Number of Physicians and Marginal Valuation

used only for critical purposes such as organ operations. Thus the valuation of those services is high.

In contrast, when the number of physicians is large, sufficient services can be provided for critical purposes and the medical services provided by an additional physician will be used for non-critical purposes such as wound treatment. Thus the valuation of these additional services is low. Moreover, it may happen that when there are too many physicians in the market some of them have too few patients and too much vacant time even while their clinics are open. This is because many patients (consumers) actually need to spend their precious time to receive treatment and thus do not consume medical services for unimportant purposes. The valuation of such physicians' time is very low. (Vacant time may have some value, since it enables treatment of emergency cases.)

The following comment might apply to this argument about the relationship between number of physicians and marginal valuation. When the number of physicians increases in the market and their incomes are expected to decrease, physician-induced demand may arise (Evans, 1974; Fuchs, 1978; Tokita, 1995). This is defined as unnecessary demand for medical services generated by physicians themselves making use of patients' ignorance in order to prevent their own incomes from falling. (When the number of physicians is small, demand for medical services may be manipulated in the opposite direction.) If physician-induced demand is prominent and unnecessary services are provided, marginal valuation expressed in terms of "points" in the Japanese medical system is not necessarily the true social marginal valuation.

Nishimura (1987) suggests that physician-induced demand does exist in Japan. It should be noted, however, that physicians cannot induce demand limitlessly. Consumers are not completely ignorant of medicine, and they constantly exchange information about which physicians provide proper services. Even if physician-induced demand exists, it is limited partly because physicians have to consider their reputations and long-term relationships with their patients (Dranove, 1988). Moreover, the empirical study for Canada by Ferguson and Crawford (1989) shows that an increase in the ratio of physicians to population does not give rise to physician-induced demand. Arrow (1963) points out that those who engage themselves in medical services are required to have a high level of ethics. As far as physician-induced demand is concerned, ethics seems to be functioning reasonably well. The analysis in this chapter assumes that physician-induced demand does not exist.

4.1.3 Internal Rate of Return and Optimality

Because marginal valuation shows how highly the market or society evaluates the services provided in a year by an additional physician, one method to express its value in the real economy is to equate it with the average annual income of physicians. This is because the income of a physician is the valuation by society of his/her services.[3]

This marginal valuation normally increases with economic growth under a condition that the number of physicians is constant. This is firstly because consumers become willing to pay more than previously for the same medical services as their income grows. In other words, the same medical services will be evaluated more highly owing to income growth. The second reason derives from technological progress in the medical industry. Newly developed methods of treatment can cure diseases which could not be cured before. Moreover, they enable each physician to supply more services than before. Thus, when there is economic growth, the income of each physician increases every year. If the number of physicians is small, say N_1, high income grows, whereas if it is large, say N_2, low income grows every year. Hence, those who are currently physicians or very likely to become physicians want the total number of physicians not to be too large in order to keep their incomes high.

Of course, this is not a judgment from the standpoint of the welfare of society as a whole. Then how can we determine the optimal number of physicians from the standpoint of social welfare? It is this question that we can answer using the internal-rate-of-return method.

The basic idea is that if training costs for a physician are high, the number of physicians should be kept small so that high marginal valuation is maintained. A large number of physicians would generate a wasteful usage of human resources because medical services would be supplied even to purposes with low valuation. In contrast, if training costs for a physician are low, a wasteful usage of human resources will not arise even if medical services are extensively supplied by a large number of physicians to purposes with low valuation. In short, the optimal number of physicians should be determined by comparing training costs for a physician and the marginal valuation or income a physician can achieve. Further, this comparison should be undertaken by considering a time-series of training costs and incomes from the beginning of training to the time of retirement.

The internal-rate-of-return method is used to see how high the stream of marginal valuations is in comparison with that of training costs. If the measured social internal rate of return under a certain number of physicians is higher than that to other investment opportunities, an increase in the number of physicians will enhance social welfare because the marginal valuation is high relative to training costs. In contrast, if the measured social rate of return is lower, a decrease in the number of physicians will enhance social welfare.

The private internal rate of return to medical education as compared with the social rate of return shows how attractive investment in medical education is from the standpoint of an individual. An individual can use the former for his/her decision to invest in medical education. It can be used for policy making as well to determine the level of public subsidies to medical education and the level of income tax. More specifically, if the private rate of return is so low at the optimal number of physicians that the number of applicants for the medical occupation is small, government should induce more to apply by expanding public subsidies and/or lowering the rate of income tax for physicians. In contrast, if the private rate of return is too high, the opposite policy should be enforced.

It is worthwhile to mention biases that will arise when measuring social rates of return. The biases which are important here concern external economies and the psychological satisfaction of consumers. External economies of medical services include prevention and treatment of epidemic and hereditary diseases, which give external economies to potential patients.

Important psychological satisfaction or a sense of security on the part of consumers derives from the mere fact that medical services are being supplied. This is the benefit consumers obtain when they have medical specialists for most diseases in their region even if some of the consumers do not actually suffer from many of the diseases. Because of the very presence of physicians, consumers can live with security in their region. The existence of this benefit is at least a partial reason that towns in sparsely populated regions and isolated islands invite physicians with guaranteed high incomes to live there.

Because these external economies and the amount of psychological satisfaction cannot be easily computed, they are omitted from the following analysis. Therefore, the social rates of return computed below have downward biases and the true rates must be regarded as higher.

The analysis below follows the logic of the internal rate of return. That is, it will deal first with training costs for physicians and dentists, secondly with returns to investment in medical and dental education, and finally with the internal rates of return. Before doing this, however, we would like to introduce as a comparison a view which is quite different from the internal-rate-of-return method.

4.2* A Different View on the Optimal Numbers of Physicians and Dentists

The above view about the optimal numbers of physicians and dentists derives from economic theory. But the view used for actual policy making is very different and has little relation to any persuasive economic theory. Here we examine this latter view for comparison with the internal-rate-of-return method.

This alternative view can be seen in the *Interim Opinion of the Committee for Examination of the Future Demand for and Supply of Physicians* published in November, 1984 and this Committee's final opinion published in June, 1986.[4] A similar view can also be seen in the *Interim Opinion of the Committee for Examination of the Future Demand for and Supply of Dentists* published in December, 1984 and this Committee's final opinion published in July, 1986.[5]

On the basis of almost identical logic, both these opinions insisted that there would be "excess" numbers of physicians and dentists in the future, and proposed reductions in new entry. More specifically, they proposed a reduction of at least 10% in the new entry of physicians and that of at least 20% in the new entry of dentists from about 1995 onwards. In addition, they requested those concerned to achieve these goals. These opinions were expressed in order to "maintain the optimal numbers of physicians and dentists."[6] In this section, we examine the essence of these opinions and show that they in reality lack an objective concept of "optimality."

In 1970, the Japanese Ministry of Public Welfare examined policies for the supply-demand balance of physicians and dentists. Its basic proposal was that the minimum number of physicians should be 150 per hundred thousand people and that of dentists should be 50 per hundred thousand people, and that the numbers of physicians and dentists should be increased in order to achieve these targets by 1985. In response to this policy proposal, new medical and dental schools were built and more students were admitted to existing medical and dental schools. In this way, the target for physicians was achieved two years earlier than anticipated and that for dentists five years earlier. The basic matter of concern in the above opinions was that if the numbers of medical and dental students were maintained at current levels, the total numbers of physicians and dentists would continue to grow steadily beyond the initial targets and reach the state of "excess".

When an "excess" of physicians and dentists is at issue, the demand for and supply of physicians and dentists should naturally be considered. Hence, we would like to examine how these opinions derived the demand and supply. Because similar methods are used for both physicians and dentists, we will discuss the former case as representative. As the above opinion concisely explains how the demand and supply were derived, we quote this excerpt:[7]

> *Supply.* It is expected that aged physicians will retire earlier than now. Hence the supply is derived by assuming that the group of physicians seventy years old or older will work half as much as younger physicians from 2000 to 2020. Further, the supply from 2020 on is derived by ignoring the presence of the older group of physicians. In addition, each female physician is assumed to work 80% as much as each male physician.
>
> *Demand.* The number of patients has been estimated first by multiplying the future age-grouped population by the rate of receiving treatment of each age group estimated in 1980, and secondly by considering the tendency for higher demand by the aged. Further, an assumption has been made that the number of patients per clinician will decrease by 10% from now and by 15% from 2020. The demand for non-clinical physicians is assumed to be ten thousand at present, but to be twenty thousand from 2020 on. In addition, demand for physicians has been estimated to be larger than above by 2% because of the frictional gap between demand and supply due to changes in specialized fields and regional mobility of physicians.

The above opinions say that the supply is estimated downwards and demand upwards in order to respond to an increase in the demand for physicians due to developments in medical science. It adds that even under these estimations, there will be an equilibrium of demand and supply in 2000 and ten percent excess supply in 2025.

As the above quotation reveals, the supply of physicians is estimated by adding the new entry of graduates from medical schools (or those who are likely to pass the national medical examination) at each future point in time to the stock of physicians existing at the time of estimation, by subtracting the retirement of aged physicians, and by considering different work hours due to age and sex.

On the other hand, the demand for physicians is estimated essentially by the following formula:[8]

$$\text{Demand for Physicians} = \text{Number of Patients} \times \frac{1}{\text{Number of Patients per Physician}}. \quad (4.1)$$

Of course, some adjustments are made by considering the increase in demand by older people, the necessity for non-clinical physicians[9] and so on, as can be seen in the above quotation.

Incidentally, the reason the quotation suggests that the number of patients per clinician will decrease by 10 to 15% is that "work hours will decrease in the future due to a shift to the two-weekly-holiday system and physicians will spend more time treating each patient."[10] A simple calculation shows that a shift from the system of one and a half weekly holidays to two weekly holidays implies a 9.1% reduction in the number of patients per clinician. A shift from the system of one weekly holiday to that of two weekly holidays implies a 16.7% reduction. Therefore, most of the reduction of 10 to 15% can be regarded as due to changes in weekly holidays.

The part 1/(Number of Patients per Physician) in Eq. 4.1 is a kind of input coefficient which stands for the number of physicians the medical industry uses to treat one patient. What is problematical in this estimation equation is that this input coefficient has essentially the same value as at the time of estimation (in the early 1980s), though account is taken of the reduction of 10 to 15% due to changes in holidays. In other words, the future demand for physicians is computed here essentially on the premise that the number of patients per physician in the early 1980s should be maintained with minor changes.

This method of estimation may be justified to some extent if the number of patients per physician in the early 1980s is "optimal" in some sense, but is baseless otherwise. Though "optimality" is the most important problem in determining the number of physicians, the above opinions do not discuss this problem at all. The problem of economic "optimality" was not considered either in the policy examination in 1970 by the Japanese Ministry of Public Welfare, which was mentioned at the beginning of this section. We have seen that the opinions examined in this section, unlike the internal-rate-of-return method, lack a concept of "optimality".

4.3 Costs

The purpose of this section is to estimate private and social costs of medical and dental education. There is a great difference especially in private costs between private and national (public) institutions. Available data enables us to compute private costs for both types of institutions. However, social costs for national institutions cannot be estimated as it is impossible to obtain data about budget allocations to medical and dental departments within national universities. Hence, this section computes only social costs for private institutions. Fortunately, it is said that there is no significant difference in the social costs of medical and dental education between private and national institutions.

As we saw in Chap. 2, we need data for the stream of costs and benefits in order to compute the internal rate of return to a specific type of education. There we noted that actual computation is usually based on cross-sectional data over age-groups at a particular point in time. We choose here the year of 1982 as the time of estimation, because the author could obtain unpublished data only for that year and almost all other necessary data are available for that year. This point in time is almost the same as the year in which the above opinions measured the input coefficient in Eq. 4.1.

We first examine private costs for private medical institutions. See Table 4.1. (Information about the Japanese yen exchange rate is provided in Appendix C.) Tuition and fees per student can be computed from data collected by the Ministry of Education, *Average Tuition and Fees in the Departments of Medical and Dental Sciences at Private Universities*. Medical education in private universities differs from other types of higher education in that students have to pay not only tuition and entrance fees but also fees for facilities, experiments, and completion of education, which are very large amounts. (This is also the case for private dental education.) Especially large are the fees for completion of education which are paid in the first year.[11] Data for costs of books, stationery, and commuting can be obtained from the Ministry of Education, *Survey of Student Life*.

We can obtain information about forgone earnings mainly from the Ministry of Labor, *Basic Survey of Wage Structures*. From this data we can compute the average before-tax annual earnings of male (senior) high-school graduates for each age group for all firm sizes in all industries. Subtracting tax generates after-tax earnings.[12] Data for male workers are used here because most physicians and dentists are males. In

Table 4.1. Costs per student of medical education in private institutions.

(yen)

Year	1	2	3~6
Tuition and Fees			
Tuition	1,802,197	1,802,197	1,802,197
Entrance Fees	900,987		
Facility Fees	1,166,579	849,280	849,280
Experiment Fees	288,855	288,855	288,855
Completion of Education Fees	4,444,243		
Books and Stationery	160,700	160,700	160,700
Commuting Costs	61,800	61,800	61,800
Forgone Earnings			
Before-Tax Wage for a Male Senior High-School Student	1,649,500	1,649,500	2,265,200
After-Tax Wage for a Male Senior High-School Student	1,533,990	1,533,990	2,065,780
(−) Income from Part-time Work	−233,700	−233,700	−233,700
Subsidies	3,171,680	3,171,680	3,171,680
Private Costs	10,125,651	4,463,122	4,994,912
Social Costs	13,412,841	7,750,312	8,366,012

order to compute net forgone earnings, the average income from part-time work must be subtracted from the above average after-tax earnings. The only information available about part-time income is that it equals 233,700 yen if averaged for all college students. This information is obtained from the *Survey of Student Life* mentioned above and is used to compute net forgone earnings.

In this way we can compute the (average) private costs of medical education for six years in private institutions. The simple total of the costs to be paid in terms of money in six years is 24.640 million yen, while the net forgone earnings equal 9.929 million yen. Thus the simple total of the private costs amounts to 34.568 million yen. This is an enormous amount even today and was all the more so in 1982. We can confirm that it is very difficult for a student from an average household to receive medical education in a private institution.

How high are the social costs of medical education in private institutions? As private costs are already computed, social costs can be estimated simply by making adjustments for forgone earnings and public subsidies. For forgone earnings we have only to use pre-tax earnings, data for which can be obtained from the *Basic Survey of Wage Structures*. Subtracting the above-mentioned part-time income from these earnings produces net forgone earnings as part of the social costs. The amount of social subsidies can be computed on the basis of the *Survey of the Structure of Revenues and Expenditures in 1982*, data compiled by the Japanese Association of Private Medical Institutions.

This procedure reveals the average social costs of medical education for six years. The simple total of costs to be paid in terms of money in six years is 43.669 million yen, while net forgone earnings equal 10.958 million yen. Thus the simple total of social costs amounts to 54.627 million yen per student. To put it differently, additional social costs of more than 50 million yen are necessary to make a physician of a (senior) high-school graduate.

Next we examine private costs for private dental institutions. The data to be used are almost the same as those used to measure private costs for private medical institutions. The only difference is that information about facility fees from the second to the sixth year is now obtained from the *Table of Tuition and Fees for Private Dental Institutions* compiled by the Japanese Association of Private Dental Institutions. Table 4.2 shows average private costs of dental education for six years in private institutions. The simple total of costs to be paid in terms of money in six years is 25.828 million yen, while net forgone earnings equal 9.929 million yen. Thus the simple total of private costs amounts to 35.757 million yen. This total exceeds that of medical education only by 1.189 million yen, so the two totals can be regarded as almost the same.

The social costs of dental education in private institutions can be estimated in a similar way as for medical education. But as data for public subsidies we use the *Survey of Public Subsidies Per Student in 1982* compiled by Japan Private Institutions Promotion Foundation, which was the only data available to the author. Table 4.2 also shows the social costs of dental education for six years. The simple total of the costs to be paid in money over six years is 31.521 million yen, while net forgone earnings equal 10.958 million yen. Thus the simple total of social costs amounts to 42.479 million yen. This total is less than the total for medical education by 12.148 million yen, the difference being almost equal to the difference in public subsidies.

Table 4.2. Costs per student of dental education in private institutions.

(yen)

Year	1	2	3~6
Tuition and Fees			
Tuition	2,075,333	2,075,333	2,075,333
Entrance Fees	510,000		
Facility Fees	1,768,333	861,176	861,176
Experiment Fees	20,000	20,000	20,000
Completion of Education Fees	5,336,667		
Books and Stationery	160,700	160,700	160,700
Commuting Costs	61,800	61,800	61,800
Forgone Earnings			
Before-Tax Wage for a Male Senior High-School Student	1,649,500	1,649,500	2,265,200
After-Tax Wage for a Male Senior High-School Student	1,533,990	1,533,990	2,065,780
(−) Income from Part-time Work	−233,700	−233,700	−233,700
Subsidies	949,000	949,000	949,000
Private Costs	11,233,123	4,479,299	5,011,089
Social Costs	12,297,633	5,543,809	6,159,509

Table 4.3. Costs per student of medical and dental education in national institutions.

(yen)

Year	1	2	3~6
Tuition and Fees			
Tuition	216,000	216,000	216,000
Entrance Fees	100,000		
Books and Stationery	118,400	118,400	118,400
Commuting Costs	59,700	59,700	59,700
Forgone Earnings			
After-Tax Wage for a Male Senior High-School Student	1,533,990	1,533,990	2,065,780
(−) Income from Part-time Work	−233,700	−233,700	−233,700
Private Costs	1,794,390	1,694,390	2,226,180

Finally, we compute the private costs of medical and dental education in national institutions. We do not compute social costs for national institutions as this is difficult for the reason mentioned before. Because of institutional reasons, private costs of medical and dental education are the same in Japanese national universities, so we measure both at the same time. All necessary information can be obtained from data already mentioned except that for tuition and fees for which the *Abstract of Education Statistics* by the Ministry of Education can be used (see Table 4.3).

The simple total of costs to be paid in terms of money in six years is 2.464 million yen, while net forgone earnings equal 9.929 million yen. Thus the simple total equals 12.394 million yen, which is only slightly higher than one third of the private costs of private medical and dental education. The reason is obviously that tuition and fees in national institutions are almost negligible as compared with those in private institutions.

4.4 Returns

As for costs of medical and dental education, different data were available for private and national institutions, and the measured private costs were actually different between the two. However, separated data for returns are not available, so we compute returns under the assumption that there is no difference between graduates from private and national institutions for either physicians or dentists. For computation we use mainly data from the *Facts about Wages in the Private Sector* by the National Personnel Authority and the *Basic Survey of Wage Structures* by the Ministry of Labor.

We start with medical education. *Facts about Wages in the Private Sector* shows the average before-tax annual wages of employed physicians grouped by age. As stated earlier, each of these wages can be regarded as the marginal valuation of (the services provided by) a physician in a year. The social returns to medical education at each age can be obtained by subtracting the average before-tax annual wages of male (senior) high-school graduates from the above wages of physicians of the same age. It must be noted that the age groupings are different between *Facts about Wages in the Private Sector* and *Basic Survey of Wage Structures*. We compute returns by assuming that physicians in the same age group receive the same wages.

What should be noted in this computation is the fact that there is an intern system for physicians which requires them to work as trainees for two years immediately after graduation from medical school for relatively low wages. The government provides subsidies for this program every year. The wages of interns are not publicized, but it is said that they are very close to the wages of male (senior) high-school graduates of the same age, so we assume here that they are the same. According to the *General Account Budget in 1982* from the Ministry of Public Welfare, there was a total expenditure in 1982 of 3,424,436,000 yen for subsidies for clinical training of the total of 4,774 interns. This implies that the public expenditure per intern equaled about 717,000 yen. This amount is a negative social "return". Because the wages of interns are (almost) the same as those of male high-school graduates and public subsidies are provided by government, this two-year period is actually a training period.

The social returns computed in this way are shown in the column of "Social Returns to Medical Education" in Table 4.4. Annual social returns after the two-year intern period are within the range of about 5.4–11.8 million yen and almost increase with age. The ratio of annual social returns to average annual wages for male (senior) high-school graduates is, for example, 2.0 for the age group of 36 to 39 and 2.3 for the age group of 52 to 54. Thus, the average income of employed physicians is likely to be more than three times as high as that of male high-school graduates.

The stream of private returns in the column of "Private Returns to Medical Education" in Table 4.4 has been computed by applying almost the same method as above to after-tax wages. Annual private returns after the two-year intern period are within the range of about 3.6–7 million yen and increase with age.

Let us next examine returns to dental education. We can apply again the same method as above, but wage data for employed dentists in the *Facts about Wages in the*

Table 4.4. Returns to medical and dental education.

(yen/year)

Age \ Returns	Private Returns to Medical Education	Social Returns to Medical Education	Private Returns to Dental Education	Social Returns to Dental Education
24	0	−717,300	3,912,103	5,305,473
25	0	−717,300	3,161,003	4,614,573
26~27	3,636,982	5,373,702	3,161,003	4,614,573
28~29	4,377,560	6,210,000	3,551,381	4,890,291
30~31	3,831,920	5,555,200	3,005,741	4,235,491
32~34	4,697,215	6,821,535	3,454,220	4,769,070
35	4,148,215	6,134,535	2,905,220	4,082,070
36~39	5,368,129	8,486,649	4,398,585	6,436,185
40~43	5,062,840	8,087,240	2,761,414	3,940,334
44	5,483,585	8,954,185	5,722,327	9,475,077
45~47	5,358,165	8,792,685	5,596,907	9,313,577
48~49	6,311,719	10,892,689	2,403,250	3,415,280
50~51	6,399,119	10,911,489	2,490,650	3,434,080
52~54	6,282,438	11,030,158	4,161,342	6,512,082
55	6,947,338	11,793,058	4,826,242	7,274,982
56~59	5,993,209	9,994,179	4,610,185	7,127,125
60~64	6,776,739	10,984,879	5,393,715	8,117,825
65~	7,031,139	11,291,879	5,648,115	8,424,825

Private Sector has only a small number of samples and lack reliability. Yet, since the average wages in 1982 shown in this data do not differ greatly from those for corresponding age groups in several years around 1982, the rates of return that will be computed in the next section do not seem to deviate much from the true rates of return.

In contrast to the case of physicians, dentists do not have an intern system. Thus they can be considered to work as full-fledged dentists immediately after graduation. The returns computed in this way are shown in the last two columns of Table 4.4. Annual social returns are in the range of about 3.4–9.5 million yen, whereas annual private returns are in the range of about 2.4–5.7 million yen. Private returns to the average physician are higher than those to the average dentist by more than a million yen per year.

The oldest age group of the data in the *Facts about Wages in the Private Sector* is the group of 56 and older. What is the best assumption about the retirement age of physicians and dentists? The longer they are assumed to work, the higher the rates of return to be computed in the next section will be. However, the formula for internal rates of return suggests that the returns in the few years near the time of retirement have only minor effects on the computed internal rates of return. As it is said that the group of physicians older than sixty-five are much less active than younger physicians and many hospitals set the retirement age of full-time physicians at sixty-five, it is assumed here that all physicians and dentists work till sixty-five and then retire.[13]

The above estimation of returns were based on the wages of employed physicians and dentists. There is no guarantee that the returns for medical practitioners, who are self-employed, are the same as above. Since income data concerning medical practitioners classified by age are not available, we cannot compute returns for them.

However, we can obtain data as to the average incomes of medical practitioners for 1981 from the *Survey Report on the Medical Economy in 1981* compiled by the Central Association of Social Insurance and Medicine and show them here for reference. The average annual income of practicing physicians was 21.987 million yen in 1981, whereas that of practicing dentists was 19.020 million yen. According to the *Facts about Wages in the Private Sector*, the average annual wage of employed physicians was 10.828 million yen in 1982, whereas that of employed dentists was 8.640 million yen.

Therefore, if income data for medical practitioners classified by age were available, the returns computed in the same way as above would be much larger. However, a considerable part of the difference can be interpreted as the risk premium. In other words, since the income of a medical practitioner is uncertain, no one will enter this career unless the mean income is much higher than that of an employed physician or dentist.

4.5
Evaluation of the Measured Rates of Return

4.5.1
Computation Results of the Internal Rates of Return

As we estimated the streams of costs and returns of medical and dental education in the previous two sections, we are now ready to compute the internal rates of return to these types of education. Internal rates of return which do not consider economic growth can be computed using almost the same equation as Eq. 2.4. The only difference arising here is that medical and dental education requires six years rather than four years of study. Therefore, the equation to be used here becomes the following:

$$C_1 + \frac{C_2}{1+r} + \cdots + \frac{C_6}{(1+r)^5} = \frac{R_7}{(1+r)^6} + \frac{R_8}{(1+r)^7} + \cdots + \frac{R_T}{(1+r)^{T-1}}. \quad (4.2)$$

The sought after internal rates of return can be obtained by making T correspond to sixty-five years of age, substituting the social and private costs and returns of medical and dental education in private and national institutions into $C_1, C_2, \ldots, C_6, R_7, R_8, \ldots, R_T$, and solving the resultant equations.

The computation results are shown in the 0% column in Table 4.5. A comparison between the private internal rate of return to medical education in private institutions and that in national institutions shows that the latter is about twice the former. Since private returns are assumed to be the same for both, this difference is solely due to the difference in private costs. As public subsidies bear a large portion of the costs of medical education in national institutions, the private rate of return to this education becomes extremely high. On the other hand, a comparison between the private internal rate of return to dental education in private institutions and that in national institutions reveals that the latter is about 2.4 times the former. This difference is larger than that in medical education.[14]

Table 4.5. Internal rates of return to medical and dental education.

(%)

Rate of Return	Education Type	Institution Type	0% Rate of Economic Growth	3% Rate of Economic Growth
Private	Medical	Private	8.7	12.0
Private	Medical	National	17.1	20.6
Social	Medical	Private	8.5	11.8
Private	Dental	Private	7.7	11.0
Private	Dental	National	18.1	21.7
Social	Dental	Private	9.2	12.4

Next we would like to find the difference in the private rate of return between medical and dental education in private institutions. Table 4.5 shows that the internal rate of return to medical education is higher than that to dental education by one percentage point. The reason this difference is so small in spite of the fact that the simple total of the private costs of the latter is higher than those of the former only by 1.2 million yen and annual returns to the former are higher than those to the latter by more than a million yen is that physicians have to receive clinical training for two years immediately after graduation and in this period receive almost the same wages as those for high-school graduates of the same age. Computation results of internal rates of return are very sensitive to returns (and costs) at early stages.

A comparison of the private rates of return between medical and dental education in national institutions shows that the latter is one percentage point higher than the former. Since the private costs are the same between medical and dental education in national institutions, only the difference in the returns generates the difference in the internal rates of return. As stated above, it is the existence of the intern system for physicians that makes the rate of return to medical education lower than that to dental education even though the average annual wages of physicians are higher than those of dentists by more than a million yen.

Finally, we will compare the social rates of return between medical and dental education in private institutions. The two rates are fairly close with the latter being higher by only 0.7 percentage points. There are mainly two reasons for the lower social rate of return to medical education in spite of the fact that physicians earn more than dentists. The first is the existence of the intern system as mentioned above. The second is that training for physicians is more expensive than for dentists. As we saw in Sect. 4.3, the simple total of social costs of medical education exceeds that of dental education by 12.150 million yen. In addition, the intern program requires public subsidies.

The internal rates of return used in the above argument have been computed by directly applying Eq. 4.2 to cross-sectional data for 1982. As discussed in Chap. 2, such rates of return would be realized if there was no economic growth. In other words, they were obtained by assuming that the costs of medical/dental education and the wage differences between physicians/dentists and general workers will not vary over time. Since these values will actually vary over time in the real economy as mentioned in Sect. 4.1, we also need to see internal rates of return which take economic growth into consideration. If we assume that costs and returns grow annually at a constant rate, internal rates of return under this assumption can be computed using a relation which is formally the same as Eq. 2.8. Table 4.5 also contains internal rates of return which have been computed under the assumption that costs and returns grow annually at the rate of 3%. It is evident that these rates are very high and a discussion similar to the above also holds in this case.

We pointed out that there are large income differences between employed physicians/dentists and medical practitioners. Though most are likely to be risk premiums, the rates of return shown in Table 4.5 may be lower than those for medical practitioners even after considering these premiums. Therefore, the rates in Table 4.5 can be interpreted as the lower bounds of the rates of return to medical and dental education. Incidentally, according to the *Survey of Physicians, Dentists, and Pharmacists* by the Ministry of Public Welfare, in 1982 39% of all physicians were practitioners, whereas most of the others were employed. On the other hand, 65% of all dentists were practitioners and most of the others were employed dentists.

4.5.2 Discussion

As stated before, private internal rates of return are indices that can be used for individual decision making as to investment in medical or dental education. In other words, those rates show how attractive such education is as an investment object for individuals. Thus, it is worthwhile to compare the private rates of return shown in Table 4.5 with rates of return to other investment opportunities for individuals.

First, we consider the interest rate for bank term deposits, which have been the most popular investment opportunity for Japanese people. The rate of interest for this investment opportunity was 6% in 1982 (Economic Planning Agency, *Economic Statistics Abstract*). It should be noted that this is a nominal rate, and thus the real rate, which considers increases in the consumer price index, is lower. In fact, the real rate of interest for bank term deposits was almost 0% if averaged over the past several decades. In contrast, the internal rates of return shown in Table 4.5 are real rates, since they have been computed using cross-sectional data. Therefore, the private rates of return to medical and dental education in Table 4.5 were much higher than the real interest rate of bank term deposits so that investment in such education was very advantageous.

It may be necessary to explain why the interest rate for bank term deposits was so low. For a long period, interest rates were regulated to very low levels in Japan. This was called the low-interest-rate policy.[15] One purpose of this policy was to enable small financial institutions to gain enough profits to avoid bankruptcies and thereby protect depositors. This principle of avoiding small financial institutions becoming bankrupt is called the convoy system. Another purpose was to give priority to large corporations in the allocation of the capital collected at such low interest rates. It should be added, however, that there is a factor besides the low-interest-rate policy which tends to lower the interest rate for bank term deposits. This derives from the nature of bank term deposits, which have difficulty responding flexibly to changing rates of inflation and economic growth.

Another alternative investment possibility for individuals is higher education other than medical and dental education. We mentioned rates of return to general higher education in Sect. 2.4 in Chap. 2 and will discuss those for Japan in detail in the next chapter. Here, we would like to point out only what is useful for the present comparison.

When no account is taken of economic growth, the private internal rate of return for male Japanese students in private universities was 6.7% in 1982. It should be added, however, that this rate is computed under the assumption that general workers continue to work until the age of fifty-nine, though we have assumed that physicians and dentists work until the age of sixty-five.[16] It is realistic to differentiate retirement ages between physicians/dentists and general workers, because the former tend to work more years. Should there be little difference in retirement ages, no serious problem would arise in the present comparison, since the returns at those older ages have little influence on the computed internal rates of return.

It is clear that private rates of return to both medical and dental education in private institutions exceed that to general higher education (6.7%). Therefore, it can be proposed that medical and dental education in private institutions is an economically advantageous object of investment, even though a student has to bear enormous private costs to receive it.

A comparison between general higher education and medical/dental education in national institutions is much more striking. The private rates of return to the latter types of education are 17 to 18% when no account is taken of economic growth, and are slightly higher than 20% when the rate of economic growth is assumed to be 3%. These returns to medical and dental education are so high that we can easily understand how attractive these types of education are from an individual standpoint. It should be noted that returns are even higher when considering the possibility that some physicians and dentists become practitioners. Incidentally, among those who were admitted to medical institutions in 1982, 62% were enrolled in national or public (prefectural) institutions, while among those who were admitted to dental institutions in the same year, 28% were enrolled in national or public institutions (Ministry of Education, *Basic School Survey*). Summing up, the fact that medical and dental education is so attractive an investment opportunity from the standpoint of an individual has generated the feverish competition for enrollment in medical and dental education.

It is social rates of return that are criteria for determining whether numbers of physicians and dentists are excessive or not. The social rates of return shown in Table 4.5 cannot be said to be low. They are no lower than 8.5% in real terms when no account is taken of economic growth, whereas they equal about 12% in real terms when the rate of economic growth is assumed to be 3%. These rates are sufficiently high that there is no waste in resource allocation from the standpoint of society as a whole. Therefore, investment in medical and dental education is still quite advantageous. In other words, the numbers of physicians and dentists are still less than optimal and thus should be increased.

A question may arise as to what are the optimal numbers. An analysis such as the above indicates only the direction of policy (whether to increase or decrease the numbers), but does not suggest how many physicians or dentists should be added or reduced. As stated earlier, the purpose of this chapter is to argue the basis for achieving optimality, so we do not specifically estimate optimal numbers of physicians and dentists.

To undertake such an estimation with high accuracy would require a large volume of detailed data. If the necessary data were available the optimal numbers could be estimated, basically by extending the above analysis. What we should do further is to first vary the numbers of physicians and dentists around the current numbers and then estimate the corresponding changes in the costs of medical and dental education and those in the marginal valuations of physicians and dentists. This process would enable us to estimate the social rates of return corresponding to different numbers of physicians and dentists. Thus we would be able to determine the optimal numbers of physicians and dentists corresponding to the target social rate of return.

Finally, we would like to discuss questions concerning private rates of return. As we have seen, the actual private rates of return to medical and dental education in national institutions are abnormally high. In response to the fact that physicians and dentists earn extremely high earnings, one of the opinions examined in Sect. 4.2 expresses the following:

> There is an estimate that an average employed physician earns three to four times as much as an average general worker and an average practicing physician earns six to seven times as much. However, these high earnings induce competent students to choose to become physicians or dentists. Moreover, such high earnings are not irrational if account is taken of the long period of training and severe working conditions.[17]

What matters here is whether such large earnings differences are necessary. Everyone may allow that the more competent the physicians and dentists, the better the society will be. But other industries also need competent human resources. Competent scientists, engineers, and managers will contribute to society in no lower degree than physicians and dentists.

If the medical (dental) industry tries to secure high earnings or high incentives to invite competent students by artificially limiting the number of physicians (dentists), then the human resource allocation of the economy will be very unlikely to be optimal. In other words, pecuniary incentives that are too high tend to induce those who may have an aptitude for other occupations to choose to be physicians or dentists. If pecuniary incentives were lower, the human resource allocation would be improved because the above individuals would engage themselves in other more suitable occupations and because medical and dental occupations would be filled by those who have a really strong aptitude for these occupations but may not be so good at competing for admissions to medical or dental schools in the current system.

It should be added that a long period of training is common among professionals, and some occupations have working conditions more severe than those for physicians and dentists. The keen competition itself for admission to medical and dental institutions suggests that the "long period of training" and the "severe working conditions" are not burdensome.

High private rates of return have another problem in resource allocation. Even a large amount of investment in preparation for entrance examinations into medical or dental institutions pays off for an individual when rates of return are high. Thus a large amount of waste is likely to arise from the standpoint of society as a whole. If private rates of return were much lower, fewer individuals would spend so much money or effort preparing for these entrance examinations.

We can think of about three policies that would correct the high rates of return we saw above. First, it is necessary to increase the numbers of physicians and dentists. Other things being equal, this policy will reduce not only social but also private rates of return.

If private rates of return are too high at socially optimal numbers of physicians and dentists, either of two policies should be enforced; to reduce public subsidies to medical and dental education, or to increase income tax for physicians and dentists. If the capital market was perfect, these two policies would have the same effect of reducing private rates of return.

However, since it is in reality unlikely to be perfect, the two policies tend to have different effects. A reduction of public subsidies will prevent those students who have difficulty financing investment costs from going to medical or dental school, but an increase in the income tax rate will not generate such a problem. As there are many who are suitable to be physicians and dentists in terms of aptitude and personality among those who have difficulty financing investment costs, an increase in the income tax rate is preferable for the optimal allocation of human resources.

In short, because training costs for physicians and dentists are very high, government should bear most training costs and then impose a high tax rate on the incomes of physicians and dentists. It should be added that the abnormally high tuition and fees of private medical and dental schools are not consistent with the above-mentioned opinions that students with high intelligence should receive medical and dental education.

Notes

1. This chapter is based on Arai (1986).
2. As we saw in Chap. 2 (see Note 11), the resource allocation in perfectly competitive markets is Pareto optimal (under certain conditions).
3. For instance, when the total number of physicians equals N_1 in Fig. 4.1, the marginal valuation and income of any particular physician equal w_1. This is because when any particular physician exits from this market (or when the number of physicians decreases by one), the value the market (society) loses equals w_1 under an assumption that all physicians are identical and thus substitutable. This is equivalent to saying that the social valuation of any physician is equal to w_1.
4. Both are compiled in Ministry of Public Welfare (1986b).
5. The former is compiled in Ministry of Public Welfare (1985). See Ministry of Public Welfare (1986a) for the latter.
6. See page 6 of the *Interim Opinion of the Committee for Examination of the Future Demand for and Supply of Physicians* and page 7 of the *Interim Opinion of the Committee for Examination of the Future Demand for and Supply of Dentists.*
7. See page 3 of the *Interim Opinion of the Committee for Examination of the Future Demand for and Supply of Physicians.*
8. The number of patients depends basically upon the following three factors: (1) the population, (2) the rate of receiving treatment, and (3) the disease structure which affects treatment days and treatment intervals (page 16 of the *Interim Opinion of the Committee for Examination of the Future Demand for and Supply of Physicians*).

9. This number of ten thousand non-clinical physicians equals about 5.5% of the total number of physicians in 1984 (*source*: Ministry of Public Welfare, 1986b).

10. See page 18 of the *Interim Opinion of the Committee for Examination of the Future Demand for and Supply of Physicians.* In contrast, the *Interim Opinion of the Committee for Examination of the Future Demand for and Supply of Dentists* considers the number of patients per clinical dentist independently of the matter of week holidays.

11. The exact nature of these fees is not clear as they are only vaguely described in the source. It is possible that they are "required donations".

12. The author owes Mr. Takatoshi Kikuchi the following computation of the amounts of tax.

13. The quotation is from page 14 of the *Interim Opinion of the Committee for Examination of the Future Demand for and Supply of Physicians.* However, this opinion suggests that many physicians no younger than sixty-five are actually working. According to the *Interim Opinion of the Committee for Examination of the Future Demand for and Supply of Dentists* (page 14), most dentists regard seventy as the proper average age of retirement for dentists. If these are taken into consideration, the rates of return computed below are biased slightly downwards.

14. Maurizi (1975) and Burstein and Cromwell (1985) estimated private rates of return to medical and dental education in the United States. The former estimated private rates of return to dental education at eight points in time from 1948 to 1970. The estimated rates are between 13.6% and 25.5%, and more recent rates tend to be higher. On the other hand, the latter estimated private rates of return for physicians, general practitioners, and dentists at thirteen points in time from 1967 to 1980 (at six points in time for dentists). The rates of return were estimated respectively before and after adjustment for working hours. (It should be noted, however, that this estimation did not use earnings data classified by age, and thus rates of return were computed basically by applying the earnings averaged over all ages to an equation similar to Eq. 2.16. Moreover, it did not consider economic growth either.) According to the estimates, the rates of return for physicians were between 10.2% and 12.1% before adjustment for working hours and between 12.6% and 15.5% after adjustment. On the other hand, those for general practitioners were between 16.3% and 19.0% before adjustment and between 12.1% and 14.5% after, while those for dentists were between 13.5% and 16.3% before adjustment and between 14.8% and 15.7% after. These rates are higher than the private internal rates of return to medical and dental education in private institutions in Japan. See also Mennemeyer (1978).

15. See *Financial Institutions in Japan* by the Bank of Japan for the low-interest-rate policy.

16. It should be added further that before-tax wages are used in the computation of the private rate of return to general higher education.

17. This is the author's summary of a part from page 29 to page 30 of the *Final Opinion of the Committee for Examination of the Future Demand for and Supply of Physicians.*

Chapter 5
Causes of Changes in the Enrollment Rate

We saw in Chap. 1 that the percentage of students going to college has greatly changed over time. How can we explain these changes? This chapter will answer this question. Applying the internal-rate-of-return method yields the simple answer that the changes are due to those in the (expected) private internal rate of return to investment in higher education. However, computing private rates of return over some period and comparing them with the percentages of students who went to college reveal that the question is not so simple.

This chapter will show in Sects. 5.1 and 5.2 that the private internal rate of return is not always sufficient to explain the percentage of students going to college. A reason for this is that as the capital market is actually imperfect, whether an individual's household has its own funds for investment (in higher education) becomes a crucial factor in his/her college-going decision making as argued in Chap. 2.

It will be shown in Sects. 5.3, 5.4, and 5.5 that there are also other reasons. For instance, tuition and fees, forgone earnings, and wage differences between college and senior high-school graduates, each of which is a constituent of the internal rate of return, have different effects on college-going decisions from those assumed in the internal-rate-of-return method. In these sections, we will analyze in detail factors generating the changes in the percentage of students going to college by taking account not only of all these constituent factors but also others that are ignored in the internal-rate-of-return method.

Section 5.6 will discuss the relationship between the percentage of students going to college and the percentage of students applying for admission to college. Some researchers insist that the latter concept is more suitable when analyzing demand for higher education, but we will argue that it is theoretically and empirically more suitable to consider the former.

Some notes follow. First, the analyses in this Chapter will focus only on the percentage of male students going to four-year college or university, because the case of female students is not only more complex but also suffers from a scarcity of data.

Second, in this Chapter we will use a few short expressions for frequently used terms. The internal rate of return which is appropriate to analyzing individual college-going decision making should be the expected private internal rate of return. Because this rigorous expression is too long, we will often use such expressions as "the rate of return" and "the internal rate of return". Further, "tuition and fees" is represented by the simpler expression of just "tuition". "The percentage of (male) students going to college" is also a long expression. Hence, we will use the expression "enrollment rate" to mean the above. For the percentage of (male) students applying for admission to higher education, we will use the expression "application rate".[1]

5.1 Internal Rate of Return and Enrollment Rate

5.1.1 Changes in the Rate of Return

In this section, we will examine whether a simple rate-of-return analysis can explain the actual enrollment rate. In other words, we will examine whether the expected private internal rate of return to higher education is a determinant of the enrollment rate in the real economy. For this purpose we first compute a time-series of rates of return over some period and then examine if they can explain the enrollment rates in this period.

When actually computing rates of return, we are obliged to focus only on pecuniary costs and benefits as we did in Chap. 4. Further, we need some other simplifying assumptions. In accordance with the discussion in Chap. 2, we assume that individuals anticipate rates of return on the basis of the cross-sectional structure of investment costs and wages that can be observed at the time of their decision making.

As to expectations of economic growth, either of the following two simple but standard assumptions are used, as suggested in Chap. 2. The first is that no economic growth is expected and thus all investment costs and wages observed at the time of decision making are expected to be maintained. The second is that all investment costs and wages are expected to grow at a constant rate. If we use the first assumption, the expected rate of return is computed from Eq. 2.4. On the other hand, if we use the second, it is computed from Eq. 2.8, though we need to specify the level of the constant rate of economic growth.

We undertake here an empirical study covering a period of about twenty years from the mid-1960s. There was a remarkable change in the enrollment rate in the middle of this period which makes it a very interesting period to study.

This empirical study makes further simplifications in order to cope with difficulties of data availability and to save research costs. As for investment costs, we consider only tuition and gross forgone earnings (forgone earnings before the reduction of part-time income) per student, which are the major costs of higher education. Data for costs of books and stationery, commuting costs, and part-time income are available for every alternate year from the *Survey of Student Life* by the Ministry of Education. But these amounts are quite small compared with tuition and gross forgone earnings. Moreover, as the sum of the costs of books and stationery and commuting costs is almost equal to part-time income, they can be considered to cancel each other out in the computation process of internal rates of return.

As for tuition, we use the average amount per student in private institutions. If the enrollment rate depends on the rate of return, the latter must be the rate of return for private institutions, because most "peripheral students" go to private institutions in Japan. (In 1975, 79.7% of new students were enrolled in private institutions. Here "peripheral students" are defined as those who make college-going decisions quite near the time of high-school graduation.) The tuition per student in private institutions can be computed from the data in the *Survey of the Financial Situations of Private Schools* and the *Basic School Survey*, both of which are compiled by the Ministry of Education.

Data for forgone earnings are obtained from the *Basic Survey of Wage Structures* by the Ministry of Labor. Here forgone earnings are regarded as equal to the annual average wages or earnings of male senior high-school graduates in each age group from ages 18 to 21 in all firm sizes in all industries (the earnings include bonuses). Strictly speaking, after-tax wages should be used for forgone earnings, but before-tax wages are used here to save computation costs.

Next, we would like to examine returns to higher education. The wage difference between college and (senior) high-school graduates can be computed in the same manner using the same data as for forgone earnings. It is assumed here that all workers work until the age of fifty-nine and then retire. Adjusting retirement age by two or three years would not significantly change resultant internal rates of return. It should be noted that though the computation method used here overestimates both forgone earnings and returns by the amount of income tax, these cancel out to some extent in the process of computing internal rates of return. When we assume that all investment costs and wages will grow at a constant rate, this rate of growth is assumed to equal the real rate of wage growth averaged over the past three years at the time of decision making.

The private internal rates of return computed in this way are shown in Table 5.1 and Fig. 5.1. The rate of return *B*, which does not consider economic growth (or assumes

Table 5.1. Rate of male university enrollment and private internal rate of return.

(%)

Year	Rate of Enrollment (*A*)	Rate of Return under Zero Economic Growth (*B*)	Rate of Return under Economic Growth (*D*)
1965	20.7	8.85	11.97
1966	18.7	8.35	12.33
1967	20.6	8.38	13.02
1968	22.1	8.32	16.77
1969	24.7	8.38	18.09
1970	27.2	8.42	19.45
1971	30.3	8.25	16.58
1972	33.5	7.67	16.77
1973	35.1	7.17	16.03
1974	37.5	7.24	13.74
1975	40.4	7.50	10.77
1976	40.9	7.43	8.04
1977	39.6	7.38	8.80
1978	40.8	7.05	9.14
1979	39.4	6.88	9.33
1980	39.3	6.69	8.16
1981	38.6	6.75	7.75
1982	37.9	6.71	7.48
1983	36.1	6.62	8.23
1984	36.4	6.44	8.27
1985	38.6	6.58	8.05
1986	34.1		

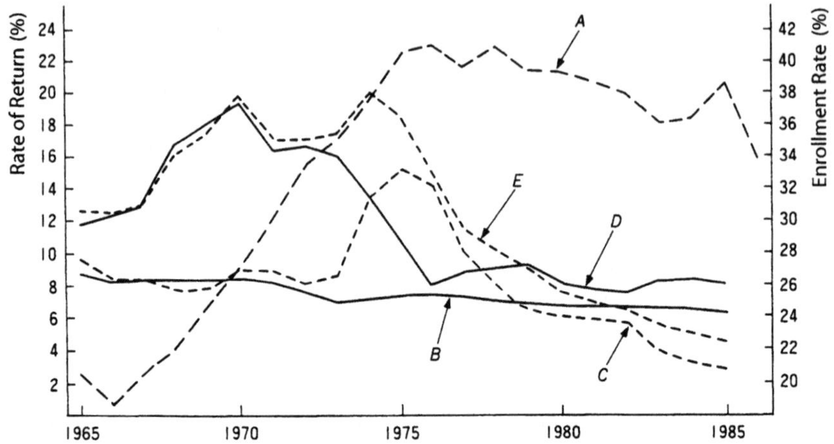

Notes: A = Enrollment Rate B = Rate of Return under Zero Economic Growth
$C = B -$ Interest Rate D = Rate of Return under Economic Growth
$E = D -$ Interest Rate

Fig. 5.1. Private Internal Rate of Return and Rate of Male University Enrollment

zero expected growth), is decreasing almost monotonically from 8.85% in 1965 to 6.58% in 1985. If individuals are assumed to expect all investment costs and wages to grow at the real rate of wage growth averaged over the past three years, the expected rate of return D varies greatly, and achieves a peak of 19.45% in 1970 and a trough of 7.48% in 1982.

Figure 5.1 also shows the differences between these rates of return and the real interest rate of one-year bank term deposits averaged over the past three years, which can be regarded as the rate of return to the alternative investment opportunity.[2] C in the Figure equals the difference between B and this interest rate, whereas E equals that between D and the interest rate.

On the other hand, the percentage A of male students who went to four-year college (university) increased very rapidly till the mid-1970s and then decreased slightly. In the following, A will be often referred to as the enrollment rate.

5.1.2
Relationship Between Rate of Return and Enrollment Rate

The Table and Figure show the following: First, the rates of return are quite high. B is higher than 6% and D is higher than 7% in all years. C and E are also quite large. The average level of C is higher than 6% even after the mid-1970s when the enrollment rate reached its peak. The average of E is even higher. As pointed out in the previous chapter, the interest rate offered by banks was kept very low by regulation. From the standpoint of most individuals, however, bank term deposits were the most favorable investment opportunity. Thus it is meaningful to compare this interest rate with the private rate of return.

This observation reveals that as far as the absolute level of the rate of return is concerned, higher education was still an advantageous investment even after the mid-1970s. This fact becomes an important piece of evidence showing that it is difficult to explain the decline in the enrollment rate using rates of return.

Next we examine whether the variations in the rate of return can explain those in the enrollment rate. It should be noted that the above internal rates of return were computed from average investment costs and average wage differences. The actual (expected) rate of return is likely to vary among individuals, because for example some expect to receive high wages and others low wages. If the average rate of return varies over time, the "upper bound" and "lower bound" of rates of return are also likely to vary in a similar manner. When the average rate of return is high, for instance, the "lower bound" is also high and more individuals may go to college. Hence, the variations in the average rate of return might explain those in the enrollment rate.

To see if this is the case, let us first focus on *B*. As a whole, *B* is decreasing, which is contrary to the general trend of *A*. It is true that there is a positive correlation between *A* and *B* after the mid-1970s, but the correlation before that is negative. Therefore, we cannot generally conclude that the enrollment rate increased (decreased) because the rate of return to higher education increased (decreased).

As investment in higher education depends on rates of return to other investment opportunities, let us now focus on *C*. In Fig. 5.1 *C* greatly deviates from *B* around 1975 due to a sharp decline in the real rate of interest caused by the jump in consumer prices from the first oil shock. In contrast, the deviation in the few years up to 1985 is due to stable consumer prices. In other years, *C* is close to *B*.

It seems that *C* can explain *A* if only the period after 1972 is considered, because both change similarly in this period. In particular, *C* seems able to explain quite well the sharp rise in the enrollment rate up to 1975 and its subsequent decline. However, *C* cannot explain *A* in the period up to 1972. In addition, it does not seem to be so persuasive to use the jump in consumer prices at the time of the oil shock to explain the enrollment rate. If the period of the oil shock is excluded, *C* tends to decrease contrary to the general trend of *A*.

Next let us examine *D*. As a whole, *D* also tends to decrease against the general pattern of *A*. However, there is a high positive correlation between *A* and *D* with a time lag of six to seven years. In other words, if the graph of *D* is shifted to the right by six to seven years in Fig. 5.1, the new graph of *D* will look quite similar to *A*. Thus, if it is proposed that college-going decisions were made on the basis of the rate of return shown by *D* six to seven years before the age of (senior) high-school graduation and these decisions were not changed once made, then this proposition based on a rate-of-return analysis cannot be statistically rejected.

Yet, the author's basic idea differs from this. It is true that individuals in no small numbers, in fact the main group of college-going students, decide to go to college six or seven years before the age of high-school graduation. However, those whose decisions influence annual changes in the enrollment rate are not in this core group but in the "periphery" or "margin" of the whole population of students going to college. These students make college-going decisions at a point in time quite close to high-school graduation.

Incidentally, if the time lag for D is shortened to about three years, the positive correlation will disappear. Moreover, if we use the rate of wage growth (or economic growth) averaged over a much longer period of time than three years, e.g., a high constant rate of wage growth during the period of high economic growth (the period up to the beginning of the 1970s) and a low constant rate of wage growth after that period, the new curve for D would be decreasing and would as a whole have an opposite movement to A.

Finally, we would like to look at E. As a whole, E is barely correlated with A. There is again a high positive correlation between A and E with a time lag of five to seven years, but the same argument holds as for D.

All these considerations lead to a conclusion that neither absolute levels of the private internal rate of return nor its changes enable a simple rate-of-return analysis to explain the level of the enrollment rate or its variation. This conclusion is in stark contrast with that proposed by Mattila (1982), who analyzed determinants of the enrollment rate using time-series data for American males from the mid-1950s to the end of the 1970s.

Table 5.2, from Mattila's paper, shows the changes in the index of the rate of return to higher education, which has been computed as B above. He does not show specific levels of the rate of return, but rather represents them using an index where the value in 1956 is 100. Thus, though the table does not inform us of the absolute levels of the rate of return (he reports that they are between 10% and 13%), it reveals the changes in the rate of return. According to the Table, the rate of return increased steadily from 1959 to 1968–69 and then decreased for about ten years.

On the other hand, Fig. 5.2 shows the enrollment rate of American male students. According to this Figure the enrollment rate generally increased till about 1969 and then decreased. A comparison between Table 5.2 and Fig. 5.2 reveals that the rate of return and the enrollment rate changed almost analogously. With this fact and a variety of other computation results, Mattila concludes that the internal rate of return is the most important determinant of the enrollment rate.[3]

Table 5.2. Rate of return index for American males.

(1956 = 100)

Year	Rate of Return Index	Year	Rate of Return Index
1956	100.0	1968	115.7
1957	96.3	1969	115.5
1958	94.3	1970	114.3
1959	93.9	1971	111.8
1960	94.8	1972	107.7
1961	96.7	1973	102.2
1962	99.6	1974	96.3
1963	102.8	1975	95.5
1964	105.8	1976	94.3
1965	108.7	1977	93.9
1966	112.2	1978	94.1
1967	114.3	1979	94.9

Source: Mattila (1982).

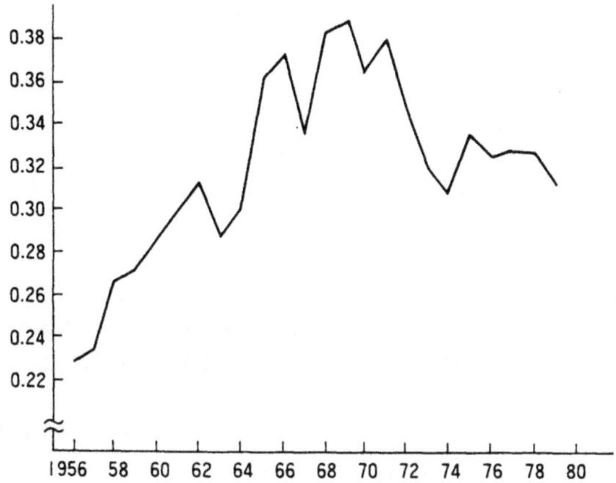

Fig. 5.2. Enrollment Rate of American Males. Source: Mattila (1982)

It should be noted, however, that when the average rate of return is between 10% and 13%, investment in higher education is unlikely to be disadvantageous even to those who face low rates of return. For instance, an ordinary (not extremely rich) individual who can enjoy 70% of the average rate of return (thus 7% to 9.1%) finds it profitable to invest in college education. (Very rich individuals might have investment opportunities which will yield higher returns.) Therefore, what determines the enrollment rate may not be the rate of return itself even in the United States.

5.2 Capital Market Imperfection and the Enrollment Rate

One of the reasons a simple rate-of-return analysis gives rise to the above difficulties at least in the case of Japan is that its assumption about availability of funds for investment by individuals is unrealistic. As we saw in Chap. 2, the internal-rate-of-return method assumes capital market perfection. If the real capital market is imperfect as in most countries, cases will arise in which individuals cannot invest in higher education because of insufficient funds, even though the private rate of return is high.

Incidentally, the above difference between Japan and the United States in the relationship between the rate of return and the enrollment rate may be due firstly to the fact that the majority of Japanese students are enrolled in private institutions whereas the reverse is true for the United States, and secondly to the difference in systems of education loans and financial aids.

More specifically, college-going behavior may be more sensitive to changes in returns to higher education where most are public institutions and thus average tuition fees are very low, such as the case of state universities in the United States. Moreover, as a variety of education loans and financial aid programs have long been more highly developed in the United States than in Japan, the sensitivity of college-going behavior to changes in returns must have been higher in the former.

It is easy to modify the analysis in Sect. 5.1 by considering availability of funds for investment under capital market imperfection. What we need to do is simply to introduce a variable for family income, because that variable greatly affects availability of funds as seen in Chap. 2. The signaling models under capital market imperfection discussed in Chap. 3 also suggest that an increase in family income is likely to induce individuals to go to college. That is, those models imply that the enrollment rate is likely to increase when more individuals face low signaling costs because of increases in family income. Of course, higher education needs to be sufficiently attractive in terms of costs and benefits in any model to induce individuals to invest in it.

Columns (1) through (9) in Table 5.3 show the results of a regression analysis by the ordinary least squares method which considers the above points about capital market imperfection. (See Appendix B for the theory of regression analysis.) The dependent variable in this regression analysis is the male enrollment rate, which is the same as *A* in the previous section.

The independent variables from *RR* to *RRGWIR* have already been used. More specifically, *RR* is the rate of return computed assuming zero economic growth, thus it is equal to *B* in Table 5.1 and Fig. 5.1. *IR* equals the real interest rate of one-year bank term deposits averaged over the past three years and represents the real market (lending) rate of interest. *GW* is the real rate of wage growth averaged over the past three years. *RRIR* equals the difference between *RR* and *IR*, and thus is the same as *C* in Fig. 5.1. *RRGW* is the rate of return computed assuming wage (economic) growth and thus equals *D* in Table 5.1 and Fig. 5.1. Similarly, *RRGWIR* is equal to the difference between *RRGW* and *IR* and thus is the same as *E* in Fig. 5.1. All these variables are represented in terms of percent.

W is a variable for family income. We use here regular workers' average monthly real wages in units of 10,000 yen at the 1980 price level.[4] In this and our subsequent empirical analyses, all values of independent variables from which the influence of price changes should be eliminated are transformed into real values using the consumer price index.

On the assumption that investment decisions are made one year before graduation from high school, each independent variable in Table 5.3 has a lag of one year. The sample size is twenty-one years covering the period from 1966 to 1986.

Let us examine the regression results in Table 5.3. (The numbers in parentheses under the coefficients of the independent variables indicate the corresponding *t*-values.)

Result (1) is obtained from the simplest model specification which has only the rate of return *RR* and family income *W* as its independent variables. The coefficient of *RR* equals 8.968 and thus is positive. The *t*-value of 4.42 implies that the coefficient is significant. On the other hand, the coefficient of *W* equals 2.530 and is again positive. The *t*-value of 8.33 also implies that the coefficient is significant.

Result (2) derives from a regression model which modifies the above specification by adding another independent variable *IR* or the market rate of interest. Introduction of *IR* changes the coefficients of *RR* and *W* and also the corresponding *t*-values, but each is still positive and significant. The coefficient of *IR* is negative and signifi-

Table 5.3. Determinants of the enrollment rate (I).

	(1)	(2)	(3)	(4)	(5)	(6)	(7)	(8)	(9)	(10)
CONST.	−88.207	−44.761	−2.396	−80.302	−5.672	−26.827	−5.033	−7.540	−7.967	11.035
RR	8.968	4.795		7.894		2.630				
	(4.42)	(2.46)		(3.87)		(1.67)				
IR		−0.560				−0.648	−0.747			
		(−3.61)				(−5.44)	(−7.72)			
GW				0.300		0.421		0.470		
				(1.66)		(3.74)		(4.43)		
RRIR			0.765					0.741		
			(5.92)					(8.16)		
RRGW					0.556		0.486			
					(2.59)		(4.66)			
RRGWIR									0.626	
									(8.74)	
W	2.530	1.948	1.378	2.480	1.522	1.786	1.505	1.536	1.570	1.616
	(8.33)	(6.83)	(16.96)	(8.51)	(9.81)	(8.15)	(20.01)	(22.85)	(22.70)	(28.31)
PT										−0.073
										(−11.33)
SER	2.15	1.66	1.81	2.05	2.65	1.25	1.28	1.27	1.36	1.09
R^2	0.918	0.953	0.942	0.929	0.875	0.975	0.972	0.973	0.967	0.979
$\overline{R}^2$	0.908	0.945	0.935	0.916	0.861	0.969	0.967	0.968	0.963	0.976
F	100.12	115.71	114.93	74.15	62.82	156.46	198.07	202.93	264.93	416.36
D.W.	0.96	1.29	0.98	0.95	0.50	1.88	1.74	1.77	1.49	1.70

Notes: The time-series analysis from 1966 to 1986. *t*-values are in parentheses.
RR = rate of return under zero economic growth, *IR* = interest rate in real terms, *GW* = rate of wage growth, *RRIR* = *RR* − *IR*, *RRGW* = rate of return under economic growth, *RRGWIR* = *RRGW* − *IR*, *W* = family income, *PT* = private university tuition.

cant. This implies that an increase in the rate of return in the alternative investment opportunity reduces the enrollment rate. Though *IR* is a regulated interest rate, it can be considered to have the property of the rate of return to the alternative investment opportunity because of this result.

Result (3) is obtained by replacing *RR* in (1) by *RRIR*. This model specification is introduced in order to examine whether explanatory power increases if, in place of the rate of return to higher education, its advantageousness relative to the alternative investment opportunity is used as an independent variable. As a matter of fact, all the statistics including *t*-values and R^2 are better in (3) than in (1).

Result (4) derives from the introduction of *GW* into the regression model for (1). Though the significance of the coefficient of *GW* is not very high, this result is consistent with the theory in Chap. 2 which suggests that when the rate of wage (economic) growth is high, the rate of return to higher education becomes high and thus investment in college education becomes advantageous.

Result (5) is obtained by combining *RR* and *GW* into one independent variable *RRGW* in the regression model for (4). This result also shows that the enrollment rate is high when the rate of return related to wage (economic) growth is high, as predicted by theory.

Similarly, all the results up to (9) are consistent with the theories we have considered. Hence, when the independent variable *W* for availability of funds is introduced, the rate of return *RR* and other independent variables derived from it (whose names have *RR*) seem to have unquestionably positive effects on the enrollment rate. Further, the effects of *IR* and *GW* satisfy theoretical sign conditions and are significant. In addition, all the coefficients of family income *W* are positive and highly significant, which implies that availability of funds is a very critical determinant of investment in higher education. Among the above results, those with fewer independent variables generally have smaller *D.W.* statistics, although only the *D.W.* statistic for (5) is very small.

According to the above analysis, it is impossible to reject the hypothesis that the rate of return has a positive effect on the enrollment rate if the availability of funds for investment in higher education is considered.[5] We would like to propose here, however, that this hypothesis does not have a very strong foundation as far as the Japanese case is concerned.

Let us look at result (10) in Table 5.3. This is obtained from a regression model which has *W* and *PT* as independent variables. *PT* is the simple sum of real tuition per student for four years in private institutions. *PT* is computed from cross-sectional data and is expressed in terms of 10,000 yen (at the 1980 price level). This specification is introduced to test a very simple hypothesis that the enrollment rate depends only on tuition and the availability of funds. This is a rather extreme hypothesis especially in the sense that the decision makers are considered to ignore pecuniary returns.

In the result of (10), the coefficient of *W* is positive and that of *PT* negative, and their significance is very high. This suggests that when a variable for availability of funds is introduced, the enrollment rate can be explained fairly well without using a variable for the rate of return but using the variable for tuition, which is merely a constituent of the rate of return.

In fact, though (10) has only two independent variables, R^2 and $\bar{R}^2$ are larger there than in any of the regression results from (1) to (9). By the property of the internal rate of return, an increase in tuition reduces the internal rate of return if other things are equal. Therefore, it may be said that while the enrollment rate actually depends on family income and tuition as in (10), this fact is tested in (1) through (9) slightly inaccurately or under slightly inadequate specifications.

The conclusion of this section can be summarized as follows: If a variable for availability of funds for investment in higher education is introduced, the rate of return to higher education surely has a positive and significant effect on the enrollment rate. However, the explanatory power of this model is weaker than a similar model with the rate of return replaced by tuition, which is merely a constituent of the rate of return.

5.3 Models That Do Not Use Rates of Return

As the internal rate of return is not so powerful in explaining the enrollment rate at least in the case of Japan, we will in this section and the next discuss models that do not use rates of return. Before starting, however, we would like to summarize the problems inherent in analyses that try to explain the enrollment rate using the internal rate of return. They have several shortcomings.

First of all, such analyses do not consider non-pecuniary costs or returns. It is true that theoretical models can consider these, but empirical studies have difficulty doing so. This is because even if data on non-pecuniary costs or returns are available (such data will actually be used later in this Chapter), they cannot be transformed into pecuniary values and thus rates of return with non-pecuniary elements cannot be computed.

Incidentally, the fact that medical and dental education is popular today is probably not only due to the high private rates of return to these types of education but also due to the high unmeasurable satisfaction generated by the high social status of medial and dental occupations. (This high satisfaction itself is largely due to the fact that the numbers of physicians and dentists are regulated. In general, as the number of workers engaged in an occupation increases, their social status decreases if other things are equal. This is similar to the fact that the marginal valuation discussed in Chap. 4 is decreasing in the number of physicians.)

Secondly, the internal-rate-of-return method is unlikely to sufficiently approximate real college-going decision making. It is highly improbable that general students and their families engage in such complex computation as that in the internal-rate-of-return method. They might do some computation, but it is probably very intuitive or rough. In the first place, very few of them actually know the concept of the internal rate of return. In addition, the computation of the internal rate of return undertaken in economics itself makes some artificial assumptions especially about expectations, and thus may not be sufficiently persuasive. It is likely that different individuals have different expectations. What should be emphasized here is that the internal-rate-of-return method for investment decisions is merely a model or a hypothesis. In other words, it is nothing but one approach to explain reality.

Thirdly, individuals may not place as much weight on the investment costs of forgone earnings as human capital theory insists. When human capital theory was being developed, there was controversy as to whether forgone earnings should be included in the costs of investment in education. At present most economists recognize them as costs not differing from tuition. However, this widely accepted view may not be accurate.

Fourthly, there may be other determinants of the enrollment rate that were not considered in the previous two sections. For example, what is important in many other countries is recruiting by the army. Other examples of determinants are changes in the education system, the unemployment rate, and so on. Thus, a simple application of the internal-rate-of-return method does not produce persuasive results.

There are time-series analyses which, without using the rate of return, have considered determinants of the percentage or absolute number of male students who went to college. They include Campbell and Siegel (1967), Galper and Dunn (1969), Radner and Miller (1970), Lehr and Newton (1978).[6] These empirical studies have undertaken regression analyses by introducing such independent variables as family income, average tuition, the rate of increase in the army size, the number of discharges from the army, and the rate of unemployment. According to the results of these studies, the effects of these variables are respectively positive, negative, negative, positive, and positive, with all these effects being significant.

The meanings of the effects of family income and average tuition are self-evident. It is also quite obvious that fewer people go to college if the size of the army increases and the reverse is the case if more are discharged.

The unemployment rate can be considered to have the following two effects on college-going decision making: First, if the unemployment rate is high, high-school graduates find it difficult to obtain jobs, so the expected forgone earnings decrease which induce more to go to college. Secondly, even if some jobs are available to high-school graduates, they may not be very desirable. This implies that the expected returns to higher education increase when the unemployment rate is high and that more will go to college, since the returns to higher education equal the wage and psychological satisfaction gained by graduating from college minus those gained by obtaining an unsatisfactory job as a high-school graduate. Because of these two effects, a high rate of unemployment will induce more to go to college.

In Japan, Fujino (1986) has performed a time-series analysis without using the internal rate of return. His model specification is that the enrollment rate depends on the average wage of regular workers (a proxy for family income), the average tuition of private institutions, and the enrollment rate in the previous year.

The last independent variable is introduced to show the demonstration effect on the demand for higher education.[7] A demonstration effect means that an individual's (consumption) behavior is influenced by that of others. An example is the case in which one buys a big car because a neighbor has bought a big car. The demonstration effect here means that when many high-school graduates go to college in a year, many of the high-school graduates next year who have observed this will also go to college.

The empirical study by Fujino covers the period from 1961 to 1982 and has obtained results as expected, i.e. the wage of regular workers has a positive effect on the enrollment rate, tuition has a negative effect, and the enrollment rate in the previous year has a positive effect.[8]

These empirical studies are more advanced than the internal-rate-of-return method in that they introduce independent variables which are not considered in the latter. But they are weaker in the sense that they do not have independent variables for returns to higher education or forgone earnings. There is no *a priori* reason to ignore these factors before performing empirical analyses.

In the next section, we will undertake empirical analyses which improve these models. Though details will be discussed at that time, we will mention here the four main improvements.

Firstly, we will introduce an independent variable for the wage difference between college and senior high-school graduates as pecuniary returns to higher education.

Secondly, we will also introduce an independent variable for a kind of non-pecuniary returns. That is, we will consider the difference in probability between college and senior high-school graduates of being promoted to section chief. The effect of this independent variable is interesting because Japanese seem to be sensitive to promotion. Since promotion generally involves increased status and satisfaction as well as a wage increase, this independent variable contains both psychological and pecuniary aspects of which the psychological is probably more important. An empirical analysis relying on the internal-rate-of-return method cannot incorporate such a non-pecuniary factor as that stated above.

Thirdly, we will consider forgone earnings as investment costs. The effect of forgone earnings is especially interesting if compared to that of tuition.

Fourthly, we will examine the effect of the new system in Japan of professional schools. In 1976, exactly when the enrollment rate peaked, professional schools (*senmon gakko*) began to admit students, so these schools may have become substitutes for colleges or may have begun to play a partial role in college education.

5.4 Testing Models That Do Not Use the Rate of Return

This section tests several hypotheses on college-going decisions by the ordinary least squares method. As in the previous section the dependent variable in all the following regression models is the enrollment rate. The analyses of this section are divided into two groups according to the periods of analysis. The first group analyzes the period from 1966 to 1986 (Table 5.4) and the second from 1971 to 1986 (Table 5.5). The first group of analyses do not introduce the independent variable for promotion difference because data are not available for all the years in this period.

Let us first look at Table 5.4 and explain the meaning of each independent variable: *PT* is real tuition as defined in Sect. 5.2 which explains that this is based on a simple sum of tuition in four years observable in cross-sectional data. The reason we use a simple sum is not only that it is easy to compute but also that the real rate of interest of bank term deposits averaged over the past thirty years or so is almost 0%. *FG* is real forgone earnings in units of 10,000 yen for staying in college for four years. As in the case of *PT*, this is based on the simple sum of the values of cross-sectional data in the *Basic Survey of Wage Structures* by the Ministry of Labor.

*BN*39, *BN*49, and *BN*59 are the total wage differences in units of 10,000 yen between college and (senior) high-school graduates from the age of graduation from college to the age of 39, 49, and 59, respectively. These are also simple sums based on cross-sectional data from the *Basic Survey of Wage Structures*. We consider these three kinds of wage differences because the wage differences of older workers may not be good indicators of wage differences in the distant future. Using *BN*39, for example, as an independent variable for the wage difference between college and high-school

Table 5.4. Determinants of the enrollment rate (II).

	(11)	(12)	(13)	(14)	(15)	(16)	(17)	(18)	(19)	(20)	(21)	(22)
CONST.	10.163	10.041	9.268	9.809	10.365	8.717	10.739	11.276	9.872	11.093	11.271	11.331
PT	−0.101	−0.094	−0.098	−0.098	−0.090	−0.092	−0.100	−0.091	−0.094	−0.101	−0.091	−0.097
	(−7.35)	(−5.76)	(−7.82)	(−5.58)	(−5.89)	(−6.18)	(−6.11)	(−6.15)	(−6.68)	(−7.65)	(−6.51)	(−7.88)
FG	−0.047	−0.043	−0.052	−0.043	−0.036	−0.044	−0.043	−0.035	−0.042	−0.044	−0.035	−0.045
	(−2.12)	(−1.37)	(−2.59)	(−2.36)	(−1.51)	(−2.43)	(−2.25)	(−1.54)	(−2.24)	(−2.46)	(−1.60)	(−2.52)
BN39	0.0018	0.0022	0.0037									
	(0.29)	(0.37)	(0.79)									
BN49				0.0007	0.0005	0.0014						
				(0.28)	(0.17)	(0.63)						
BN59							0.00012	−0.00000	0.00049			
							(0.10)	(−0.00)	(0.45)			
W	3.030	2.903	3.210	2.876	2.680	2.921	2.883	2.653	2.889	2.911	2.653	3.023
	(4.29)	(2.88)	(5.34)	(4.84)	(3.52)	(5.04)	(4.47)	(3.56)	(4.55)	(5.18)	(3.69)	(5.54)
GW	0.551	0.518	0.498	0.534	0.507	0.448	0.554	0.531	0.450	0.571	0.531	0.502
	(2.79)	(2.91)	(3.01)	(2.35)	(2.25)	(2.39)	(2.25)	(2.18)	(2.21)	(3.16)	(3.14)	(3.08)
UN	0.994			1.146			1.269			1.334		
	(0.52)			(0.69)			(0.77)			(0.91)		
DUM		0.806			1.059			1.278			1.277	
		(0.39)			(0.51)			(0.64)			(0.80)	
SER	0.95	0.95	0.92	0.95	0.96	0.93	0.95	0.96	0.94	0.92	0.92	0.91
R^2	0.988	0.987	0.987	0.988	0.987	0.987	0.987	0.987	0.987	0.987	0.987	0.987
$\bar{R}^2$	0.982	0.982	0.983	0.982	0.982	0.983	0.982	0.982	0.983	0.983	0.983	0.983
F	184.5	182.9	232.7	184.5	181.5	229.2	183.5	181.2	226.3	235.8	232.9	297.7
D.W.	2.35	2.33	2.32	2.37	2.34	2.33	2.35	2.32	2.28	2.34	2.32	2.21

Notes: The time-series analysis from 1966 to 1986. *t*-values are in parentheses.
FG = forgone earnings, *BN39* = wage difference up to 39 years of age, *BN49* = wage difference up to 49 years of age, *BN59* = wage difference up to 59 years of age, *UN* = unemployment rate, *DUM* = dummy variable for the existence of professional schools. See also the notes to Table 5.3 for the definitions of other independent variables.

graduates implies that we have assumed that the wage difference up to age 39 is a proxy indicator for the lifetime wage difference.

W and *GW* have been defined before. To repeat, *W* measures availability of funds. *GW* is the average rate of wage growth and can be interpreted as a rate of economic growth. A high level of *GW* may imply that forgone earnings (and indirectly tuition too) are expected to increase, and thus may have a negative effect on college-going decisions. However, its positive effect is likely to be stronger because individuals expect that availability of funds will increase and/or because they become optimistic about future economic conditions in general.

UN stands for the percentage of male workers unemployed, and uses data from *Labor Force Survey* by the Statistics Bureau. *DUM* is a dummy variable to test the effect of the existence of professional schools. The value of *DUM* equals 1 from 1976 to 1986 and equals 0 in other years.[9] It is assumed that college-going decisions are made one year before the time of graduation from high school. Thus, each independent variable has a one-year time lag except *DUM*, which does not need a time lag because the existence of the system of professional schools is known a year before.

Table 5.4 shows the regression results from twelve specifications. The specifications are basically determined by eliminating independent variables which do not have significant effects.

In all these results, *PT* has a negative and highly significant effect on the enrollment rate. If the total amount of tuition in four years increases by 10,000 yen (at the 1980 price level), the percentage of students going to college will decrease by about 0.1%. If tuition increases by 10,000 yen per year, the percentage will decrease by about 0.4%. The coefficients of *FG* are also all negative and many are quite significant. This result shows that forgone earnings cannot be ignored when considering college-going decisions.

Interestingly, there is a large difference in the coefficient between *PT* and *FG*. In many specifications, the coefficients of *FG* are slightly less than half of those of *PT*. This implies that even if the total investment cost increases by 10,000 yen, its negative effect on the enrollment rate will differ according to whether it arises in tuition or whether it arises in forgone earnings. The effect in the latter case will be slightly less than half that in the former. It can be shown by statistical tests that in all twelve results this difference is significant (at the significance level less than 1%). We can therefore propose that individuals make more of tuition than forgone earnings for a given amount of cost. This result is fairly consistent with that obtained by Fuller, Manski, and Wise (1982) who have applied a different model to United States data.

Paying tuition uses up the same amount of income. In contrast, forgone earnings can be comparatively easily borne because they are costs that arise when failing to use an earnings opportunity.[10] This is a partial reason for regression models using the internal rate of return having weak explanatory power.

Next let us examine the effects of *BN*39, *BN*49, and *BN*59. In the nine specifications which include one of these independent variables, almost all of their coefficients are positive but none are significant. This seems to suggest that individuals do not consider pecuniary benefits when making college-going decisions.

Because, if true, this result is of great importance, the author has tried regression analysis using similar but slightly different independent variables. *BN*39, *BN*49, and

BN59 in Table 5.4 were computed on the basis of monthly earnings and yearly bonuses in the *Basic Survey of Wage Structures*. In contrast, the new independent variables are computed on the basis of only monthly earnings, only contract wages,[11] and contract wages plus bonuses from the age of college graduation to the age of 39, 49, or 59. The data are again obtained from the *Basic Survey of Wage Structures*.

Regression analysis similar to that in Table 5.4, however, reveals that none of the coefficients of these new independent variables have significant effects. This result confirms the above finding, i.e., that the college-going behavior of Japanese people does not seem to be sensitive to expected future pecuniary benefits. This is also a factor that reduces the explanatory power of models that use the internal rate of return.

W has again positive and significant effects in Table 5.4. The effects of *GW* are also positive and significant as predicted before. The coefficients of *UN* are positive but insignificant. Hence, the unemployment rate does not seem to influence Japanese males' college-going behavior.[12] Both theoretically and empirically, there is a negative relationship between *UN* and *GW*. Thus, specifications have been tried which do not include *GW*, but it has been found that even there *UN* does not have a positive effect.

The coefficients of *DUM* are not significant. If the emergence of the professional school system restrained some people from going to college, the coefficients of *DUM* would have to be negative and significant. Therefore, as far as this period of analysis and males are concerned, professional schools did not play a substitute role for colleges.[13]

It should be noted that R^2 and $\bar{R}^2$ in all of these twelve results are higher than those in Table 5.3. Thus the explanatory power of the models that do not use the internal rate of return is quite large.

Which hypothesis is consistent with the above result that the enrollment rate is insensitive to the future pecuniary benefits of higher education? A conceivable hypothesis is that the pecuniary benefits expected by decision makers are not values that can be observed in actual wage data but rather are subjective values that are relatively high and fuzzy in a sense (thus they do not vary much). Theoretically speaking, almost everyone can know objectively the costs of investment in higher education, especially tuition and fees. However, the benefits are hard to predict because they concern the distant future. Therefore, it is quite natural to have the above result that college-going behavior does not depend on expected benefits computed under the particular assumptions we made.

Next let us turn our attention to Table 5.5. New independent variables are introduced in this Table, though the dependent variable remains the same. One of them is *PS*, which is a variable for the difference in promotion probability between college and (senior) high-school graduates. To obtain this, the proportion of section chiefs (*kacho*) was first computed in the group of college graduates who work for firms with 1,000 employees or more in all industries and who are younger than 40 but no younger than 35. Then the same proportion for high-school graduates was also computed. *PS* is the difference between these two proportions expressed in terms of percent. Data are available from the *Basic Survey of Wage Structures* from 1970.[14]

The larger the value of *PS*, the more likely it is that a college graduate will become a section chief when he is relatively young as compared with a high-school graduate. It should be noted that if a much older age stage was chosen, the difference would be negative and would not be a suitable indicator for benefits of higher education. It

Table 5.5. Determinants of the enrollment rate (III).

	(23)	(24)	(25)	(26)	(27)	(28)	(29)	(30)
CONST.	3.569	9.367	4.006	15.251	36.051	39.717	10.377	12.210
PTFG	−0.0842	−0.0552	−0.0689	−0.0536	−0.0706	−0.0623	−0.0688	−0.0522
	(−3.20)	(−3.88)	(−2.94)	(−3.36)	(−3.26)	(−4.60)	(−3.06)	(−4.05)
BN39	0.0076	0.0039						
	(1.10)	(0.58)						
BN49			0.0019	−0.00096				
			(0.29)	(−0.17)				
BN59					−0.00396	−0.00438		
					(−1.37)	(−1.64)		
PS	0.253	0.374	0.303	0.414	0.360	0.392	0.341	0.400
	(1.88)	(3.73)	(1.73)	(3.38)	(3.38)	(4.80)	(3.10)	(4.60)
W	3.986	2.798	3.427	2.709	3.279	2.924	3.361	2.681
	(3.98)	(6.70)	(3.81)	(6.63)	(4.08)	(8.03)	(4.04)	(7.55)
GW	0.507		0.382		0.180		0.323	
	(1.30)		(0.90)		(0.50)		(0.91)	
SER	1.19	1.23	1.25	1.24	1.15	1.11	1.20	1.19
R^2	0.894	0.876	0.882	0.872	0.900	0.897	0.881	0.872
$\bar{R}^2$	0.840	0.831	0.823	0.826	0.850	0.860	0.837	0.840
F	16.80	19.38	14.92	18.78	17.93	24.00	20.32	27.24
D.W.	2.30	2.56	2.26	2.50	2.42	2.64	2.25	2.51

Notes: The time-series analysis from 1971 to 1986. *t*-values are in parentheses.
PTFG = sum of private university tuition and forgone earnings, *PS* = probability difference in promotion to section chief. See also the notes to Tables 5.3 and 5.4 for the definitions of other independent variables.

should also be noted that the ratio of the two proportions is not a suitable indicator for benefits.

Another new independent variable in Table 5.5 is *PTFG*, which is defined as the sum of *PT* and *FG*. Since *PS* is highly negatively correlated with *PT*, the author has combined these two independent variables for costs into one.

According to the regression results shown in the Table, the coefficients of *PS* are positive and quite significant in most specifications. Thus it can be proposed that the difference in promotion probability affects the enrollment rate. This fact also reduces the usefulness of an explanation that uses the internal rate of return.

The effect of the difference in probability between college and high-school graduates being promoted to subsection chief (*kakaricho*) has also been analyzed, though the result is not shown in the Table. In contrast to the previous difference, this does not have a significant effect on the enrollment rate. The reason is probably that it is not so difficult to be promoted to subsection chief.

To briefly mention other results, *PTFG* has an effect as expected, and again none of *BN39*, *BN49*, and *BN59* has positive and significant effects. The latter is also true even if different wage data are used for these variables as before. As for *W* similar results have been obtained again, but the significance of the effect of *GW* has decreased.

5.5 Factors Generating Changes in the Enrollment Rate

Here, we will summarize and interpret the results of all previous sections. First of all, it has been shown that the enrollment rate cannot be explained by the simple internal rate of return nor by the more complex one that takes account of wage (economic) growth and the market rate of interest (the interest rate of bank term deposits).

It is true that results are obtained which are consistent with existing economic theories when independent variables for the internal rate of return and availability of funds (family income) are simultaneously introduced. However, the explanatory power of such models is weaker than that of the model which, instead of the former independent variable, introduces merely tuition, a constituent of that independent variable. One of the serious problems of a regression model which uses the internal rate of return is the fact that pecuniary benefits in the ordinary sense barely affect college-going decisions.

Therefore, the internal-rate-of-return method has difficulty at least in Japan in explaining the enrollment rate. This implies that we need to discount the usefulness of this method in explaining reality. It should be emphasized, however, that this conclusion highlights the difficulty this method has in explaining the college-going behavior of individuals in general and does not negate its usefulness in normative analysis, policy making, and persuasion. For instance, if social rates of return to medical and dental education are high, investment in these types of education should be increased. When the private rate of return to a particular type of education is high, it is also meaningful to inform those who do not know of this fact. Further, in the case of a very popular type of education such as medical education, the internal-rate-of-return method can be used to determine whether the popularity reflects real advantageousness of the education, or to determine the levels of tuition and income tax.

The previous section examined regression models which do not use the internal rate of return and obtained the following results: (1) Tuition has a negative and highly significant effect (on the enrollment rate). (2) Forgone earnings have a negative and significant effect, which is slightly less than half that of tuition if compared per money unit. (3) The pecuniary benefits as expressed by the wage difference between college and (senior) high-school graduates do not have a significant effect. (4) Availability of funds as represented by family income has a positive and significant effect. (5) The rate of wage (economic) growth has a positive and significant effect. (6) The difference in probability between college and high-school graduates being promoted to section chief, a kind of non-pecuniary benefit of higher education, has a positive and significant effect, but the probability difference of being promoted to a subsection chief is not significant. (7) The effect of the unemployment rate is not significant in Japan. (8) The emergence of the system of professional schools did not have a significant effect. Among these results, (2), (3), and (6) point out the shortcomings of the method which explains the enrollment rate by means of the internal rate of return.

On the basis of these findings, we would like to examine why the trend in the enrollment rate changed in the mid-1970s. We divide the period we have considered into two sub-periods, from 1966 to 1976, and from 1976 to 1986. The enrollment rate increased by 22.2% in the first sub-period, but decreased by 6.8% in the second sub-period. The independent variables which have significant effects as shown above changed in these sub-periods as follows: *PT*;(0.90, 2.11), *FG*;(1.96, 1.05), *W*;(1.94, 1.15), *GW*;(1.06, 0.52), *PS*;(1.02, 0.36), *PTFG*;(1.19, 1.19), where each of the first components is the ratio of the value in 1976 to that in 1966 (1971 in the cases of *PS* and *PTFG*), while each of the second components is the ratio of the value in 1986 to that in 1976. It should be noted that all monetary values have already been transformed into real values taking account of consumer price changes.

Tuition *PT* decreased slightly in the first sub-period, but more than doubled in the second. In fact, it increased every year in the second sub-period. Hence, as far as tuition is concerned, the low or decreasing level in the first sub-period encouraged more people to go to college, while its rapid increase in the second sub-period restrained enrollments.

Family income *W* increased greatly in the first sub-period, but only barely increased in the second. Thus, this factor augmented the enrollment rate in the first sub-period and stagnated it in the second.

The rate of wage growth had also quite different effects in the two sub-periods. Though not shown clearly in the above ratios, *GW* was about 6 to 7% in the first sub-period, but declined to 1 to 2% in the second. Thus it had a similar effect to those of *PT* and *W*.

The difference in promotion probability also declined dramatically in the second sub-period, mainly due to a decline in the proportion of section chiefs among college graduates in the age group under consideration. As a matter of fact, the proportion was about 30% at the beginning of the 1970s, but declined drastically in the second sub-period to 11%. There is not a clear tendency in the case of high-school graduates, but the proportion decreased by 1 to 2% from the beginning of the 1970s to 1986. This relative decrease in psychological satisfaction from higher education discouraged enrollment.

In contrast to other independent variables, forgone earnings *FG* increased in the first sub-period and stagnated in the second. *PTFG* increased slightly in the two sub-periods which restrained investment in higher education.

These observations lead to the following conclusion about the changes in the enrollment rate: The rapid increase in the enrollment rate in the first sub-period occurred because the positive effects of the decline in tuition and the doubling in family income surpassed the negative effect of the doubling of forgone earnings. The decline in the enrollment rate in the second sub-period was due to the doubling in tuition, the small increase in family income, the decrease in the rate of wage growth, and the large drop in the probability difference of being promoted to section chief.

5.6 Enrollment Rate and Application Rate

5.6.1 Application Models

The above analyses and those quoted above are not above criticism in that they do not explicitly consider the behavior of suppliers of higher education services. In other words, because there are actually students who apply for admission but fail to be enrolled, the above enrollment rate may measure the supply of higher education rather than the demand for it. What is implicitly assumed in the above analyses, however, is that the supply of higher education services depends mainly on the demand. Put differently, each private institution has incentives to admit as many applicants as possible so far as it can achieve its education goal with those students or so far as those students have academic ability no lower than the minimum it requires (Fujino, 1986).

In contrast with this view, there is a view which considers that the percentage of students who applied for admission is a better dependent variable in regression analysis than the percentage of students who were actually enrolled, if the demand for higher education is to be the focus of analysis. On the basis of this latter view, the percentage of students applying for admission is used as the dependent variable in the analyses by Yano (1984), Nakata and Mosk (1987), and Tanaka (1994). Let us call these regression models application models and those in the previous sections enrollment models. In the following, the percentage of students applying for admission to higher education will be called the application rate. We would like here to examine the results of these application models.

Using data covering the period from 1958 to 1980, Yano (1984) has demonstrated that the application rate is almost determined by availability of funds, tuition for private institutions, the acceptance rate of new high-school graduates (a new high-school graduate's probability of being enrolled), and a dummy variable for the period from 1975 to 1978. More specifically, he has shown that these variables have respectively positive, negative, positive, and positive significant effects. It was found, however, that as for women's application for junior college education, the above second and third independent variables do not have significant effects. His interpretation is that the tuition is low and the acceptance rate of new high-school graduates is high for junior college education. The dummy variable is introduced to improve Durbin-Watson ratios and is interpreted as reflecting an uneasiness that existed for some time after the first oil shock.

He has also examined the effects of other independent variables such as the ratio of effective labor demand to effective supply as a measure of labor market tightness,[15] the difference in the starting wage between college and high-school graduates as a measure of the benefit of higher education, and the starting salary of high-school graduates as a measure of forgone earnings, but found that their effects are not significant.

Using a similar idea, Nakata and Mosk (1987) have undertaken a time-series analysis covering the period from 1959 to 1980 to identify determinants of the male application rate. The basic independent variables they used are firstly direct college costs for tuition, books, stationery, and commuting; secondly real family disposable income per capita; and thirdly the percentage of college graduates aged 20 to 24 working in large firms (of 1,000 or more employees). This third variable, unique to their analysis, is introduced to measure a favorable effect of college education by which graduates enjoy the better fringe benefits and retiring allowances provided by large firms. (This favorable effect derives from the fact that large firms may prefer to employ college graduates over high-school graduates.)

Their regression results have almost confirmed that the effects of these three independent variables on the application rate are respectively negative, positive, and positive. Their study has also introduced the independent variable for the acceptance rate and showed that its effect is positive and significant. It is shown in addition that the internal rate of return does not have a significant effect on the application rate but does have a positive and significant effect on its variations (annual changes in the application rate).

Tanaka (1994) has also performed a regression analysis for the period 1970 to 1990 with the application rate as the dependent variable and the internal rate of return, availability of funds, tuition, etc. as the independent variables.

His results can be summarized as follows: the internal rate of return with time lags of either four or three years and more has a positive and significant effect on the application rate. (Since this analysis considers distributed lags for all independent variables, the internal rate of return in a particular year affects the application rates for many future years.)

This analysis used either family income, family savings, or family assets for the availability of funds, and found that each can have a significant effect depending on regression specifications but that the effect of family income is the strongest.

It was further found that tuition is an important determinant of the demand for higher education but its effect is less significant than that of family income. This result is probably due to the fact that this analysis also has the internal rate of return as another independent variable.

It should be added that this analysis actually uses a logit transformation of the application rate rather than the application rate itself as the dependent variable. It is noted in this study, however, that the regression results would barely differ even if such a transformation was not undertaken.[16,17]

5.6.2 Differences Between Application Models and Enrollment Models

As already stated, the basic difference between these empirical analyses and ours lies in the difference in the dependent variable. Using the enrollment rate as the dependent variable can be interpreted as analyzing how large a proportion of individuals of enrollment age apply for admission to higher education and actually have academic ability no lower than the minimum required by higher education. In contrast, using the application rate as the dependent variable is likely to include the demand for higher education by those individuals whose academic abilities are lower than this minimum.

Higher education, as a service in the economic sense, has an important property that cannot be found in other ordinary commodities. That is, anyone can purchase the latter by paying the price. In order to purchase the former, however, one has not only to pay the price but also to show (at least in today's Japan) that one has high academic ability. Using the application rate means analyzing demand for higher education with little consideration of this property.

The important differences between application models and enrollment models are illustrated in Fig. 5.3. The horizontal axis of this Figure shows the levels of academic ability of individuals of enrollment age. Of the two distributions depicted in the Figure, the upper one indicates how many individuals of enrollment age have each level of academic ability. On the other hand, the lower one indicates how many individuals of enrollment age who apply for admission to higher education have each level of academic ability. It should be noted that these two are simplified expressions of frequency distributions. Ideally, they should be depicted as histograms, but are expressed as if they were probability density functions for continuous variables. Hence, the number of individuals of enrollment age whose academic abilities are in the levels from x_1 and x_2, for example, can be shown by the shaded area between x_1 and x_2 in the Figure.

Let the areas of A, B, C, and D equal a, b, c, and d, respectively. A stands for a group of individuals who are enrolled in college. That is, they are applicants who can exhibit

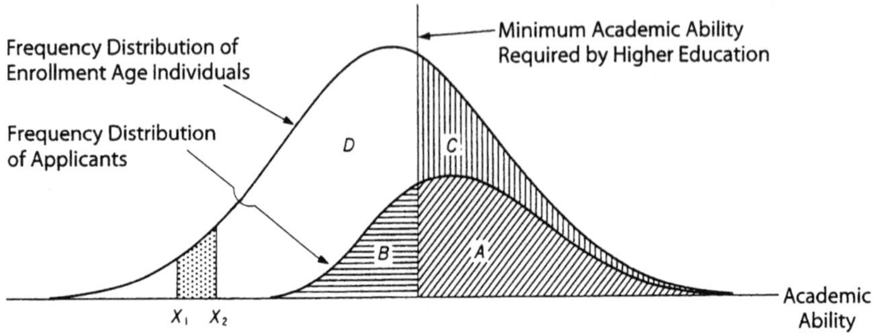

Fig. 5.3. Enrollment Rate and Application Rate

in entrance examinations academic abilities no lower than the minimum required by higher education. Thus the enrollment rate equals $a/(a + b + c + d)$. On the other hand, the application rate equals $(a + b)/(a + b + c + d)$: the group of individuals who apply but fail to be admitted is expressed by *B*. Group *C* indicates the individuals who have sufficiently high abilities but do not apply because of lack of funds or other reasons.

The reasons given by enrollment models for the existence of the group of individuals *B* who fail in entrance examinations are firstly that there is uncertainty as to the results of entrance examinations and secondly that applicants have imperfect information about their own academic abilities. (To be exact, true academic ability should be distinguished from the academic ability exhibited in entrance examinations, but a simplified explanation is given here to save space.)

In contrast, application models regard *b* as the excess demand for higher education. It should be noted that these models do not emphasize the minimum academic ability for admission. They regard the number of individuals actually enrolled in higher education, which corresponds to *a* in the Figure, as predetermined exogenously or by policy. In short, enrollment models analyze how various factors change the boundary between *A* and *C*, while application models analyze how similar factors affect the frequency distribution of applicants (or *A* and *B*) without paying attention to the minimum academic ability required.

In comparison with the demand for ordinary commodities, the demand for higher education shown by the above application rate has an important characteristic. The former is determined by the price of a commodity and each consumer's preferences and income, whereas the latter is determined not only by these factors but also by the probability with which an individual can pass at least one entrance examination. Those who face low probabilities will not apply for admission even if they have sufficient funds, because preparation in the form of hard work for entrance examinations is likely to generate merely mental and pecuniary loss as well as time loss.

This implies that in order to explain the application rate we need to introduce the acceptance rate (in the previous year, for instance) as an independent variable. (The acceptance rate is defined as the proportion of applicants who are enrolled.) In fact, the regression models by Yano (1984) and Nakata and Mosk (1987) have introduced the acceptance rate and demonstrated that its effect on the application rate is positive and significant. However, if there is any constraint on the supply of higher education services (by policy, for instance) as pointed out by the application models themselves, the acceptance rate is influenced by this supply constraint. Thus, those models cannot escape supply constraint even though they initially intended to analyze the pure demand for higher education free from supply constraint. This point is also mentioned by Yano (1984).

In contrast, the above enrollment models regard the individuals who take entrance examinations as those who are certain that they have academic abilities no lower than the minimum required by higher education, who want to go to college, and who have sufficient funds including financial aids. (Of course, those applicants whose academic abilities are found to be lower than the minimum or who cannot exhibit their true abilities in entrance examinations fail to be admitted.) Therefore, enrollment models seem to be theoretically clear.

It should be added that enrollment models express only one simplified approach to reality. We cannot completely deny that the minimum academic ability may change over time or that it may be influenced by government policies. Thus, using the enrollment rate as the dependent variable of regression analysis may not be faultless.

However, as far as the period after the mid-1970s is concerned, in which the enrollment rate stagnated or decreased slightly, it cannot necessarily be insisted that the enrollment rate changed in this way because the supply of higher education services was restricted by policy. An impressionistic reason is that the average academic ability of students in those years was decreasing as was pointed out by many college educators. Kikuchi (1981, 1982) emphasizes that the stagnation in the enrollment rate after the mid-1970s can be explained to a large extent by family income and the price of higher education. This is a view which is partly consistent with our above results based on an enrollment model.[18]

Another difference between our enrollment model and the application models by Nakata and Mosk (1987) and Tanaka (1994) is whether or not the internal rate of return is used as an independent variable. Because the distinction between the analysis of the level of the application rate and that of its variations is not clear in Nakata and Mosk (1987), we would like to focus on Tanaka (1994). One of the characteristics of his analysis is that the internal rate of return has a positive and significant effect on the application rate. This result does not necessarily contradict our results in Sects. 5.1 and 5.2 for the following reasons.

Firstly, our analysis in Sect. 5.2 showed that the internal rate of return has a positive and significant effect on the enrollment rate if an independent variable for family income is introduced. (The dependent variables are different for these two analyses. But since an identity exists in the form of: enrollment rate = application rate × acceptance rate, they would become essentially the same analysis if the acceptance rate was constant. As a matter of fact the enrollment and application rates have varied quite similarly.)

Secondly, our results in Sect. 5.1 are similar to Tanaka's. That is, by considering distributed lags for all independent variables, he found that the application rate is affected positively and significantly by the levels of the internal rate of return only four (or three) or more years before. (It should be noted that in our observations the enrollment rate was correlated with the internal rate of return five to seven years before.) However, his result does not mean that the internal rate of return is a determinant of the application rate. This is because his analysis does not explain why the levels of the internal rate of return near the time of graduation from high school do not have a positive and significant effect on the application rate. Near the time of graduation from high school, an individual is completely free to abandon plans made four or more years before to go to college.

Notes

1. A large portion of this chapter is based on Arai (1990b).
2. The data for this interest rate are obtained from the *Economic Statistics Abstract* by the Economic Planning Agency.
3. Whitfield and Wilson (1991) have undertaken a regression analysis for the United Kingdom by introducing the internal rate of return as an independent variable and have found its effect significant. Their analysis uses other independent variables such as the unemployment rate, social class, and so on.
4. This is from the *Monthly Labor Statistics Abstract* by the Ministry of Labor. This data is also used in the analysis by Fujino (1986), which will be quoted below.
5. Mattila (1982) also estimates regression models which introduce the independent variable for family income and other independent variables. The results indicate that not only the internal rate of return but also family income can have a positive and significant effect on the enrollment rate.
6. Other studies include Handa and Skolnik (1972, 1975), Pissarides (1981), and McPherson and Schapiro (1991).
7. This variable is also intended to express the existence of distributed lags. A distributed lag model is used when the effect of an independent variable is considered to appear over several periods. An example is the case in which the income of a particular year is considered to affect not only the consumption of that year but also that of one and two years later. Thus, in this model the enrollment rate of a particular year is influenced by the levels of income and tuition in the past several years. A regression analysis of distributed lag models can be undertaken by introducing the dependent variable in the previous year (period) as an independent variable. Distributed lag models are explained in any standard textbook on econometrics such as those cited in Appendix B.
8. Kaneko (1986) provides another study. His regression analysis explains the rate of logit change in the enrollment rate P, i.e., $\Delta P/P(1 - P)$, by the average expected returns ratio (which is defined as the ratio of the returns to higher education to its costs, and thus is similar to the internal rate of return), family income, and the cohort size (the number of students in the third year of senior high-school education). It was found by the analysis that these three independent variables have respectively positive, positive, and negative significant effects on male enrollment rate. This regression model differs from others in that it deals with changes in the enrollment rate. It may be said that this is a kind of internal-rate-of-return analysis because it uses a concept close to the internal rate of return.
9. A method of examining the effect of the existence of the professional school system on the enrollment rate is to introduce an independent variable which takes on the value of 1 when the system exists and the value of 0 when it does not exist. Such a variable is called a dummy variable.
10. The fact that the effect of forgone earnings is smaller than that of tuition is also confirmed in the results of cross-sectional analyses by Bishop (1977) who has used micro-data from the United States and by Tannen (1978) who has used state-grouped data from the United States. Kodde and Ritzen (1984) have developed a theoretical model which indicates that forgone earnings and tuition have different effects on the demand for education when education has consumption benefits and when the capital market is perfect.
11. The difference between "monthly wages (earnings)" and "contract wages" is that the former include overtime pay.

12. Other studies which have analyzed the relationship between unemployment and college-going decisions include Handa and Skolnik (1975) and Whitfield and Wilson (1991). According to the former, the effect of the number of unemployed workers on the number of students advancing to colleges in Ontario, Canada is significant but very small. Its effect on the number of students advancing to graduate schools was also analyzed, but is found to be insignificant. According to the latter study of the United Kingdom, the unemployment rate has a positive and significant effect on enrollment in higher education.

13. Firms, specially those in the manufacturing industries, tend to regard graduates from professional schools as lower specialists than those from colleges, and require them to quickly exhibit their abilities in limited fields without providing additional training for them (Kosugi, 1993).

14. The service industry is not included in the data prior to 1976 but is included afterwards. For the three years from 1976 through 1978 both kinds of data are available, and we can find that the difference in the proportion is slightly larger when the service industry is excluded. For this reason, adjustments have been made by multiplying the difference in the proportion prior to 1976 by 0.94, where 0.94 is the ratio obtained by comparing the data from 1976 through 1978. The essence of the argument would be the same even if such adjustments were not made.

15. See Note 4, Chap. 6 for the definition of this ratio.

16. When P is the application rate, its logit transformation is expressed as $\ln[P/(1 - P)]$, where ln is the natural logarithm. When a rate (or a probability) is directly used as the dependent variable, the value of the regression equation will not necessarily be confined to between 0 and 1 depending on the values substituted into the independent variables. The logit transformation avoids such inconveniences. When the values of a rate (application or enrollment rate here) which actually matter are not close to 0 or 1, similar regression results will be obtained whether the rate is directly used or whether its logit transformation is used as the dependent variable. The former approach is often adopted, because it is simpler and also because it can provide direct information about the effect of a unit increase in the value of an independent variable on the dependent variable. The enrollment rate was directly used as the dependent variable in our regression analysis above and in that by Nakata and Mosk (1987).

17. The simulation analysis by Ogura and Wakai (1991) also uses the application rate as the dependent variable. In their model, the application rate of new high-school graduates depends on the ratio of the total education cost (tuition + food costs + "daily costs") to the wage index, the proportion of parents with college degrees, and the wage differential between college and high-school graduates.

18. Kaneko (1986) points out that institutions requiring relatively low minimum academic ability have considerable excess capacity and that this plays the role of a buffer in the adjustment of demand for and supply of higher education. To see the effect of a supply constraint, he has introduced into his empirical analysis an independent variable for cohort size. The result of this analysis suggests that the stagnation in the enrollment rate after the mid-1970s was due mainly to family income and not to cohort size. Because the cohort size in about ten years after the mid-1970s was smaller than before (see the *Abstract of Education Statistics* by the Ministry of Education), it cannot be maintained that the cohort size or supply constraint generated the stagnation.

Chapter 6
Individual Attributes and College-Going Behavior

The analyses in Chap. 5 were based on time-series data. It is difficult in such analyses to demonstrate the attributes of individuals who go to college and to contrast them with the attributes of those who do not. Hence, in this chapter we would like to consider this problem using cross-sectional data.

First we will analyze the Japanese case on the basis of prefectural data which are easily obtainable. The individual attributes that will be considered are the availability of funds for investment, proximity to institutions, father's educational background, mother's educational background, parents' occupations, mother's participation in the labor force, and so on. We will investigate how these attributes affect male college-going behavior, female college-going behavior, and female junior college-going behavior. (Because the percentage of males going to junior college is very low, their behavior will not be analyzed in this chapter.) These three kinds of college-going behavior will be analyzed separately because some of the above attributes have different effects in the three cases.

In Sect. 6.1 we will observe the enrollment rates or percentages of students going to university and junior college in all prefectures and confirm that there are large differences in the rate among prefectures. (Japan is divided into forty-seven regions called prefectures in English. See Fig. A.4 in Appendix C.) A few cross-sectional analyses will also be examined in this section. Sect. 6.2 will discuss our hypotheses and the data used to test them. Sect. 6.3 will examine the results of our cross-sectional regression analysis.

In the subsequent two sections we turn our attention to two very interesting topics, the effects of parents' educational background on their children's college-going behavior, and the sex difference in college-going behavior. For the first topic, we will argue in Sect. 6.4 that the effect of the father's educational background is different from that of the mother's and that these effects tend to change with economic development. For the second topic, we will examine in Sect. 6.5 a variety of reasons for the historically observed large difference between sexes in the enrollment rate. We will further discuss the reasons for the recent rapid increase in the rate of female enrollment.

As the first three sections of this chapter will undertake different analyses for four-year and two-year institutions, we will explicitly distinguish them when necessary as universities and junior colleges respectively.[1]

6.1
Enrollment Rates in the Prefectures

First we would like to observe enrollment rates or the percentages of students going to university and junior college in all prefectures. These rates can be computed from the *Basic School Survey* by the Ministry of Education as in the previous chapter. Note, however, that these data should be used with a minor reservation in mind. Strictly speaking, the survey does not have data for the number of new students from each prefecture who were enrolled. What the survey actually contains is data for the number of new students from senior high schools located in each prefecture. There are small differences between the two, especially in prefectures which contain, or are close to, large cities, but these differences seem negligible.

In the first three sections of this chapter we will focus our analysis on enrollment rates in 1981. The reason is that for some independent variables in the regression models in Sects. 6.2 and 6.3 we will use data that can be obtained from the *Population Census of Japan* for 1980.

Fig. 6.1 shows the rate of male university enrollment for each prefecture. The prefecture names on the horizontal axis are arranged from the lowest rate to the highest. The rate varies from just above 20% to just below 55%. The top three prefectures in terms of this rate are Tokyo, Hiroshima, and Kanagawa with rates of 54.3%, 49.8%, and 47.4%, respectively. The bottom three are Aomori, Okinawa, and Iwate with 21.4%, 21.9%, and 24.4%, respectively.

Similarly, Fig. 6.2 shows the rates of female university enrollment by prefecture. The rate varies from a value slightly above 5% to slightly above 20%. The top three prefectures in this case are Tokyo, Okayama, and Kagawa with 21.2%, 17.9%, and 17.5%, respectively. The bottom three are Hokkaido, Okinawa, and Kagoshima with 5.5%, 5.6%, and 6.1%, respectively.

Fig. 6.3 shows the rates of female enrollment in junior college. The rate varies from slightly above 10% to slightly above 30%. The top three are Nara, Hiroshima, and Hyogo with 30.5%, 28.6%, and 28.0%, respectively. The bottom three are Aomori, Yamagata, and Iwate with 10.2%, 10.9%, and 12.4%, respectively.

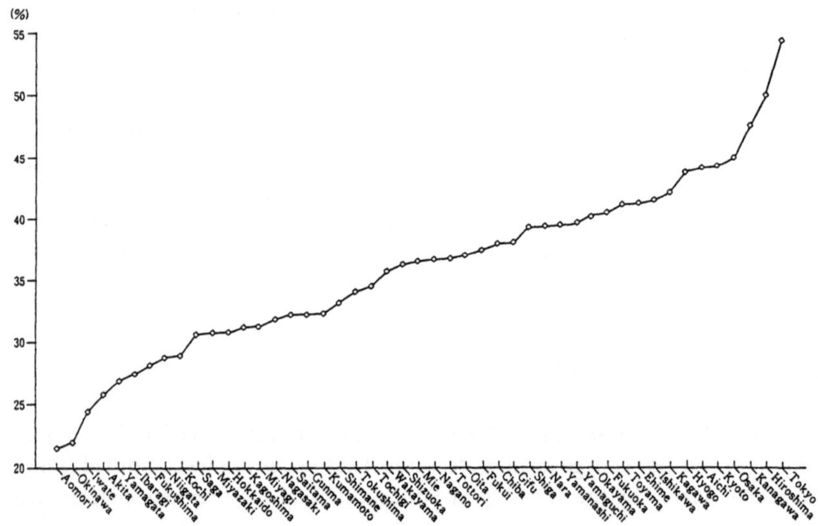

Fig. 6.1. Rates of Male University Enrollment by Prefecture

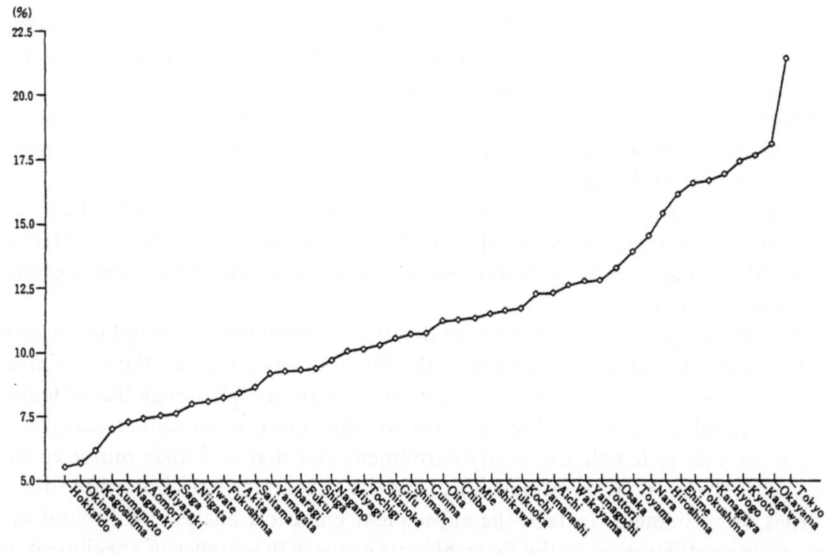

Fig. 6.2. Rates of Female University Enrollment by Prefecture

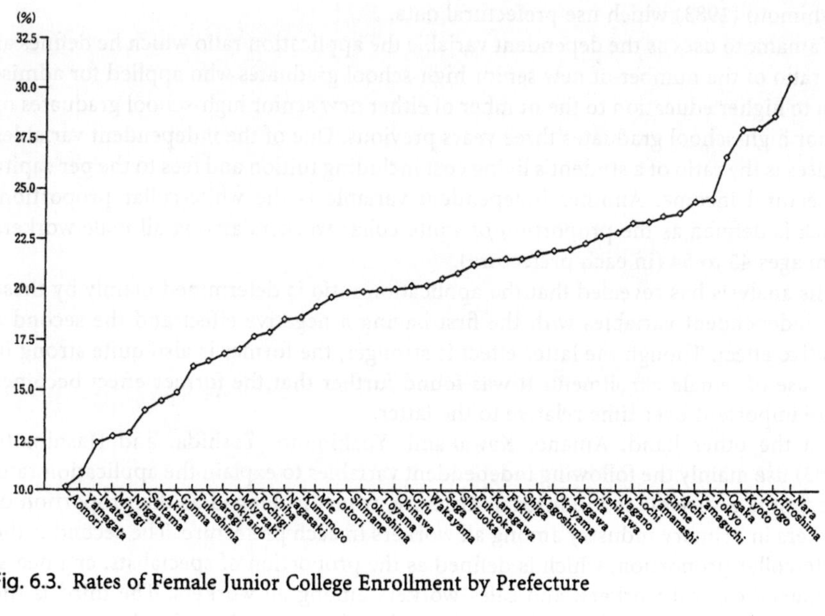

Fig. 6.3. Rates of Female Junior College Enrollment by Prefecture

These observations reveal that the differentials in the enrollment rate by prefecture amount to two to four times. As we saw in Chap. 1, the sex differential in the rate of enrollment in university is more than double. The sex differentials are especially high in prefectures where average enrollment rates are low. It can be seen further that the rate of male university enrollment in Tokyo is about ten times that of female university enrollment in Hokkaido.

The first three sections of this chapter will analyze factors determining in Japan the rates of male enrollment and of female enrollment in university and the rate of female enrollment in junior college. This will be equivalent to showing why the above prefectural differentials exist.

If these three types of enrollment were determined similarly, we would not have to examine each separately. We can see in the Figures, however, that there are many prefectures where the rate of male university enrollment is high though that of female university enrollment is low. We can also see that there is no salient correlation between the rate of female university enrollment and that of female junior college enrollment. Therefore, it seems desirable to analyze separately the above three different types of enrollment. In fact, the subsequent empirical analysis will reveal that there are some differences in the determinants of these three types of enrollment, so this approach will prove appropriate.

Before starting our analysis, let us review a few related empirical studies such as those by Yamamoto (1979) and Amano, Kawakami, Yoshimoto, Yoshida, and Hashimoto (1983) which use prefectural data.

Yamamoto uses as the dependent variable the application ratio which he defines as the ratio of the number of new senior high-school graduates who applied for admission to higher education to the number of either new senior high-school graduates or junior high-school graduates three years previous. One of the independent variables he uses is the ratio of a student's living cost including tuition and fees to the per capita prefectural income. Another independent variable is the white-collar proportion, which is defined as the proportion of white-collar workers among all male workers from ages 45 to 54 (in each prefecture).

His analysis has revealed that the application ratio is determined mainly by these two independent variables with the first having a negative effect and the second a positive effect. Though the latter effect is stronger, the former is also quite strong in the case of female enrollment. It was found further that the former effect becomes more important over time relative to the latter.

On the other hand, Amano, Kawakami, Yoshimoto, Yoshida, and Hashimoto (1983) use mainly the following independent variables to explain the application rate. The first is a variable for industrial structure, which is defined as the proportion of workers in primary industry among all workers in each prefecture. The second is the white-collar proportion, which is defined as the proportion of specialists, engineers, managers, clerical workers, and sales workers among all workers. The third is the college graduate proportion, which is defined as the proportion of college graduates among the whole prefectural population.

Their results show that these independent variables have respectively negative, positive, and positive significant effects on the application rate, but that family income barely affects it. They note, however, that the significance of these effects vary over time. For instance, the college graduate proportion had a significant effect only in the final years among the several years analyzed.

They show further that the rate of university enrollment is affected mainly by per capita prefectural income and the geographical location of each prefecture, with the former having a positive effect and the latter a negative effect. The latter independent variable is defined as whichever is shorter of the distance from Tokyo or Osaka, the two largest cities in Japan. (Many colleges concentrate in or near these two cities.) In addition, their study considers an independent variable called capacity, which they define as the ratio of enrollment in universities or junior colleges of each prefecture to the number of senior high-school graduates from that prefecture. They show that the effect of this independent variable is positive and significant and that the explanatory power of a regression equation with this independent variable is larger.

6.2 Hypotheses, Independent Variables, and Data

This section proposes several hypotheses, to be tested in the next section, concerning the determinants of individual college-going behavior. This section will discuss in addition the independent variables to be introduced and which data to use to test the hypotheses.

Since we will use the *Population Census of Japan* for 1980 as key data as mentioned before, we use data for 1980 for almost all independent variables. Because the dependent variable (enrollment rate) is based on data for 1981, using these data amounts to assuming that college-going decisions were made in 1980. Even if these decisions had been made a few years earlier, regression results would not significantly differ since the relative differentials in most independent variables among prefectures are supposed to be quite stable over a short period of time. Regressions will be undertaken with respect to the three types of enrollment mentioned before.

Two interpretations are possible as to the concept of enrollment rate in cross-sectional analyses. One is the same as before and implies the percentage of students who had at least the minimum academic ability required by higher education and who applied for admission. The other is that the enrollment rate means the percentage of "winners" in the competition for admission to higher education among all students of enrollment age. In other words, this second interpretation refers to those applicants who achieved relatively high scores in entrance examinations.

Even if the supply of higher education services is completely fixed (by policy) as some researchers might like to insist, the second interpretation makes our analysis meaningful, whereas the first does not. This is because the analysis will reveal the attributes of individuals who survived in the competition for admission. In short, the first interpretation assumes that supply of higher education services depends on demand, whereas the second assumes supply is exogenously fixed. Of course, our analysis will also be meaningful even if the reality is somewhere between.

Our first hypothesis is basic and standard and is concerned with the availability of funds for investment. We have already examined theories that an individual's family income (or wealth) has a positive effect on college-going behavior under capital market imperfection. This held not only in human capital theory in Chap. 2 but also in some signaling models in Chap. 3. Further, the time series analyses in the previous chapter also supported this hypothesis. For instance, when family income increased rapidly the enrollment rate also increased dramatically in Japan. This chapter will investigate whether this hypothesis also holds in a cross-sectional analysis. In other words, we will examine if high income prefectures have higher enrollment rates.

For the data for family income, we use prefectural wages from the *Basic Survey of Wage Structures* by the Ministry of Labor. More precisely, we use the average annual wage of male workers aged from 40 to 54 (in each prefecture), where the annual wage is defined as the monthly wage times twelve plus annual bonuses. This age class is chosen because it includes most fathers of students facing college-going decisions. Because these data show wages paid to those who work in each prefecture and because some workers work outside the prefecture they live in, the prefectural wage does not strictly equal the (average) wage of fathers of students living in each prefecture. However, this difference seems negligible.

Since there are regional differences in consumer price, it is desirable to consider these when comparing prefectural wages. Here, we will adjust these wages using the *National Survey of Prices* by the Statistics Bureau. It should be added, however, that because this survey was not undertaken in 1980, we use data for 1982 under the assumption that relative regional prices are quite stable over a short period. The independent variable so defined is called *AWR*.

The second hypothesis is concerned with proximity to institutions. If a college is located nearby, the investment cost of higher education (or signaling cost) is lower and incentives to receive higher education increase. There are actually cost differences between commuting to college from home and living alone to commute. Students living alone may have to bear higher costs in actuality, not only for mobility and communication but also for rent and food. In economic theory and simplified empirical analyses, however, these differences tend to be ignored.

Proximity to institutions may generate differences other than in investment costs. There may be a difference in motivation to go to college between those who live near a college and those who have never seen a college. The former may often see a campus and college students, and are likely to have a stronger desire to advance to higher education. This is due to a kind of demonstration effect and also relates to desire to study. These effects are probably most prominent in countries that are neither highly nor less developed.

As it is difficult to accurately measure proximity to college, we will use an approximation in the form of the number of institutions in a prefecture per fixed number of people of enrollment age. For the cases of male and female enrollment in university, we use the total number of people of enrollment age in the denominator (in ten thousands). For the case of female enrollment in junior college, we use the number of females of enrollment age in the denominator (in ten thousands). (Since the proportions of males and females are the same in all prefectures, counting only one sex or both in these calculations will not cause biased results.) This proximity variable is called *NOIPC*. Data for the number of institutions are available in the *Basic School Survey* by the Ministry of Education, and for the number of people of enrollment age in the *Population Census of Japan* for 1980 compiled by the Statistics Bureau.

The third hypothesis is that individuals who have a highly educated father are more likely to go to college. Fathers' educational background affects children's college-going decisions through various mechanisms. First, highly educated fathers are likely to have intelligent children for a genetic reason, though this is only a matter of probability and thus not all their children are necessarily intelligent enough to receive higher education. Secondly, such fathers are likely not only to give their children good advice about study and school continuation, but also to arrange study environments for them. Thirdly, those fathers are certainly aware of (pecuniary and mental) benefits of higher education and have ample information about higher education in general. Fourthly, highly educated fathers may place higher value on benefits in the distant future and may not feel that the present costs of education are very burdensome. Moreover, because children, especially sons, tend to consider fathers their role models, children of highly educated fathers are more likely to receive higher education.

Data for fathers' educational backgrounds are available in the *Population Census of Japan* for 1980. This is the reason we have chosen the year 1981 for the data for the dependent variable. As above, we assume that the fathers of college-going decision makers are distributed uniformly between ages 40 to 54. Some of these people, however, were educated under the old education system, so in order to make fathers' educational background an independent variable, we need to transform the distribution of different educational backgrounds into one index using a specific assumption. We will use here a method of making all types of educational backgrounds, whether old or not, correspond to those in the current education system and compute a weighted average of the number of years of education under the current system.

The *Census* shows for each prefecture the distribution of five types of school graduates, a small number of persons who are presently attending schools, and a negligible number of people who have never attended school. We compute a weighted average of the years of fathers' education for each prefecture by assigning the following number to each type of school graduate: 9 to graduates who reached only the minimum compulsory education level, 12 to those from senior high school (including former middle school), 14 to those from junior college or equivalent institutions, 16 to those from university or graduate school, and zero to those who have never attended school. (We exclude those who are presently attending school from this computation.)

These numbers do not necessarily imply that these types of people have actually been educated for those numbers of years. But for the present purpose, this method of transformation will be appropriate. The variable obtained in this way is denoted by *YEDFA*.

The fourth hypothesis is that an individual with a highly educated mother is more likely to go to college. The ways in which the mother's educational background influences children's college-going behavior are almost the same as those for the father's.

There may be, however, some differences in the intensity or quality of the influence. An important conceivable difference is that contact time between mother and children is normally much greater than that between father and children. In other words, mothers spend more time with their children. Hence, children are likely to receive a stronger influence from their mothers. It is also likely that while fathers have a stronger influence on the basic plan of study, mothers have a stronger influence on details of the children's behavior. The method of computing mothers' average years of education in each prefecture is the same as that of fathers', but we assume that mothers are distributed uniformly between ages 40 to 49. The independent variable obtained in this way for mothers' academic background or average years of education is denoted by *YEDMO*.

The fifth hypothesis is concerned with parents' occupations, since people who are engaged as managers, officials, and professional and technical workers are more likely to send their children to college. One basis of this hypothesis is that these parents tend to understand more fully than others the importance of an educational career that includes a college degree. Their own educational careers are likely to include a college degree, but even those whose educational careers do not include a college degree are likely to recognize from their experience the advantage of college education. These tendencies may be strong, especially when a college education as a signal enables one to be assigned at a young age to a position which is advantageous for future career development (see Sect. 7.1.2). It can be added that parents in the above occupations are likely to be lovers of the concept of college education who want their children to experience this regardless of what occupations they take up in the future.

Data for the percentage of those engaged in these occupations are available in the *Employment Status Survey* for 1982 compiled by the Statistics Bureau. There is no data available for the year 1980, the closest available being 1982. The independent variable obtained in this way is denoted by *PRMNG*.

The sixth hypothesis is that a mother's labor force participation positively affects her children's college-going behavior. Two kinds of effects are conceivable. The first is that when she works, she is more likely to recognize the benefit of higher education because she can more closely observe those who are actually working. The second is that labor force participation leads to higher availability of funds for investment in higher education.[2] This empirical analysis uses the women's labor force participation rate in each prefecture to test the effect of mothers' work on their children's college-going behavior.[3] Data for women's labor force participation are available in the Census data previously mentioned. The range of age for mothers is the same as that for *YEDMO*. The variable obtained in this way is denoted by *PARTR*.

The seventh is the signaling hypothesis. According to most signaling models in Chap. 3, higher education does not enhance students' productive capabilities. The academic career of college graduation simply conveys to firms information about the job applicant's pre-college capability. Though we will discuss several other tests of the signaling hypothesis in Chap. 7, here we would like to try a simple test as suggested by Wolpin (1977).

Wolpin suggested that if those who do not have to transmit information about their productivity do not invest in higher education, that education simply plays a role of providing signals. A typical example of those who do not need to transmit information is people who are planning to be self-employed. Though Wolpin suggested this idea, he did not undertake a rigorous statistical test. From the simple observation that average years of education for the self-employed are only slightly fewer, he concluded that the signaling hypothesis is not very persuasive.

We would like to test here the signaling hypothesis using Wolpin's idea, although a satisfactory test is difficult to undertake because it is difficult to identify those who are planning to be self-employed. Furthermore, even those who plan to be self-employed may have reasons to invest in higher education, even if higher education is simply a screening process.

Firstly, there are very few self-employed workers who work completely independently: most must have regular traders or trade partners especially in Japan. Thus they have incentives to transmit information about their abilities to those who trade with them. Secondly, there is the risk that one might not be able to be self-employed even if one wants to. There is also the risk that one's enterprise will go bankrupt. Hence, one may invest in higher education in preparation for these risks. Thirdly, a college degree may become a good signal when choosing a spouse.

With these reservations in mind, we consider two candidates for the independent variable used to test the signaling hypothesis. Both are concerned with the size of the group of people who plan to be self-employed. One is the weight of individual proprietors' incomes in total prefectural income in 1980, which is denoted by *INPR*. The other is the proportion of self-employed workers among all working persons in each prefecture, which is denoted by *SEMP*. These two variables are expressed in terms of percent. Data for the former are available in the *Annual Report on Prefectural Accounts* compiled by the Economic Planning Agency, and for the latter in the *Employment Status Survey* for 1982 mentioned previously.

The rationale for using these data is that if the present weight or proportion is large in a prefecture, the future proportion of self-employed workers is expected to be also large, because the economic environment in that prefecture encourages self-employment and because the children of self-employed workers are more likely to be self-employed. Though *INPR* is not directly concerned with the number of self-employed people, it has the advantage of representing the importance of self-employment in each prefecture: even if the number of self-employed workers is large, the future number cannot be expected to be also large if the present income per self-employed worker is not large. If the signaling hypothesis and this test method are correct, both *INPR* and *SEMP* are expected to have negative effects on the enrollment decision.

The eighth hypothesis is that students living in or near large cities have advantages and thus are more likely to obtain admission to universities or junior colleges. These advantages include a variety of services they can enjoy when preparing for entrance examinations such as lectures and practice examinations for particular institutions offered by several well-known preparatory schools. This specialized instruction allows the students from large cities to score more highly in entrance examinations than students who attend only regular high schools. Furthermore, these preparatory schools provide their students with high quality information regarding entrance examinations, partly because they collect data from the large number of students who attend or who take the practice examinations.

Well-known preparatory schools tend to be located in large cities and assist students there to pass entrance examinations. High-school students who do not live in or near large cities have relative difficulty making use of such services. Thus their total costs (the sum of time, mental, and pecuniary costs) to acquire a certain level of academic ability are larger. (Otherwise, no one would attend preparatory schools or take their practice examinations.) As stated before, the cost of preparing for entrance examinations can be regarded as a cost of higher education. Hence, the costs of investment in higher education or signaling costs are lower for those who live in or near large cities.

In order to test this hypothesis, we use a dummy variable which takes on a value of one if the prefecture contains a very large city and zero if otherwise. Here "a very large city" refers to one of Tokyo, Osaka, Nagoya, Kyoto, Yokohama, Kobe, Kitakyushu, Kawasaki, Fukuoka, or Hiroshima. (See Fig. A.4 in Appendix C.) All of these cities, with the exception of Tokyo, are special cities chosen by a government ordinance (*seirei shitei toshi*). This independent variable is denoted by *LCDUM*. Sapporo in Hokkaido is also a large city as designated by the government ordinance, but it is excluded from the above list because it is not very large compared with the area and/or population of Hokkaido as a whole.

The ninth hypothesis is that fewer students apply for admission to higher education if labor markets are tighter when college-going decisions are made. This means that when senior high-school students face sellers' markets and can easily find desirable jobs, they start working without choosing to go to college. Time-series analyses in the previous chapter also tested a similar hypothesis. Time-series analyses seem more proper to test this kind of hypothesis because there are normally regional differences in labor markets. Here we would like to try an incidental test to see what result will be obtained in a cross-sectional analysis.

We use here the ratio of effective labor demand to effective supply for both sexes to measure the tightness of labor markets.[4] The data are available in the *Annual Report on Labor Markets* by the Ministry of Labor. There are a variety of dates (by month or year) for which data for the ratios are available. In this chapter we have chosen the fiscal year 1979 for our analysis, i.e., we use the annual average of the ratio in that year (for each prefecture). One reason for this is that, fortunately, the degree of correlation between the ratios in adjacent months or years is very high. Another reason is that if we assume that college-going decisions are made about one year before graduation from senior high school, the ratio in 1979 seems more appropriate than that in 1980. The author actually applied average ratios in both 1979 and 1980 to some of the specifications discussed below and found that that of 1979 is more supportive of the hypothesis we are going to test. The independent variable defined in this way is denoted by *DSMF*.

6.3 Testing the Hypotheses

We are now ready to test by regression the several hypotheses considered above. As we use prefectural data, the sample size of our regression analysis is forty-seven. Before proceeding to the tests, we would like to specify regression models. We will try several specifications based on different combinations of the independent variables.

Since *INPR* and *SEMP* are two similar candidates to test the signaling hypothesis, we will use either in one specification. As to parents' academic background, we have two independent variables, *YEDFA* and *YEDMO*. It might be interesting to introduce both in the same specification to see which effect is stronger. But the author has found from a number of experiments that we cannot test both effects at the same time because there is a high correlation between the two variables. Hence, in the following, we will use either of the two variables in one specification. This high correlation is reasonable because highly educated people tend to choose highly educated spouses. It is likely that we could avoid this problem if we used micro-data about individuals.

The regression results based on ordinary least squares are shown in Tables 6.1 through 6.3. The dependent variable of the equations in Table 6.1 is the rate of male university enrollment, that of Table 6.2 the rate of female university enrollment, and that of Table 6.3 the rate of female junior college enrollment.

In all the Tables, the same specifications are undertaken, i.e., equations with the same equation number are under the same specification. In equations (1) through (4),

Table 6.1. Determinants of the rate of male university enrollment.

	(1)	(2)	(3)	(4)	(5)	(6)
CONST.	−88.97	−130.3	−115.7	−132.3	−106.2	−116.9
AWR	0.007827	0.009247	0.006595	0.007888	0.006996	0.006070
	(2.66)	(3.18)	(2.40)	(2.78)	(2.34)	(2.15)
NOIPC	−0.07338	−0.4352	−0.1092	−0.3911	0.4730	0.3964
	(−0.11)	(−0.67)	(−0.18)	(−0.64)	(0.81)	(0.72)
YEDFA	3.922	6.126			7.932	
	(1.13)	(1.79)			(2.91)	
YEDMO			7.593	7.695		10.06
			(2.69)	(2.80)		(3.91)
PRMNG	1.421	1.432	1.191	1.421		
	(1.78)	(1.86)	(1.85)	(2.23)		
PARTR	48.82	52.22	44.02	46.24	41.56	33.72
	(4.03)	(4.54)	(3.87)	(4.17)	(3.54)	(3.29)
INPR	−0.09095		−0.06790		−0.1212	−0.1441
	(−0.47)		(−0.38)		(−0.61)	(−0.81)
SEMP		0.4615		0.2784		
		(1.62)		(1.09)		
LCDUM	3.553	4.040	3.572	4.083	3.104	3.514
	(1.57)	(1.83)	(1.72)	(1.97)	(1.34)	(1.64)
DSMF	0.6039	0.3726	1.116	1.265	−0.8096	0.1971
	(0.23)	(0.15)	(0.48)	(0.56)	(−0.32)	(0.08)
SER	3.67	3.56	3.42	3.38	3.77	3.53
R^2	0.779	0.792	0.808	0.813	0.761	0.791
$\bar{R}^2$	0.733	0.748	0.768	0.774	0.718	0.753
F	16.75	18.10	20.00	20.67	17.70	21.05

Notes: *t*-values are in parentheses.
AWR = family income, *NOIPC* = number of institutions per enrollment age population, *YEDFA* = average years of education of fathers, *YEDMO* = average years of education of mothers, *PRMNG* = proportion of parents engaged as managers, officials, and professional and technical workers, *PARTR* = mothers' labor force participation rate, *INPR* = weight of individual proprietors' incomes, *SEMP* = proportion of self-employed workers, *LCDUM* = dummy variable for a large city, *DSMF* = measure of labor market tightness.

INPR and *SEMP* are used alternatively. Similarly, *YEDFA* and *YEDMO* are used alternatively in the six equations in each Table. In equations (5) and (6), *PRMNG* and *SEMP* are excluded, because *PRNMG* is correlated with parents' academic background and because, as we will see, *SEMP* has an effect opposite to the prediction of the hypothesis to be tested. (*t*-values are shown in the parentheses under estimated regression coefficients.)

Let us first examine the effect of *AWR* or family income. This variable has positive effects as expected and their significance is relatively high in all three types of enrollment. (For the rate of female university enrollment, there are two specifications in which the significance is low.) Therefore, as in the time series analyses in the previous chapter, this cross-sectional analysis shows that high family income is again an important factor prompting students to go to college.

Proximity to institutions or *NOIPC* does not have a significant effect in the case of male university enrollment in Table 6.1. This implies that as far as Japanese males are concerned, college-going decisions are not affected by additional mobility and living

Table 6.2. Determinants of the rate of female university enrollment.

	(1)	(2)	(3)	(4)	(5)	(6)
CONST.	−51.00	−69.42	−93.23	−93.83	−66.91	−93.97
AWR	0.004014	0.004789	0.002397	0.003229	0.003248	0.002062
	(1.95)	(2.39)	(1.32)	(1.75)	(1.51)	(1.11)
NOIPC	0.1343	−0.07722	0.1775	0.007905	0.6381	0.5000
	(0.30)	(−0.17)	(0.45)	(0.02)	(1.51)	(1.38)
YEDFA	0.7410	1.752			4.439	
	(0.30)	(0.74)			(2.26)	
YEDMO			6.185	5.577		7.758
			(3.30)	(3.11)		(4.57)
PRMNG	1.311	1.248	0.7595	0.8352		
	(2.35)	(2.36)	(1.79)	(2.01)		
PARTR	28.12	28.28	24.66	24.17	21.42	18.09
	(3.32)	(3.57)	(3.27)	(3.34)	(2.54)	(2.68)
INPR	0.1208		0.1775		0.09291	0.1289
	(0.88)		(1.51)		(0.65)	(1.10)
SEMP		0.4211		0.3595		
		(2.15)		(2.15)		
LCDUM	0.8357	1.165	0.5160	0.8842	0.4217	0.4791
	(0.53)	(0.77)	(0.38)	(0.65)	(0.25)	(0.34)
DSMF	0.006147	−0.5345	0.04291	−0.4173	−1.297	−0.5431
	(0.00)	(−0.31)	(0.03)	(−0.28)	(−0.72)	(−0.35)
SER	2.57	2.45	2.27	2.20	2.71	2.33
R^2	0.589	0.626	0.680	0.697	0.529	0.653
$\bar{R}^2$	0.502	0.547	0.612	0.634	0.445	0.591
F	6.81	7.95	10.09	10.95	6.26	10.48

Notes: *t*-values are in parentheses.
See the notes to Table 6.1 for the definitions of the independent variables.

costs due to studying apart from parents. It also implies that the demonstration effect mentioned above does not hold. In the case of female university enrollment in Table 6.2, equation (5) shows fairly high significance of the effect of *NOIPC*.

In the case of female junior college enrollment in Table 6.3, many specifications show significant effects of *NOIPC*. (Low significance appears only when *SEMP* is simultaneously used.) This implies that whether there is a junior college nearby is an important factor when a female student makes a decision about advancing to junior college. This is probably due to the fact that the presence of an institution nearby reduces the costs of investment in education, though the demonstration effect may work to some extent. The demand for junior college education seems especially elastic with respect to location-related costs.

According to the empirical study of a case in the United States by Christensen, Melder, and Weisbrod (1975), males' college-going decisions do not depend on proximity of institutions, but females' decisions are significantly affected by this factor. Amano, Kawakami, Yoshimoto, Yoshida, and Hashimoto (1983) show that the rates of female enrollment in university and in junior college are more strongly affected than male enrollment by the capacity of higher education in each prefecture, where the capacity is defined as the ratio of admissions to high-school graduates in each prefecture. (The admissions include those from other prefectures.) Though *NOIPC* is con-

Table 6.3. Determinants of the rate of female junior college enrollment.

	(1)	(2)	(3)	(4)	(5)	(6)
CONST.	23.74	−49.96	−24.39	−75.86	3.528	−24.76
AWR	0.005765	0.008108	0.004427	0.007318	0.005157	0.004343
	(2.13)	(3.22)	(1.59)	(2.87)	(1.84)	(1.55)
NOIPC	2.436	0.6501	2.559	0.4604	3.425	2.986
	(2.04)	(0.56)	(2.01)	(0.39)	(3.00)	(2.44)
YEDFA	−5.104	−1.183			−0.8047	
	(−1.59)	(−0.40)			(−0.31)	
YEDMO			0.5439	1.944		1.939
			(0.18)	(0.75)		(0.69)
PRMNG	1.492	1.575	0.7267	1.226		
	(2.09)	(2.43)	(1.18)	(2.26)		
PARTR	16.05	23.51	17.32	23.07	8.640	11.17
	(1.43)	(2.33)	(1.50)	(2.30)	(0.78)	(1.07)
INPR	−0.2098		−0.1193		−0.2483	−0.1711
	(−1.14)		(−0.63)		(−1.30)	(−0.92)
SEMP		0.7843		0.8380		
		(2.97)		(3.36)		
LCDUM	0.7970	1.639	0.1693	1.471	0.5674	0.3413
	(0.39)	(0.86)	(0.08)	(0.79)	(0.26)	(0.16)
DSMF	−2.172	−2.145	−2.999	−2.449	−3.966	−3.745
	(−0.90)	(−0.98)	(−1.23)	(−1.16)	(−1.68)	(−1.58)
SER	3.42	3.14	3.53	3.12	3.57	3.55
R^2	0.545	0.618	0.515	0.622	0.492	0.497
$\bar{R}^2$	0.449	0.538	0.413	0.542	0.401	0.407
F	5.69	7.68	5.05	7.82	5.40	5.51

Notes: *t*-values are in parentheses.
See the notes to Table 6.1 for the definitions of the independent variables.

cerned with the number of institutions, capacity is concerned with the number of those admitted. However, our results here are almost consistent with all these preceding findings.

Next let us examine the effect of *YEDFA* or fathers' educational background. We note first that all the coefficients of *YEDFA* are positive in the case of male university enrollment. The significance of this effect is high if *PRMNG* is excluded as in (5), but is low if it is included (especially in (1)). This is because there is a correlation between fathers' academic background and occupation. We can find similar results in the case of female university enrollment. However, the *t*-value is smaller in this case than in the previous case of males in each corresponding equation. This suggests that fathers' educational background affects sons' educational attainment more strongly than daughters'. In contrast with these results, fathers' educational background does not have a positive or significant effect on female junior college enrollment. This is probably because it is relatively easier to be enrolled in junior college than in university.

Mothers' educational background has a positive effect on all three rates of enrollment. Further, this effect is significant in any specification in the cases of male and female university enrollment, whereas for female junior college enrollment the significance is rather low. Thus, as in the case of fathers' educational background, mothers' does not affect daughters' decisions to go to junior college. Comparisons of the corresponding equations in Tables 6.1 and 6.2 reveal that the *t*-values of the estimated coefficients of *YEDMO* in Table 6.2 are higher than those in Table 6.1. This suggests that contrary to the case of fathers' educational background, mothers' affects daughters' decisions more strongly than sons'.

Let us turn our attention to the following three pairs of equations in Table 6.1: the first is (1) and (3), the second is (2) and (4), and the third is (5) and (6). The specifications of the two regression models in each pair are the same except that *YEDFA* and *YEDMO* are used alternatively. In these pairs we can compare the effects of fathers' and mothers' educational background on male university enrollment.

In any of these specifications, the effect of mothers' educational background is stronger than fathers' as far as the *t*-values are concerned. Moreover, the specifications which include *YEDMO* have better values in such statistics as *SER*, the coefficient of determination, etc. Exactly the same things hold in the case of female university enrollment in Table 6.2. Therefore, regardless of the sex of children, mothers' educational background has a stronger effect on children's university enrollment than fathers'.[5] Because the effects of parents' educational background on children's college-going behavior are an interesting issue, we would like to discuss it in more detail in the next section.

PRMNG or the proportion of managerial, official, professional, and technical workers has a positive and significant effect in almost all specifications in the three Tables. There are no prominent differences in the effect of this independent variable among the three types of enrollment. The fact that there are no prominent differences in this effect between sexes or between university and junior college may support not only the hypothesis that these workers place a high value on the benefits of college education for most jobs but also the hypothesis that they are lovers of the concept of college education.

Micklewright (1989) analyzed educational attainment by those who had completed compulsory education in the United Kingdom. According to his study, parents' occupations (or social classes) are also an important factor in the decision making as well as parents' educational background and the student's sibship size. He showed further that the effect of that factor mostly remains, even if such an independent variable as the student's academic ability is introduced into the analysis.

PARTR or the rate of mothers' labor force participation has a positive and significant effect as far as male and female enrollment in university is concerned (see Tables 6.1 and 6.2), but the effect is much weaker in the case of female junior college enrollment. A comparison between Tables 6.1 and 6.2 shows that the significance of this effect is slightly higher in the case of male university enrollment, perhaps because by participating in the labor force mothers feel that a college education is more important in the case of males than females.

According to Willis and Rosen (1979), if American mothers worked when their children were six to fourteen years old, the probability that these children go to college increases significantly. However, whether mothers worked when their children were younger than six does not have a significant effect. (The effects of mothers' labor force participation at other ages are not analyzed.)

We have different results as to the effects of *INPR* and *SEMP*. The effect of the former independent variable is negative in Tables 6.1 and 6.3 as the basic signaling theory predicts, though it is not significant. (This effect is positive in Table 6.2). The effect of the latter independent variable is positive in all the Tables and in most specifications highly significant which does not support the signaling hypothesis. This may be partly because our usage of data was inappropriate or partly because those who are planning to be self-employed actually need education signals.

The coefficients of *LCDUM* or the dummy variable for large cities are all positive, but are relatively significant only in the case of male university enrollment (Table 6.1). Thus males who live in or near large cities and use a variety of services to prepare for entrance examinations have advantages in the competition for university admission. Those who do not initially live in or near large cities can make use of services provided by preparatory schools if they move into such cities to become *ronin* (high-school graduates who study for entrance examinations). But their costs are quite high because they have to live away from their parents. The effect of *LCDUM* is small in the case of female junior college enrollment (Table 6.3), mainly because the competition for admission to junior college is not very keen. It is not obvious why this effect is weak in the case of female university enrollment (Table 6.2). A conceivable reason is that far fewer female students become *ronin* in order to use the above services.

Finally, let us examine the effect of *DSMF*. In most specifications for male university enrollment (Table 6.1), the coefficients of this independent variable are positive contrary to the prediction of the corresponding hypothesis, though the significance is low. Hence, it can be proposed that the tightness of labor markets does not affect male college-going behavior. This result is consistent with that of the time-series analysis in the previous chapter. The effect is also insignificant in the case of female university enrollment (Table 6.2), but more specifications have negative coefficients. Thus, there may be some female students whose college-going decisions are influenced by the tightness of labor markets. In the case of female junior college enrollment (Table 6.3), however, all coefficients of *DSMF* are negative. Since those in (5) and (6) are nearly significant, they support the corresponding hypothesis. Therefore, the tightness of labor markets may be an important factor in the case of female students who decide whether to go to junior college.

Since women tend to have shorter working periods or their careers tend to be discontinuous, their (junior) college-going behavior is likely to be influenced by temporary factors. In contrast, males are almost certain to work until the time of mandatory retirement, so their decisions as to investment in education tend to be made from a long-run perspective. For this reason their decisions are not affected by temporary conditions in the labor market.[6]

The above analysis has dealt with college-going decisions for Japanese students in 1980. As we see in the next section, different empirical results can sometimes be obtained for different points in time for the same country. Thus, we may also obtain different results for Japan if we use data for different points in time. Japan has faced structural changes in many areas since 1980 and is now facing even greater changes, which may have influenced the college-going behavior of Japanese students. However, the above analysis seems to show quite convincing results concerning college-going behavior in the year of 1980 as a cross section of Japanese history.

6.4 Effects of Parents' Educational Background

6.4.1 Results of Several Empirical Studies

Because the effects of parents' educational background on their children's college-going behavior are such an interesting issue, we will obtain a deeper understanding in this section by referring to empirical studies undertaken abroad. We will first survey several empirical studies and then propose our hypotheses after taking them into consideration.

It should be noted before starting the survey that some of the empirical studies below use years of education as the dependent variable and thus not all consider the effects of parents' educational background on their children's college-going behavior. However, we may regard them as similar to those on college-going behavior. It should also be noted that most of the following empirical studies use years of education to measure the educational background of each parent.

It should be added that some of the empirical studies cited below do not necessarily aim at analyzing the above issue as the primary purpose. In other words, some of the results have been obtained as byproducts of research for other purposes. Moreover, since some of the data used have been collected not primarily to analyze the above issue, the research results may not be sufficiently general (or are about special groups of individuals) and may have unsatisfactory aspects.

Behrman and Wolfe (1984) analyzed determinants of the years of education of Nicaraguan females from ages 15 to 45 in 1977 and 1978. According to their analysis, the educational background of both father and mother have positive and significant effects on their daughters' years of education. It was found further as in the previous Japanese case that the effect of the mother's educational background is stronger in terms of the magnitude of both the regression coefficient and t-value.

Lillard and Willis (1994) have studied the effects of parents' educational background on their children's years of education using data for Malays who were born between 1910 and 1980. Since the average years of education increased in this period from about two to ten years, this study is concerned mainly with primary and secondary education. According to their study, the educational background of both father and mother have positive and significant effects on their children's years of education.[7] It was also shown that the father's educational background has a stronger effect on sons' years of education and that the mother's has a stronger effect on daughters'.

Heckman and Hotz (1986) undertook an empirical study on Panama for which they used household data obtained in 1983 by random sampling. According to their regression analysis which also introduced independent variables for age, regions, etc., both the father's and mother's educational backgrounds have almost similar effects on sons' years of education. (However, so far as only the correlation is concerned, the correlation between sons' years of education and mother's is larger than between sons' and father's.)

They found in addition that the effect of the father's educational background on children's years of education is smaller for younger generations. In other words, the correlation between a father's education and his father's is higher than that between a father's and his son's. They show similarly that the correlation between the father's education and his son's is larger in Panama than that in the United States in 1962. This implies that factors other than parental education become more important in educational attainment or school continuation for newer generations. (A very important factor in developing countries is emergence of compulsory education.)

Using data for 1973 for white American males of various ages, Mare (1980) analyzed how a male's social background affects his school continuation decision at each education level. According to his analysis, the mother's schooling has a positive and significant effect on all decisions from completion of elementary education to attendance in graduate education. In contrast, the father's has a positive and significant effect only on the decisions from completion of elementary education to attendance in college education. In other words, the father's schooling does not affect the decision as to completion of college education or attendance in graduate education. In addition, the effect of the mother's educational background is stronger than the father's at any education level in terms of the magnitude of the coefficient and *t*-value. However, the father's occupational Duncan socioeconomic index has a positive and significant effect on each decision from completion of high school to attendance in graduate school.

On the basis of data for American whites for about the mid-1980s, Butcher and Case (1994) analyzed determinants of years of education for males and females. One of the characteristics of their study is that they divide their sample into two groups according to age; older individuals from 45 to 65 who received school education relatively long before, and younger people from 24 to 44 who received school education relatively recently.

What is prominent in the regression results for the older group is that the effect of the mother's educational background is evidently stronger than that of the father's. However, there is no clear difference in the effects of parents' educational background between sons and daughters. The effect of the mother's educational background is also generally stronger in the results for the younger group, in particular the effect of the mother's graduation from high school is stronger than that of the father's. In comparison with the older group, however, the effect of the mother's educational background relative to the father's is weaker for the younger group.

Leibowitz (1974a) undertook a related empirical analysis using data for Americans with high IQ scores. This was follow-up data collected by a psychologist for individuals who scored in the top 1% of the national IQ distribution. (Since IQ changes over time, some individuals failed later to score in the top 1%.) According to this analysis, both the father's and the mother's educational background have almost equally positive and significant effects on their son's years of education.

There is some difference, however. This regression analysis also uses an independent variable for the child's IQ. According to the empirical result obtained by Kagan and Moss (1959), the mother's educational background has a stronger effect on the child's IQ than the father's. (Wolfe (1982) has obtained similar results.) Thus, on the whole the mother's educational background has a stronger effect on a child's years of education. (Kagan and Moss also showed that both parents' IQs have equal effects on their children's IQs.)

Similarly, Leibowitz shows that the father's and mother's educational background have both positive and significant effects on daughters' years of education, though the mother's effect is slightly stronger.

Duncan (1974) analyzed determinants of years of education using data for American men and women aged between 18 and 30 in about 1968. According to his analysis, both parents' educational background have positive and significant effects on sons' years of education, with the father's having a stronger effect. It should be added, however, that the father's educational background does not have a significant effect on sons' IQ as above, but the mother's does. He also shows that the father's educational background has a strong effect on sons' motivation. In contrast, the mother's has a very strong positive effect on daughters' years of education, but the effect of the father's is not significant though positive. (Analyses of IQ and motivation were not undertaken for daughters.)

Using follow-up data for individuals who were high-school students in Illinois and North Carolina in 1966, Kohn, Manski, and Mundel (1976) have analyzed the effects of parents' educational background on the college-going behavior of children. According to their analysis the father's educational background has a slightly stronger effect than the mother's in Illinois. Further, the probability of a child being enrolled in college jumps if the father is a college graduate or if the mother is a high-school graduate. It is found additionally that the effects of parents' educational background are smaller for high income families.

Nearly similar results have been obtained for students in North Carolina. The main differences are that the effects of parents' educational background are weaker in North Carolina than in Illinois and that the mother's educational background has a slightly stronger effect than the father's.

The empirical study by Behrman and Taubman (1985) is based on US data from 1977 to 1981 with an average birth year of 1953. According to this study, both father's and mother's educational background affect their children's years of education. However, the father's has a stronger effect on both sons and daughters.[8]

Using American data for the 1970s and 1980s, Hauser (1993) analyzed the effect of parents' educational background on their children's college-going behavior for whites, blacks, and Hispanics. (The college-going decisions were made close to the above period.) This analysis considers the household head and its spouse rather than the father and mother. The head means father for the household with two parents, while it implies either father or mother for the household with a single parent.[9]

According to this analysis, the effects of the educational background of the head and its spouse on the children's college advancement are positive and significant except in the case of the Hispanic spouse where the effect is positive but insignificant. (This analysis does not differentiate children according to sex.) Further, in the case of whites and Hispanics, the effect of the head's educational background is stronger than that of its spouse in terms of the magnitude of the regression coefficient and *t*-value. In the case of blacks, the *t*-value for the head is larger, but the coefficient is smaller.

Using similar data, Kane (1994) undertook an analogous empirical study, where the effects of both the father's and mother's educational background are explicitly measured, and found that both effects are positive and significant. However, the effect of the father's is stronger in the case of whites and weaker in the case of blacks.

6.4.2
Economic Development and Effects of Parents' Educational Background

From an observation of the above empirical studies we can propose the following two hypotheses. The first is that until a certain level of economic development (or until a certain level of family income) is reached, the mother's educational background has a stronger positive effect on her children's college-going behavior or years of education. Beyond this level, the father's has an equal or stronger effect. The second hypothesis is that as the economy develops, the effects of parents' educational background on their children's college-going behavior or years of education generally decrease.

The first hypothesis has been obtained by mutually comparing the above limited number of, but nevertheless representative, empirical studies. It has been induced from the fact that relative to the father's educational background, the mother's is (was) a more important determinant of the educational attainment (or years of education) of their children in developing countries, the former American society, and the present society of American blacks.

As the economy develops, the relative effect of the mother's educational background gradually decreases. When the economy passes a certain level, the effects of both parents' backgrounds become nearly equal or the effect of the father's becomes stronger. However, the effect of the mother's remains relatively longer on daughters' educational attainment. So far as the college-going behavior of Americans is concerned, this "turning point" seems to have occurred in about the 1960s (or for those who made college-going decisions at approximately this time). According to the empirical study in the previous section, Japanese society around 1980 was at a stage prior to the "turning point" (if it ever exists in Japan). Of course, as is usual with hypotheses in social sciences, this one may have exceptions. For instance, the above case of Hispanics may be an exception (though the estimation method may be imperfect).

As to the above second hypothesis, only Heckman and Hotz (1986) explicitly mention this rule for the case of Panama (in comparison with the United States). Intuitively, this hypothesis seems highly plausible.

It should be noted that the above two hypotheses hold when seen from a long-run perspective such as tens of years. Thus they may not hold in a short period of time. For instance, in less than ten years or for different samples collected in close years, the effects of parents' educational background may be different from those predicted by the above hypotheses.

It is mainly due to non-genetic factors that the mother's educational background has a stronger effect on children's educational attainment as stated in the first hypothesis. This is because there is almost no genetic difference between father and mother in the effect on children's IQs as seen before. An obvious difference exists between father and mother in contact time with children. In most cases, children (especially young children) spend much more time with their mother. Because children's intelligence develops as they interact and talk with their parents, it is natural that the mother's educational background affects children's educational attainment more strongly than the father's.

Leibowitz (1977) showed that a child's verbal ability significantly increases if he/she reads books with his/her mother.[10] As mentioned before, the psychological study by

Kagan and Moss (1959) demonstrates that the mother's educational background is more highly correlated with a child's IQ than the father's irrespective of the sex of the child. Similarly, Leibowitz (1974a) and Duncan (1974) show that though the mother's educational background has a positive and significant effect on children's IQ, the effect of the father's is not significant. Kagan and Moss further show that the mother's educational background is more highly correlated with a daughter's IQ than with a son's.

Moreover, Leibowitz (1974a, 1974b, 1975) and Hill and Stafford (1974) found that the IQ (and academic ability) of a child of highly educated parents increases because they spend longer periods of time together and this time is of high quality. IQ is an important determinant of academic ability (and thus the results of entrance examinations), but is not necessarily completely genetically determined.

Murnane, Maynard, and Ohls (1981) have shown in their empirical study that the mother's years of education is positively correlated with the vocabulary of children in the third to sixth grade. They conjecture that highly educated mothers are good at perceiving and satisfying particular desires of their children (they are good managers of children) and that this fact, together with their longer contact time and high quality of contact time, is an important determinant of their children's high academic abilities.

All these findings suggest that how the mother educates her young children is an especially important determinant of their future academic abilities.[11]

It should be added that there are other mechanisms through which parents' educational background affects children's academic abilities and school continuation decisions. It is worth emphasizing that parents' educational background affects the values children have. In general, highly educated parents teach children values which affirm, or instill desire for, a college education. However, sufficient analysis has not been undertaken as to how children internalize these values, their importance relative to genetic factors and contact time, any difference in influence between father and mother, and so on.

We would like to comment on the effect of a mother's educational background. Because a mother's educational background affects children's intelligence, academic records, years of education, and eventually productivity, it is necessary to reevaluate the effects of women's education. In other words, even if market-evaluated returns to women's education are low in one generation, high returns are likely to arise over two or more generations. If the two hypotheses proposed above are correct, this fact is especially important in developing countries.

Why does the effect of the mother's educational background on children's college-going behavior or years of education decrease relative to that of the father's as the economy develops? One plausible explanation is related to changes in mothers' work behavior. The increased employment opportunities (especially in the service sector) and prevalence of labor-saving capital goods and day-care centers due to economic development raise mothers', especially highly educated mothers', labor force participation rate. In particular, the rate of labor force participation increases for mothers with pre-school children.

Continuing this argument, working mothers spend less time with their children both absolutely and relative to fathers. Accordingly, the weight of market-supplied education (education by day-care centers, *juku*, new teaching materials, etc.) increases. Because of this mechanism, the relative effect of mothers' educational background on children's academic abilities and school continuation decisions is likely to decrease. It should be added that this is only one possible explanation and its plausibility may depend on the country. Further studies are necessary to provide more detailed explanations.

Next, we would like to discuss in some detail our second hypothesis, the decrease in the effects of parents' education on their children's education due to economic development. The plausibility of this hypothesis is likely to vary with types of education and levels of economic development. The dependent variable in the study by Heckman and Hotz (1986) is years of education in a developing country. These years of education are shorter than the years of compulsory education in Japan.

As the economy develops and family incomes increase to some extent, even poorly educated parents have leeway to send their children to school for some years. In addition, primary (secondary) education becomes likely to be supplied on a large scale (or almost everywhere) for low cost or as compulsory education through national policy. As this happens, education costs including commuting costs reduce and many children begin to receive education irrespective of their parents' educational background. This fact can be rephrased using the concept of demand elasticity. Namely, because the education demand of poorly educated families is income- and price-elastic, it increases dramatically when family incomes increase or education price decreases.[12] Therefore, in developing countries, the effects of parents' educational background on the demand for primary (secondary) education decrease as the economy develops.

Most of the above empirical studies show, however, that parents' educational background has significant effects on children's school continuation decisions even in highly developed countries. This is because the education at issue is a high level of education such as higher education. In the long run, the effects of parents' educational background on children's college-going decisions will decrease as in the case of primary (secondary) education in developing countries. However, higher education services cannot be purchased so easily even in today's advanced countries and thus parents' educational background significantly affects their children's college-going decisions. Moreover, if we consider the fact that unlike primary and secondary education, academic ability is an important determinant of admission to higher education, the effects of parents' educational background on college-going behavior may not disappear completely.

6.5 Sex Differences in College-Going Behavior

Historically speaking, there have been clear sex differences in college-going behavior. Until a certain stage of economic development, the rate of male enrollment far exceeds that of female enrollment in most countries. As we saw in Chap. 1, this difference still exists in Japan for university education. That is, even in recent years the rate of female university enrollment has been about half that of male enrollment. Even in terms of the total rate of enrollment in university and junior college, the women's rate exceeded men's in Japan only in 1989. However, the rate of female university enrollment is currently increasing rapidly in many advanced countries including Japan.

This section will examine mainly the factors which kept the women's rate of enrollment lower than men's, and give some reasons for the recent increase in the rate of female enrollment.

We will examine the following five factors contributing to a low rate of female enrollment. The first is the sex difference in the costs of investment in higher education. If they are higher for a woman, fewer women go to college than men. The second is the sex difference in taste or ability. If women's tastes or abilities are not suited to high wage jobs, which usually require a college education, fewer women invest in higher education because the benefits are small in comparison with the costs (including psychological benefits and costs). The third is the sex difference in work behavior or sex discrimination after graduation from college. If women expect that they will work either only temporarily or discontinuously, or if they can obtain only low wages even with a college degree, then the rate of female enrollment is low. The fourth is "sex discrimination" within households. If boys tend to be favored in college-going decisions within households, fewer women go to college. The fifth is the parents' education policy which depends on the sex composition of their children. For instance, if parents with only daughters do not strongly encourage their children to go to college, the rate of female enrollment in society as a whole will be low.

We start with the first factor. An examination of cost items for investment in higher education reveals that some items involve sex differences. There are virtually no differences in tuition, fees, and stationery costs. Gross forgone earnings are lower for women, so *ceteris paribus* this fact rather encourages them to go to college. According to the study by Steelman and Powell (1991), however, American parents feel that female college students have difficulty earning money to cover study costs by working part time. In other words, because female college students have lower part-time incomes, their net forgone earnings are likely to be higher.

Probably the most important sex difference in investment costs is any (psychological) cost to the parents and their daughter arising from living separately. In particular, the parents' psychological costs are higher for daughters than for sons. If a woman lives alone to attend college, she is likely to rent a relatively costly apartment. These discouraging effects tend to dominate the above encouraging effect due to low gross forgone earnings and lower the rate of female enrollment.

This point can be indirectly confirmed by the empirical study concerning Japan undertaken in Sect. 6.3 and the study by Christensen, Milder, and Weisbrod (1975) concerning the United States. Namely, whether an institution is located nearby is an important factor in female students' college-going decisions in comparison with male students'. One of the reasons for the high rate of female enrollment in junior colleges in Japan is that these institutions mainly focus on students coming from nearby regions. In fact, many regression results in Sect. 6.3 showed that proximity to institutions has a positive and significant effect on the rate of female enrollment in junior college.

Taking this fact into consideration, we can propose that one of the determinants of the rate of female enrollment in higher education is the regional distribution of institutions. If universities concentrate in a limited number of regions, the rate of female university enrollment is likely to be low. In contrast, if they are almost uniformly distributed (in proportion to population), the rate is likely to be higher. A probable partial reason for the low rate of female university enrollment in Japan is that these institutions concentrate in large cities. The distribution of institutions should be taken into consideration in international comparisons of rates of female enrollment in higher education.

As to the second factor of taste and ability differences, the following interpretations can hold. That is, in comparison with males, female students tend to have a taste for such fields as humanities. Thus, if they are enrolled in higher education, they are likely to major in those fields (Polachek, 1978). Since those who have majored in such fields are less likely to obtain high wage jobs, their expected returns to higher education are low. Because of these low expected rates of return, fewer women go to college. If they majored in other fields against their taste, their psychological costs would be high and the real rate of return would be low. Hence, it is more advantageous not to go to college.

Paglin and Rufolo (1990) insist that there is actually a difference in mathematical ability between sexes and that this difference partly explains the wage difference. (They show that in comparison with men's average score of 569, women's average is 488 in a GRE examination of mathematics. GRE is a type of graduate school entrance examination in the United States.) In addition, Kodde and Ritzen (1988) demonstrate that a student's records in mathematics and natural sciences in high school are highly correlated with his/her demand for higher education.

Let us now examine the third factor of work behavior and sex discrimination. There are certainly sex differences in work behavior and in earnings after graduation from college. It is very likely that these differences give rise to sex differences in the total amount of investment in education. Historically speaking, many married women engaged themselves in housekeeping or worked for family businesses and did not supply labor to markets. Even if some worked outside after marriage, they stopped working for some years for childbearing and child care. (This is also the case even today.) In this way, women's labor supply in markets has tended to be either temporary or lacking continuity.

If the period of labor supply is short, the period for harvesting the returns to education investment is short and at least the pecuniary returns become small. Interruption in labor force participation due to childbearing and child care not only shortens the total period of labor supply but also generates a loss due to depreciation and obsolescence of skills and knowledge. This will also reduce returns. Taking into consideration the low returns to female education or the future allocation of time between labor markets and home, parents invest less in their daughters' education than in their sons'. For this reason the rate of female college enrollment becomes lower than that of male enrollment.

Of course there may be women in no small numbers who want to work in the same way as men and avoid a reduction in returns to education. However, there are factors that discourage such women from investing in education. It is actually difficult in many cases for firms to tell sufficiently accurately which particular female workers intend to work in the same way as men, as discussed in Sect. 3.4 in Chap. 3. Because of this statistical discrimination, firms do not allow them so much on-the-job training nor allocate them to important positions for career development. Hence, it is likely that these women are obliged to accept low wage jobs or auxiliary jobs. This kind of statistical discrimination reduces returns to women's investment in higher education and thus discourages them from investing.

King's (1977) study showed that there was a significant sex difference in the United States in the effect of labor market experience on wages for such professionals as accountants and computer specialists even when unmarried men and women were compared. The empirical study by Ragan and Smith (1981) revealed that the past high turnover rate lowers earnings in the United States and that the wage discount for a high quit rate is larger for females.

According to the empirical study by Mincer and Polachek (1974), not less than half the wage gap between married women and men is due to sex differences in length and continuity of work.[13] Polachek (1979, 1981) also shows that the discontinuity in women's careers prevents them from being hired for professional or managerial jobs. It can be conjectured that depreciation and obsolescence in knowledge due to discontinuous careers are large in these jobs.[14]

In addition, Lazear and Rosen (1990) point out that if women have relatively more aptitude for housekeeping than men, their careers tend to be discontinuous even if they can exhibit equal productivity in labor markets. This causes them to accumulate less firm-specific human capital[15] and also restrains firms from assigning them to high salary jobs such as managerial jobs.[16]

Schuman, Ahlburg, and Mahoney (1994) show in their empirical study concerning the United States that for reasons similar to the above, female workers tend to be allocated to jobs with lower job points. (Job points measure job content, required ability, working conditions, etc. for the base of wages.) They add that sex discrimination may also be a cause of low wages for women. (See also Malkiel and Malkiel (1973), Brown, Moon, and Zoloth (1980), Groshen (1991).)

When career discontinuity is expected, women may voluntarily choose jobs for which wage reduction due to discontinuity is small. Those are usually low wage jobs.[17] Becker (1985) claims that even women who intend to work continuously may choose low wage jobs. Because women spend more energy than men on housekeeping and child care, they tend to avoid tough but high wage jobs to conserve energy in their jobs.

Next let us examine the fourth factor or "sex discrimination" within households which is in part closely related to the third factor. We make a realistic assumption that the capital market is imperfect. Then, it is possible that even when returns to female education are quite high, investment in their education is much smaller than that in male education if returns to male education are higher.

To see this, consider the very common case in which a household with a limited budget has to decide about education investment for several children. A conceivable method of resource allocation for such a household is to invest less in daughters, from whom relatively low returns are expected, and more in sons (Becker and Tomes, 1976; Becker, 1991). This method maximizes future returns under limited funds for investment. As mentioned in Chap. 2, the number of siblings has generally a negative effect on academic ability and educational attainment (Alwin and Thornton, 1984; Blake, 1989; Hanushek, 1992), but Duncan (1974) and Parish and Willis (1993) show that this effect operates more strongly on women's educational attainment than men's.

Greenhalgh (1985) proposes the following hypothesis. Suppose that sons tend to offer their parents financial support throughout life, but that daughters keep some distance from them after they marry. Then, by taking financial care of their parents throughout life, sons can return the education expenses their parents bore, but daughters cannot. Hence, parents purchase high levels of education for sons and low levels for daughters. The daughters are required to repay their education expenses within a short period by working until their marriage. This hypothesis might hold in patriarchal developing countries.

All the above are cases of "sex discrimination" within a household with some economic effects. Are there cases in which sons are favored over daughters in home resource allocation for a reason of pure taste? This is quite a subtle question and to address it we would like to utilize information from some empirical studies on food allocation within households in developing countries.

We first mention the case of "discrimination" with an economic effect. Rosenzweig and Schultz (1982) show that as the earning power of sons is higher in India, they are favored over daughters in the intra-household resource allocation and thus that their survival rate is higher. According to Behrman (1988), however, some boy-favoring food allocations are observable in India which cannot be considered a response to sex differences in expected returns in labor markets. But he adds that investment in sons may have non-market returns. Further, Behrman and Deolalikar (1990) point out that discrimination in favor of boys tends to appear especially in times of food shortage.

In contrast, Deaton's (1989) study on Cote d'Ivoire and Thailand did not find discrimination between sons and daughters in resource allocations within households. There are many other studies on this topic. From these, we may be able to conclude that sons are favored over daughters to some extent at least in some regions of South Asia.

A resource allocation method or principle that differs from the above is to treat all children equally (Behrman, Pollak, and Taubman, 1982). Education of daughters is likely to be disadvantageous in terms of pecuniary returns in labor markets, but highly educated women are likely to marry highly educated men and enjoy high family incomes. Thus parents who treat their children equally tend to provide them with equal school education. (This point is stressed by Behrman, Pollak, and Taubman (1986) and Wakisaka (1990). See also Yano (1982).)

According to Boulier and Rosenzweig (1984), in the Philippines a one-year increase in a woman's education enables her to marry a spouse with a lifetime income which is higher by 5%. (The data is for 1973, when the average years of female education were 5.8 years.) Boullier and Rosenzweig infer that there is no sex difference in years of education in the Philippines in spite of the fact that the female labor force participation rate is very low (15.5%) because education generates returns in the form of the spouse's income after marriage. (Educational background is interpreted as a dowry.)

From these analyses we can conclude that the existence of "sex discrimination" in resource allocation within a household depends on labor market conditions, tightness of the household budget, culture, and so on.

Finally, we would like to examine the fifth factor. Butcher and Case (1994) point out that the level of a woman's education is affected by the sex composition of her siblings. Their study uses data for men and women born in the United States between 1920 and 1965 and finds that women raised with only brothers received on average significantly more education than women raised with any sisters, controlling for household size. (This phenomenon is especially salient among older women who received education relatively long ago, with the significance among younger women being slightly lower.)

More precisely, even among women with the same family size and same social background, the amount of education of those with at least one sister is less than that of those without any sisters by 0.25 to 0.3 years. What is striking is that the years of education depend only on the presence of a sister and not on the number of sisters. Moreover, men's education does not depend on the sex composition of their siblings.

Why does such a phenomenon occur? This cannot be explained by parents' favoring of boys. In fact, if boys were favored under capital market imperfection, the amount of investment in a daughter with brothers would be small, controlling for sibling size. In other words, the amount of investment in a daughter with only sisters would be larger than the amount of investment in a daughter with at least one brother.

The hypothesis Butcher and Case propose is sociological and based on a reference group theory. That is, it insists that the presence of a second daughter in the household changes the reference group for the first. When there is only one daughter, the parents regard her brothers as her reference group and provide her with an equal share of the household's educational resources. In contrast, when a second daughter enters the household, the parents regard the daughters as a group separate from that of their sons and set a different target and criterion for the education of their daughters. This study adds that the influence of the presence of another sister is decreasing over time, reflecting a change in parents' values.

Brinton (1988, 1993) has analyzed sex difference in years of education in Japan through international comparison. She insists that the average years of education of Japanese women have been less than those of Japanese men because of the mutually enforcing effects of intergenerational exchange relations within households and employment practices in Japan.

If parents invest in their children's education for future returns such as old-age support, when they have some investment funds and perceive the labor market to be sex discriminatory, they place priority on their sons' education. This view is close to the above discussions concerning the third and fourth factors. She quotes the result of a questionnaire undertaken in 1979 to show that more Japanese adults prefer to have a son rather than a daughter. (However, these preferences do not mean that Japanese actually discriminate against daughters after birth.)

She also emphasizes that because of the high quit rate of female workers due to marriage and child care and because the distribution of training among employees is subject to a great deal of discretionary power by Japanese managers, female workers do not receive sufficient training which is essential for promotion in Japanese firms, where internal labor markets[18] are highly developed.

She points out several Japanese factors which cause women to be treated disadvantageously: there is lower variance in marriage age (than in the US); the age of marriage and childbearing coincides with the period of important training and experience in firms; few women have mentors; it is more important in Japan to maintain a relationship with a particular firm rather than with a particular occupation. She suggests that the low rate of participation in the labor force for highly educated Japanese women is due to these factors.

Brinton's entire works cited here are written with the nuance that any variations from the United States situation are inferior. However, Japanese society is built on the basis of a partly different principle from American society. For instance, Japanese consider that divorce has detrimental effects on children. Because this section does not seek to argue these matters we will not do so, besides mentioning that a social scientist needs to understand the whole society in order to analyze part of it.

Because of some of the above five factors, the rate of female as opposed to male enrollment in higher education was historically low in many countries. As we saw in Chap. 1, however, the rate of female enrollment is rapidly increasing all over the world. What is behind this phenomenon? Reexamination of the above factors will lead us to infer that restraint has disappeared or been weakened by increases in family income and changes in female labor markets.

In general, an increase in family income augments the rate of female enrollment more than that of male enrollment. In addition, prevalence of public pensions reduces the necessity to save for old age and increases investment in education of children. This will also promote female enrollment in higher education. According to the study on developing countries by Schultz (1985), the income- and price-elasticity of the rate of female attendance in school are higher than that of males. In other words, if family income increases or if the price of education decreases, the rate of female attendance increases more than that of male attendance. Similar results have been obtained in the study by Parish and Willis (1993) on years of education in Taiwan and in that by Rice (1987) on sex difference in the demand for post-compulsory education in the United Kingdom.

The changes in female labor markets in the United States over the past thirty years or so can be summarized as follows. Women's earning power increased with economic growth and in particular expansion of the service sector. Partly because of this, the divorce rate increased and the benefits of marriage decreased. This increase in the divorce rate necessitated self-reliance on the part of women and induced them to invest more in education to have higher earning power. Further, a decrease in the number of children prolonged the harvest period of human capital and made investment in school education and in-firm training advantageous. In addition, completion of the legal framework prohibiting discrimination made returns to female education close to those to male education.[19]

What occurred in Japan was similar to some extent. That is, labor demand expanded in the commerce, service, and financial sectors because of the recent changes in industrial structure. In response, the number of highly educated women working in these sectors increased (Kaneko, 1989). In addition, more women continued to work for the same firms (Wakisaka, 1990).[20]

Osawa (1993) points out that there was a change in the pattern of female human capital investment in Japan. Progress of the service economy and office automation have generated increased demand for highly educated female labor (their rehabilitation probability has also increased) and increases in the wages of young female university graduates relative to those of high-school and junior college graduates. Because of this, more women have had incentives to invest in university education.[21] The Equal Employment Act enforced from 1986 must also have prompted this change.

Summing up, the rate of female enrollment in higher education is currently increasing in many advanced countries firstly because family incomes have increased and secondly because environments have been set up in labor markets which make female investment in education advantageous.

Notes

1. The first three sections of this chapter are based mainly on Arai (1989).
2. The effect of a mother's labor force participation on children's school achievement and school continuation decisions depends subtly on the age of the child. According to Stafford's (1987) empirical study on the United States, if a mother works before her child goes to primary school, the child will achieve to a low standard in the early years of primary education, other things being equal. Datcher-Loury (1989) shows a similar result. (In the empirical study by Murnane, Maynard, and Ohls (1981) on primary school students from the third to sixth grades and that by Hanushek (1992), mothers' participation does not have a significant effect on their children's vocabulary or reading ability.) A mother's participation, however, does not necessarily have a negative effect on her children's school achievement as a whole or in the long run, because a working mother is likely to have fewer children and spend more funds on their education. It can be inferred that the negative effect becomes quite small after her children finish primary education. Other studies that have analyzed the relationships between a mother's participation and children's school achievement and/or school continuation include Leibowitz (1977) and Willis and Rosen (1979).
3. The population older than a certain legally determined age who have the ability to work and intend to work is called the labor force. The ratio of the labor force to the population in a specified age class is called the rate of labor force participation of that age class.
4. The effective labor demand is concerned with the labor demand considered by the Public Employment Security Office in Japan. The labor demand is called effective if the Office is still dealing with it. A similar definition applies to the effective supply. A high ratio of effective labor demand to effective supply implies that the labor market is tight.
5. For reference we would like to show the regression results obtained using either of the rates of male and female university enrollment as the dependent variable and only either of *YEDFA* and *YEDMO* as the independent variable (*t*-values are in parentheses).

	CONST.	*YEDFA*	*YEDMO*	*SER*	R^2	$\bar{R}^2$	*F*
MALE ENROLLMENT	−90.63	11.58		4.81	0.55	0.54	55.0
		(7.42)					
	−129.7		15.70	4.48	0.61	0.60	70.8
			(8.41)				
FEMALE ENROLLMENT	−41.16	4.806		2.94	0.36	0.35	25.4
		(5.04)					
	−67.85		7.510	2.52	0.53	0.52	51.2
			(7.15)				

The *t*-value of the regression coefficient is larger and the explanatory power of the regression equation is higher when *YEDMO* is used than when *YEDFA* is used. Though not directly related to the problem of education investment, similar empirical results have been obtained as to the distribution of intra-household nutrition acquisitions in Brazil. According to Thomas (1990), relative to the effect on daughters, a father's unearned income has a significantly bigger effect on sons' nutrition. In contrast, a mother's unearned income (social security benefits, interest and rent income, etc.) has a significantly bigger effect on daughters' nutrition. In addition, for both sons and daughters the mother's unearned income has stronger effects than the father's. The psychological study by Kagan and Moss (1959) shows that analogous relationships hold between parents' educational background and their children's IQs as we will see in the next section.
6. In some results of the cross-sectional analysis by Corazzini, Dugan, and Grabowski (1972) based on state data for the United States, the rate of unemployment shows a positive and significant effect on the total rate of male and female enrollment in higher education.
7. According to Tomes (1981), highly educated parents tend to invest in the school education of their children rather than leave property.

8. Similar results have been obtained concerning the effects of parents' educational background in the study by Behrman and Taubman (1986), where the average birth year of the sample is 1953, though the mother's effect appears more significantly on daughters than on sons. The father's effect is also stronger in the empirical study by Vella (1994) on Australian women who made education investment decisions in about the 1970s. Incidentally, Becker (1991) claims that the educational background of grandparents have negative effects on the education investment of their grandchildren, but significant effects could not be observed in the empirical study by Behrman and Taubman (1985).

9. Mothers are the heads in almost half of black households. The rate was less than 20% in white households during this period. For Hispanics, the rate was between 20% and 30% until the mid-1980s, but increased later to almost 40%.

10. When an independent variable "Mother reads with child" is introduced, the significance of the effect of the mother's educational background on her child's verbal ability decreases compared with when this variable is not introduced. It is conjectured therefore that part of the effect of the mother's educational background derives from reading with her child. This study also shows that the educational background of the father (more strictly, the household head) does not have a significant effect on a child's verbal ability and that the presence of an encyclopedia and labor-saving capital goods such as a clothes dryer within a household does have positive effects.

11. Rosenzweig and Wolpin (1994) point to the benefits of postponed childbearing by teenagers. Their study suggests that postponement of childbearing by two years among women who are tenth-graders would result in a 5% increase in their children's achievement test scores. Parsons (1978) is critical of too much emphasis on mothers' time spent with children. He suggests that the effect of what is actually done during that time and the effects of contacts with people other than parents are also important. The effect of neighbors on demand for education is also discussed by Bishop (1977) and Borjas (1995). See also Hill and Stafford (1978).

12. The income elasticity of demand for a good means the percentage increase in the demand for the good due to a 1% income increase. On the other hand, the price elasticity of demand means the percentage increase in the demand due to a 1% price decrease. The demand is said to be inelastic if the elasticity is less than 1, and elastic if it is larger than 1. Both income- and price-elasticity of the demand for education of highly educated families are likely to be small because they try hard to invest as much as possible in their children's education. In contrast, the elasticity is likely to be large for poorly educated families. A related analysis has been undertaken by McPherson and Schapiro (1991) which suggests that a decline in the net cost of college education (tuition minus financial aid) has a comparatively stronger effect on the demand for higher education of low income families.

13. For relationships between discontinuity of women's careers and their low wages, see also Polachek (1975), Farber (1977), Corcoran and Duncan (1979), Mincer and Ofek (1982), Cox (1984), and Goldin and Polachek (1987).

14. A similar phenomenon can also be found in the allocation of staff in American universities. McDowell (1982) points out that there are few female researchers in such fields as physical sciences where acquired knowledge is useful only in a short period of time (the speed of knowledge obsolescence is high), because the opportunity costs of child care is high in such fields. In American universities those who are research oriented tend to be sharply distinguished from those who are instruction oriented. More female staff can be found in instruction jobs where the speed of knowledge obsolescence is relatively low. See also Johnson and Stafford (1974).

15. Knowledge and/or skills acquired through on-the-job training are called general human capital if they are equally useful (productive) in many firms, and such training is called general training. On the other hand, if their usefulness (productivity) is lower in other firms than where the training was undertaken, they are called firm-specific human capital, and the training is called firm-specific training. If a worker's career is expected to be discontinuous

(his/her turnover rate is expected to be high), accumulation of firm-specific human capital is obstructed because neither the worker nor the firm wants to bear the costs of firm-specific training.

16. Sandell and Shapiro (1980) show in their empirical study that a woman's expectations of future labor force participation positively affect the amount of her on-the-job training. When a couple maximize their family income, they are likely to decide where to live in accordance with the husband's job, and thus the wife's career may be interrupted and she may not be able to choose her best available job (Frank, 1978).

17. See Polachek (1976). However, there is a criticism by England (1982). According to Ferber and Birnbaum (1981), clerical jobs in American colleges are mostly filled by women, because the depreciation of human capital due to career discontinuity is small in those jobs.

18. An internal labor market means a type of organization typically observed in a relatively large corporation. In such an organization, the allocation of human resources is determined not by the price mechanism but by a set of administrative rules and procedures. For example, when a job in an internal labor market becomes vacant, it is usually filled not by hiring in the labor market but by promoting a worker who has worked in the job below it. Wages in such an organization are not necessarily determined to equal market wages: in Japan they are likely to be determined on the basis of seniority or length of service. (See Arai (1997a) for a theoretical explanation of this fact.) Internal labor markets have high job security (such as lifetime employment in Japan). The existence of firm-specific human capital has traditionally been pointed out as an important factor generating internal labor markets. In order to promote accumulation of firm-specific human capital, which is less valuable in other firms, the firm has to offer high job security which generates internal promotions. The author considers, however, that encouragement of cooperation among workers is a more important factor generating internal labor markets at least in Japan (Arai, 1997b). For more details, see also Doeringer and Piore (1985) and Osterman (1984).

19. Beller (1982) shows that occupational differences between the sexes diminished in the United States in the 1970s because of equal employment opportunity laws. According to the empirical study by Eberts and Stone (1985) on American teachers in elementary and secondary schools, sex discrimination in promotions to administrative positions declined by more than half in the 1970s. Using federal personnel records for 1973–82, Lewis (1986) finds strikingly similar promotion probabilities for white men and women when a variety of individual characteristics are accounted for.

20. According to the empirical study on the United States by Light and Ureta (1992), in recent years firms have become able to distinguish low female quitters as easily as in the case of men on the basis of the information available at the time of hiring (academic careers, job careers, etc.), though previously it was quite risky to hire women because their quit rate was high.

21. Shimada and Higuchi (1985) point out that the labor force participation behavior of Japanese women in the post-war period was not necessarily as predicted by human capital theory. For example, the decline in the number of children occurred much earlier than the salient increases in the level of education and the rate of employed labor force participation.

Chapter 7
The Purpose and Function of Higher Education

Chap. 2 argued college-going decisions based on human capital theory while Chap. 3 those based on signaling theory. These two theories have thoroughly opposed views on the purpose or function of higher education. That is, human capital theory insists that higher education enhances the productivity of students, whereas signaling theory claims that it merely conveys information to firms about the pre-college capabilities of students. As seen in Sect. 3.6, it is possible to construct a model in which higher education simultaneously performs these two different functions. However, a question may naturally arise as to which theory is more proper or which function prevails in the real economy.

Several economists have undertaken statistical tests to answer this question. The previous chapter also tried a simple test. This chapter will examine in Sect. 7.1 the results of several representative tests undertaken so far. In addition, it will propose the present author's judgments as to the plausibility or applicability of these two theories.

The above will almost complete the initial purposes of this book. But the author would like to add in Sect. 7.2 a few notes and opinions concerning the purpose and function of higher education in Japan, which is now facing a decline in enrollment age population. The notes and opinions also relate to some aspects of the ongoing university reforms, and changes which are very likely to arise in the near future. More specifically, the last section will discuss such problems as changes in the information content of educational signals, academic abilities of students, and training for leadership.

7.1
Human Capital Theory Versus Signaling Theory

7.1.1
Basic Problems

The previous chapter tested the basic signaling hypothesis using a simple method based on Wolpin's (1977) idea. Since the emergence of this hypothesis as opposed to the human capital hypothesis, there have been several economists other than Wolpin who tried to test the relative plausibility of these two hypotheses or theories. In this section we would like to examine these test results.

What becomes important when testing the hypotheses are the differing views on the function of higher education. That is, while human capital theory insists that higher education enhances students' productivity, signaling theory claims that it merely transmits information to employers about students' pre-college capabilities.

Before examining the test results, we need to point out first that it is very difficult to reach a clear-cut and persuasive judgment as to the plausibility of each hypothesis by empirical studies. There are several reasons for this.

First, in both hypotheses each economic agent behaves in exactly the same manner. That is, in both theories each job applicant compares the benefit and cost of (higher) education and then decides education investment so as to maximize net lifetime income. On the other hand, the firm pays higher wages to highly educated individuals (college graduates) so as to maximize profits. (It should be noted, however, that a college degree signifies high capability acquired in college education in human capital theory, while it signifies high capability acquired before admission to college in signaling theory.) The process of decision making by each economic agent is the same in both theories. What matters in testing the two competing theories is not that additional education increases wage payments but why such a wage increase arises. Thus we need to clarify why highly educated individuals earn more. This task is not easily accomplished by empirical studies.

The second reason for the difficulty of obtaining a clear-cut judgment lies in the fact that there are qualitatively different signaling models. (In contrast, widely used human capital models have a high degree of qualitative homogeneity.) For example, as we saw in Chap. 3, the Spence model differs greatly from the Arrow model in assumptions and structure. This makes testing difficult. (However, many signaling models have similar features such that individual productive capability is not initially observable and that it is positively correlated with the individual's years of education.)

The third reason is that signaling models are not necessarily constructed to suit empirical analyses. The fourth is a serious reason that data which are really necessary for testing are often unavailable. The fifth is that some test results can allow different interpretations.

With these reservations in mind, let us examine in the following the statistical tests undertaken by several economists. (A note needs to be given beforehand that not all the subsequent tests are concerned with higher education.) Some of these tests use quite clever methods. Because of the difficulties discussed above, however, few of the tests are free from shortcomings. If more suitable data became available and/or improvements were made in test methods, more clear-cut judgments would be obtained.

We would like to examine first the argument by Layard and Psacharopoulos (1974). From the standpoint of human capital theory, they have raised three empirical criticisms against signaling theory. The first is that dropouts enjoy relatively high rates of return to their additional education, e.g., the partial college education college dropouts received. An interpretation of the basic Spence model is that the employer places an especially high valuation not on a job applicant's total years of education but on his/her possession of a degree. In contrast with this interpretation, college dropouts receive relatively high returns to their partial college education. Layard and Psacharopoulos support human capital theory on the grounds that even college dropouts earn comparatively more than high-school graduates owing to the productivity-enhancing function of higher education.

It is difficult to obtain data for college dropouts in Japan mainly because there are in fact few dropouts, but there are many dropouts in the United States and data for them are actually available. Empirical analyses based on such data show that private rates of return to (partial) high-school or college education obtained by dropouts sometimes exceed those obtained by those who completed their courses, after individuals' IQs, their parents' educational background, their social classes, etc. are controlled for.

For example, in the study by Taubman and Wales (1973), the rate of return to (partial) college education of dropouts equals 15% as compared with 11% for college graduates, after individuals' IQs and fathers' educational background are controlled for. The study by Rogers (1969) shows that the rate of return to (partial) high-school education obtained by high-school dropouts equals 7% as compared with 6% for high-school graduates. It also shows that the rate of return obtained by college dropouts is 12% as compared with 8% for college graduates. (Of course, higher rates of return for dropouts do not imply that they earn more than those who have completed courses. Because the total education investment of a dropout is less, his/her total earnings are smaller even if the rate of return is higher.)

The second criticism is that the effect of educational background on wages does not decrease with seniority (or age). As the length of service of a worker increases, the employer will come to have better information about his/her real productivity. Thus, if the signaling hypothesis is correct, the effect of educational background on wages should decrease. The second criticism says that this is not the case in reality.

Let us look at Table 7.1. It shows the earnings of those with each level of post-high-school education, holding constant ability not due to school education, expressed as a percentage of average high school graduate earnings, first when the sample was 33 years old and then when 47. The earnings of college graduates (B.A.), for instance, are 1.12 times as high as those of high-school graduates at the age of 33 and 1.31 times at the age of 47, with the differential (ratio) increasing by 0.19 in this interval.

This table reveals that the effect of additional education on earnings increases with age both relatively and absolutely. (Because absolute earnings at the age of 47 are normally higher than at 33, the absolute earnings difference between college and high-school graduates is larger in the former than in the latter if the earnings ratio in the

Table 7.1. Standardized earnings of those with higher education as a percentage of earnings of those who completed high school: by age (males).

	Average age		Increase in differential
	33	47	
Some College	111	117	6
B.A.	112	131	19
Some Graduate Work	115	126	11
M.A.	110	132	22
Ph.D.	102	127	25
M.D.	172	206	34
LL.B.	119	184	65

Source: Taubman and Wales (1973).

former is larger than in the latter.) The second criticism says that if the signaling hypothesis is correct, the wage ratio (or wage difference) should decrease with age, because increases in age reveal workers' real productivity more clearly and thus some high-school graduates earn more than college graduates.

The third criticism is that if screening is the main function of education, it could be done more cheaply by a simpler testing procedure. This criticism is based on an elementary question of why identification of individual productive capability is undertaken in the existing system of college education which uses an enormous amount of resources. It seems that other much cheaper methods can test individuals' basic academic ability, obedience, perseverance, or productivity. Any emergence of institutions which perform such a testing function cheaply is likely to drive out colleges, but such institutions do not exist in the real economy. According to the third criticism, this fact implies that the purpose of the existing colleges is not to screen individuals but to enhance individual productivity as in human capital theory.[1]

Riley (1979a) responds to these criticisms from the standpoint of signaling theory. As for the first, he points out that the employer in the signaling hypothesis is not interested only in whether a job applicant has a college degree. At first sight the first criticism seems plausible in the basic Spence (1973) model, but being a college dropout is nothing but a signal from which the employer obtains information about the job applicant's productivity. Hence, the high rates of return obtained by college dropouts do not contradict the signaling hypothesis. Moreover, some dropouts may have been "pulled" out of college by attractive alternatives or by high forgone earnings due to their high productivity. Thus not all college dropouts may have been "pushed" out of college by lack of academic ability or motivation (Taubman and Wales, 1973). For these reasons, it is problematical to reject signaling theory on the basis of dropouts' high wages or high rates of return.

Riley's response to the second criticism is that in a signaling equilibrium the employer finds out that on average its predictions based on educational attainment are correct. Then, one would not expect the effect of education on wages to fall even in the absence of on-the-job training. Indeed, one of the crucial roles of educational signaling in the real economy is presumably to allow employers to select the more talented individuals for jobs which involve considerable on-the-job training. Since human capital and, hence, earnings rise relatively sharply on such jobs, the observed rise in the return to years of schooling is hardly surprising.[2]

To the third criticism, Riley responds in the following way. When considering the real economy, the signaling hypothesis does not necessarily completely negate the productivity-enhancing effect of education. (As the model in Sect. 3.6 shows, Riley recognizes the plausibility of human capital theory to some extent.) The problem reduces to determining how great the costs of educational signaling are if the latter also enhances productivity.[3]

7.1.2
Several Statistical Tests

On the basis of a statistical test with the following idea, Albrecht (1981) has obtained a result skeptical about the signaling hypothesis. Suppose that in addition to educational background, information is available which indirectly discloses job applicants' productive capabilities. If educational background has a signal, the relative importance of education information for hiring decisions will decrease when information other than educational background is available to examine job applicants. The signaling hypothesis can be tested by analyzing the degree of this decrease.

Albrecht has undertaken an empirical analysis using data for recruitment of blue-collar workers by the Swedish auto manufacturer Volvo. Educational background is classified into "high" and "low" depending on whether or not job applicants graduated from gymnasium, which is a three-year institution for students from ages 16 to 19. (42% of the sample had "low" educational background, i.e., did not graduate from gymnasium.)

The information class of each applicant is identified with the source of his/her recruitment. A job applicant belongs to the high information class if he/she has a recommendation from a current Volvo employee, i.e., he/she has given the name of a Volvo employee who has informed him/her of the job opening and from whom the personnel department can solicit an evaluation. Those in the low information class have applied by searching the "Situations Vacant" announcements of the Swedish Labor Market Board or in response to newspaper advertisements. The personnel department cannot obtain evaluation information about these applicants.

An estimation of the relationship between a job applicant's characteristics and his/her probability of being hired has been undertaken by introducing such independent variables as age, nationality, residence, and sex, as well as the above variables for educational background and information class. The estimation result shows that the positive effects of additional education on the probability of getting hired are decreased in the presence of extra information (recommendation), but that these effects are quite small in magnitude. From this fact, Albrecht concludes that so far as the data used are concerned, Volvo's hiring behavior gives no support to the signaling hypothesis.

This estimation may be criticized in two ways, that it is merely a case study of a particular type of worker in a particular firm, and that the reliability of recommendation information should be questioned.

Using data collected in 1980 for Kenya and Tanzania, Boissiere, Knight, and Sabot (1985) have obtained a test result that supports human capital theory. Their test is concerned with secondary education because primary education is almost completely prevalent and less than 1% of people of enrollment age go to college in both countries. In other words, these researchers have tested whether secondary education enhances students' productive capabilities or plays a role of signaling.

A characteristic of their test method is that it has explicitly introduced a variable for the productive capability of an individual as one of the independent variables in the individual earnings function. This variable is the score of literacy (reading ability) and numeracy in an examination devised by specialists and is interpreted as the amount of human capital accumulated. (At the same time, the test has introduced an independent variable for the test score of reasoning ability. This test score is considered to measure innate ability since the test is designed so that literacy and numeracy provide no advantage.)

In their test, the effects of secondary education on wages can be divided into the signaling effect (direct effect) and the effect of secondary education on literacy and numeracy. Comparing these two effects, they conclude that the latter is larger. According to their test, the main effects of years of education and innate ability are indirect and largely play a role of augmenting literacy and numeracy. The effect of literacy and numeracy on wages are not significantly smaller in the case of blue-collar workers than in the case of white-collar workers. Further, workers with high literacy and numeracy but less education earn almost the same as those with more education. From these empirical results, they claim that human capital theory is more plausible than signaling theory in Kenya and Tanzania.

This conclusion is not very surprising, however, since basic academic ability such as literacy and numeracy is closely related to productivity in most jobs and the main purpose of secondary education is to augment such ability or productivity. Even in today's Japan, the productivity-augmenting function of education is important at least up to secondary level.

The empirical study by Kroch and Sjoblom (1994) based on US data has also generated a result which is advantageous to human capital theory. The basic characteristic of their study is that it has introduced the following two independent variables into the earnings function: one being absolute years of education and the other the individual's position (rank) in the distribution of educational attainment for his/her cohort. As average years of education increases with economic growth, graduation from high school, for instance, used to imply a superior educational background but its rank is now low in advanced countries.

If the signaling hypothesis is correct, an employer would use a job applicant's educational rank or relative years of education to infer his/her position in the distribution of abilities. Moreover, the distribution of innate abilities ought not change from cohort to cohort. The basic idea of their study is that the signaling hypothesis can be tested by examining the effect of educational rank. If the pure signaling model such as that by Spence (1973) holds in the real economy, the effect of absolute years of education in the earnings function will not be significant. On the other hand, if the pure human capital model holds, the effect of relative years of education or educational rank will not be significant. If both hypotheses are true as in the Riley (1976) model in Sect. 3.6, the estimated coefficients of these two independent variables should be positive and significant. Their tests results vary according to samples but generally support human capital theory.

The test conducted by Lang and Kropp (1986) has produced a result which supports the signaling hypothesis. Their basic idea is as follows. Changes in the years of compulsory education have been undertaken several times in states of the United States. If human capital theory is correct, such a change due to a state compulsory school attendance law would affect the educational attainment only of those who in the absence of the law would have left school prior to the minimum school leaving age. This is because each individual chooses his/her optimal level of education under the existing legal constraint. For example, those who want to acquire knowledge (human capital) obtainable in higher education will still choose to invest in higher education even if years of compulsory education are changed by law. In contrast, if the signaling hypothesis is correct, a law change of this nature would affect educational attainment in types of education other than compulsory education.

To make the story simple and clear, suppose that the education system of a country (state) consists of primary, secondary, undergraduate, and graduate education. Suppose further that only primary education was initially compulsory and that compulsory education has just been extended to the secondary level. Because of this change, the type of individual who the signaling hypothesis considers to be of low ability and who used to receive only primary education will now receive secondary education. Then, the average productivity (and accordingly wages) of workers with only secondary education will be lower than before. This is because the extended years of compulsory education will not enhance the productivity of students under the signaling hypothesis.

This will provide the type of individual who used to receive only secondary education with new incentives to receive college education. By doing so they can signal that their productivity is higher than that of those with only secondary education. Then, by a similar reason the type of individual who used to receive college education will have incentives to receive graduate education. In this way, under the signaling hypothesis an extension in the years of compulsory education will increase educational attainment of high-ability workers who are not directly affected by this extension.

Lang and Kropp have examined the changes in enrollment rates for sixteen- and seventeen-year-olds due to the extension of compulsory education to the ages of fourteen through sixteen. Their test results reject the human capital hypothesis and support the signaling hypothesis. However, they themselves allow the possibility that the same test results would be obtained even if the signaling hypothesis was not true. For instance, if the quality of compulsory education deteriorates because of an increase in years of compulsory education, the demand for high-quality education may increase and enrollment rates beyond compulsory education may increase. These enrollment rates may also increase if individuals become more informed of the benefits of additional education because of an increase in years of compulsory education.[4]

So far as the above tests are concerned, it is difficult to judge decisively which of the human capital and signaling hypotheses is correct. In particular, judgment as to higher education must be very difficult. Hence, a reasonable conclusion may be that (higher) education has both productivity-enhancing and signaling functions.

However, the present author would like to propose the following judgments taking into consideration to some extent the above test results. The first is that the lower the level of education, the more likely it is that human capital theory holds. Since the purpose of primary and secondary education is to teach for each field the basic knowledge necessary for daily life and work, the productivity-enhancing effect of such knowledge must be very large. In other words, workers who are deficient in such knowledge will face great difficulties in many occupations. The above result by Boissiere, Knight and Sabot (1985) can be considered evidence for this.

The second judgment is that the more natural-science-oriented a field of education and an occupation, the more likely it is for human capital theory to hold. Knowledge obtained in school education must be indispensable for engineers and researchers of engineering. Even if such knowledge is not sufficient in those occupations, it has a role in providing the basis or prerequisite for the greater necessary knowledge. Hence, generally speaking, a productivity-enhancing function is more important in education in natural sciences. Similarly, human capital theory is more likely to hold in the medical and dental education we considered in Chap. 4. In contrast, it is not very likely in the fields of social sciences and humanities and in related occupations that knowledge obtained in school directly relates to productive activities, and thus the plausibility of the signaling hypothesis may be high.

The third is concerned with employment rules or practices within firms. The signaling hypothesis is more likely to hold the higher the degree to which on-the-job training and/or experience immediately after hiring determine the workers' entire future career. If the human resource allocation and type of training immediately after hiring are decided according to academic background, and the subsequent career and promotions are determined in succession, individuals with high productive capabilities but without much school education have no opportunities to demonstrate them and let their employers recognize these. Under such labor market institutions, job applicants tend to make education investment decisions as in the signaling hypothesis.

As a matter of fact, many Japanese firms tend or tended to have institutions in which workers are sharply distinguished according to educational background (Shirai, 1982; Sekiguchi, 1996). More precisely, educational background *per se* is or used to be a very important determinant of starting salary, personnel allocation, promotion courses and speed, promotion limits, etc. Thus, those with different educational backgrounds are or were likely to belong to non-competing groups.

The author's fourth judgment is that human capital theory becomes more likely to hold as the economy and technology develop and become more complex. New scientific knowledge obtainable only at universities is not necessary for production activities at the initial stage of modern economic growth, but as the economy and technology become complex, many jobs will require more advanced knowledge. Thus, if a high level of knowledge is acquired in higher education, this will directly influence a worker's productivity. Most fields of natural sciences have historically experienced this process. Even in some fields of social sciences, an associated phenomenon seems to be occurring these days.

7.2 Decline in the Enrollment Age Population and the Purpose and Function of Higher Education

The above discussion has almost completed the initial goals of this book. This section adds a few economic notes on the purpose and function of Japanese higher education as these relate to the recent decline in the enrollment age population and the drastic changes that Japanese colleges are facing, matters that are currently attracting great interest. We would like to discuss such problems as changes in the information content of the education signal, academic abilities of students, and training for leadership.

Abstract of Education Statistics by the Ministry of Education shows that the Japanese population of eighteen-year-olds peaked at about 2,050,000 in 1992 and then began to decline. It is expected to be about 1,510,000 in 2000. Thus it will undergo a drastic decrease of about 26% in eight years.

However, a more drastic decrease occurred after the baby boomers (those born between 1947 and 1949) passed enrollment age. The population of eighteen-year-olds was 2,490,000 in 1966, but decreased to 1,650,000 in 1974, a decrease of about 34% in eight years. (Incidentally, the population of eighteen-year-olds continued to decrease to 1,540,000 in 1976 but was almost stationary during the subsequent ten years.) That decrease was not questioned at that time because university and junior college enrollments in those years were smaller than in 1992 and because the rate of enrollment in higher education was increasing.

Should the rate of enrollment in higher education in 2000 be the same as that in 1992 or 38.9%, enrollment would decrease by 210,000 or 26%. Thus some institutions might not be able to survive. In contrast, should the enrollment in 2000 be the same as in 1992, the rate of enrollment in higher education would be 52% in 2000, that is, the rate would increase by 13 percentage points and more than half of the population of enrollment age would receive higher education. (Since Japanese higher education has traditionally had few dropouts, most of these people would graduate.) This enrollment rate might be quite high as compared with the rates in other advanced countries.

It is almost certain that the enrollment rate will increase in Japan in the coming several years, but it is not so certain whether enrollment will decrease due to the decline in the population of enrollment age. Even if enrollment does not decrease and the enrollment rate exceeds 50%, the Japanese economy may not face inefficiency in this age of "mega-competition". In other words, if the Japanese industrial structure changes to have more weight on college graduate intensive high-tech industries, the economy may not lose efficiency even with so many college graduates.

These changes are likely to influence the purpose and function of higher education. (Some influence is already being realized.) First of all, the probable increase in the enrollment rate may change the information content of an educational background of "college graduation". That is, "college graduation" is likely to imply lower average productivity than before. It should be noted, however, that an increase in the enrollment rate does not necessarily directly bring about a decrease in average productivity. As already seen, an increase in the enrollment rate can be generated by an increase in family income or in the years of education of parents, so it does not necessarily imply that all "additional" students have lower abilities. (If an increase in the enrollment rate was caused only by shrinkage in the area of *C* in Fig. 5.3, the abilities of the "additional" students would not be a serious problem.)

The information content of the signal of college graduation will change only if some institutions facing decreases in the number of applicants begin to admit lower ability students. Should this happen, "college graduation" itself as a signal will not have as high a value as before. Thus, more important signals may be "graduation from a first-class university", "graduation from a second-class university", and so on. If human capital theory describes the reality of higher education most accurately, we need not be so pessimistic about what will happen in the near future. Because this theory implies that higher education enhances productivity, colleges can partially achieve their education goals even with low ability students in accordance with these levels of ability. In other words, since the amount of human capital per young individual will increase, the stock of human capital in the entire economy will increase accordingly.

Institutions facing a decline in applications may try to improve their financial situation by admitting foreign students and/or those who have work experience. (Because entrance examinations into Japanese colleges have traditionally been hard these individuals have had difficulty getting enrolled but the situation is now changing.) However, only those institutions which are in a favorable situation can do this. (An important condition here is the location of the institution as those located near the center of a large city will have such applicants.)

What we can predict with great confidence is that for the factors considered in the previous chapter, the rate of female university enrollment will steadily increase in the near future. Even if the rate of enrollment in higher education is constant, many institutions will be able to survive if more female students choose to be enrolled in university rather than in junior college, because then the number of students attending colleges will not decrease much. Some junior colleges may thus convert to universities to survive.[5]

Together with the decline in the enrollment age population, competition among colleges for applicants is becoming quite keen. This may encourage each institution to develop a differentiated type of education. In other words, exactly as each auto manufacturer produces differentiated products, so may each college try to produce a different type of graduate. This will benefit the entire society only if each college sets and accomplishes a proper goal from the viewpoint of society as a whole.

If, in contrast, a college changes its initial idea and tries to attract more students by negligent education or by only pleasing the students, it will harm not only society as a whole but also itself. An important example is that many universities have recently been using differentiated examination methods. This is having an adverse influence not only on higher education but also on senior high-school education.

Some senior high-school students start preparing for the entrance examinations into particular colleges or departments by focusing only on the few examination subjects required by those colleges and departments. Moreover, some senior high schools themselves are adjusting their systems to this type of preparation strategy. This must distort the fundamental purpose of senior high-school education, i.e., the purpose of teaching basic and wide knowledge (Amano, 1994). This is probably one of the reasons for the low academic abilities of college students these days.

This tendency is not desirable for the future of the Japanese economy. One of the advantages of Japanese secondary education has been to teach a high level of basic knowledge to a large number of students. (This has provided Japanese workers with the advantage of a high average level of productivity.) Given this characteristic of secondary education, Japanese higher education has played roles of human capital formation and/or signaling. Because of this, highly educated Japanese workers have been able to adjust themselves flexibly to social and economic change.

Because of the above tendency, however, some recent college students lack a basic knowledge even of subjects which are important to their major fields. This will also generate difficulties in their future occupations. As stated before, knowledge gained in senior high school has a productivity-enhancing effect in most occupations. It also fosters judgment ability necessary for a worker. In short, senior high-school education in Japan has played and should continue to play an important role in human capital formation. The author considers that the level of knowledge in senior high-school textbooks is sufficient as a prerequisite to higher education, but recent college entrants may have less knowledge in more than half of the subjects taught in senior high school.

Those who prepare for entrance examinations have traditionally been irritated by difficult questions given in entrance examinations. If first-year college students in other advanced countries took Japanese entrance examinations (in mathematics, natural sciences, etc.), they would probably obtain rather low scores.

Under the name of giving senior high-school students "leeway", the required number of subjects for entrance examinations has decreased not only in private universities but also in national universities. This implies, however, that students have to compete in a small number of subjects, and thus this causes difficult questions to be set in entrance examinations. Because students have to prepare for such difficult questions, leeway cannot be generated.

When competition is undertaken in a small number of subjects, standard questions cannot differentiate examinees, a situation which makes selection difficult. However, special training and "talent" are necessary to answer difficult questions. Hence, students who are not so good at mathematics, for example, abandon study of it at an early stage in their senior high-school education and choose to apply to enter college departments which do not require mathematics in the entrance examinations. There is a great difference between being able to understand a textbook level of mathematics and being unable to understand it almost at all due to having abandoned study of mathematics.

In this way the above type of entrance examination inhibits acquisition of basic knowledge in senior high-school education. For this reason it is desirable for colleges to give entrance examinations with more subjects. They should require students to learn a textbook level of knowledge and examine only whether their applicants have such knowledge. However, they do not have to maintain the current examination system.[6]

Of course it is important not to limit the purpose of education only to teaching a given set of knowledge. Development of originality and awareness of deeper issues is important as well. (Since originality can be generated only when basic academic ability exists, giving entrance examinations with more subjects does not contradict developing originality nor is it the same as "uniform education".)

It is also important that higher education admits those who have extraordinary talent in one field so that society can make use of their talent. We need to note, however, that individuals with such talent are really exceptional and thus that examination methods which consider many individuals to have extraordinary talent in one field will result in social loss.[7]

If the quality (productivity) of graduates from colleges with fewer examination subjects is found to be low, firms will avoid hiring such graduates. In fact this seems to be occurring in the real economy. It is necessary to note that this process has already generated invisible losses. Modern society is becoming increasingly complex and requires individuals to have basic knowledge in wider fields. In particular, the necessity for mathematical knowledge is increasing. (For example, it is now difficult to find fields in which knowledge of statistics is useless.) However, a necessary basic knowledge in most cases is never what enables one to answer difficult questions. Therefore, what senior high-school students must learn should not be determined by colleges. It should be determined to a large extent by society considering its culture and economic and social changes, though some discretion may be necessary on the part of each college. Promoting competition in a small number of examination subjects will hurt not only society as a whole but also each college in the long run.

The decline in the enrollment age population can in fact generate an opportunity to improve the above undesirable situation. Because the capacity of higher education becomes relatively large as compared with the enrollment age population, colleges do not need to screen applicants through difficult questions. Japanese higher education is now fully able to admit all applicants equipped with a textbook level of knowledge. Japan is actually in a good position to reform the currently deteriorated senior high-school education system.

The reason the decline in the enrollment age population generates an adverse effect is that colleges are trapped in a state called "the prisoners' dilemma" in game theory.[8] In this dilemma, each college actually admits low ability students because by giving entrance examinations with only a few subjects it tries to have many applicants. The same thing holds with respect to teaching in each college. Teaching that tries only to please students will hurt not only society as a whole but also the college itself and the students themselves.

Partly in relation to the decline in the enrollment age population, Japanese colleges were given in 1991 more freedom in the choice of their purposes, functions, and teaching subjects. Though the choice of specific purposes and functions is the role of each institution, the author would like to point out one socially and economically important aspect which is ignored in today's argument. This is that society needs leaders and an important purpose of higher education should be to foster leaders. (After the publication of this book in Japanese in 1995, training for leadership began to be discussed in public committees for higher education.)

True leaders need to have the ability to make proper judgments beyond self-interest and from the standpoint of society or an organization as a whole. Leaders include not only statesmen and stateswomen but also managers in public institutions and private enterprises. The quality of leaders decisively affects the efficiency or welfare of the society or organization. In other words, competent leaders bring about enormous external economies to members of the whole society or organization.

Though leaders should not be limited to college graduates, the latter are the most likely leaders for this age. Therefore, at least some colleges need to provide education with the explicit purpose of creating leaders. Lack of training for leadership in today's Japanese higher education has given rise to both a lack of competent leaders and serious scandals.

What should be noted in this argument is that training for leadership is not necessarily the same as that for specialists. Thus, if institutions which place emphasis on research and those which place emphasis on education were more sharply differentiated than they are currently, leaders need not appear from the former nor do we need to provide training for leadership only in the former. Because the signaling function is especially strong in departments of social sciences and humanities, these have a greater capability for training for leadership. If training for leadership is excluded from the purpose of higher education, the basis for public subsidies will disappear since higher education has few other external economies.

If training for leadership is a partial purpose of higher education, we find that the current Japanese methods of entrance examinations have several shortcomings. First of all, it is not desirable for leadership training that talented high-school students are obliged to acquire difficult but unimportant knowledge at one of the most important stages in life for personality development. We need to make acquisition of such knowledge unnecessary by building a multi-peak higher education structure in which several top institutions have first-class facilities.

Almost the same thing holds in the medical and dental education discussed in Chap. 4. It is not desirable to use only paper examinations to select candidates to be medical doctors and dentists, for whom a high level of ethics is required. (After the publication of this book in Japanese, some medical schools began to reconsider their examination methods.) It is also very problematical that those who are very likely to become leaders or doctors are mostly from particular regions (such as large cities) or from particular (senior) high schools which are good at training for entrance examinations into leading universities.

We saw in Chap. 6 that there are very large regional differences in enrollment rates. This suggests that there are many students who have potentially high abilities but do not go to college. If education policies inducing colleges to absorb such students are enforced, enrollment can be increased without greatly decreasing the average academic ability of college students. If suitable industrial policies are undertaken and the weight of college graduate intensive industries increases, the Japanese economy may be able to absorb all college graduates without losing efficiency. Therefore, if a variety of suitable policies are employed, Japan can still find, develop, and utilize more competent human resources and we need not be so pessimistic about the future.

Notes

1. Criticisms similar to the second and the third can also be found in Chiswick (1973).
2. See also the study by Liu and Wong (1982) for the case of Singapore.
3. Riley himself has constructed a signaling model to undertake a statistical test, which is based on a classification of occupations according to the necessity for educational signals. However, his method might invite criticism that the classification is artificial and that the differences in lifetime earnings among occupations may reflect risk premiums.
4. There are test results other than those cited here. Miller and Volker (1984) support the signaling hypothesis, while Wise (1975) and Jones and Jackson (1990) support the human capital hypothesis. See also Lazear (1977b).
5. In the 1980s, the United States faced a decline in the enrollment age population just as in Japan today. The population of eighteen-year-olds was 4,310 thousand in 1979 and decreased by about 20% to 3,430 thousand in 1990. Initially, there were predictions that many institutions would close or merge, but the number of institutions actually increased during this period. The following reasons are given for this (Kitamura, 1990): (a) Institutions facing this crisis cultivated potential demand for higher education. (Financial aid systems also became more extensive.) (b) They attracted female and adult students. (c) They switched from culture to practical education. (d) They adjusted study conditions to suit adult and part-time students. (e) They were active in developing revenue sources including business revenues.
6. For instance, a system may be devised in which senior high-school students take nationwide common examinations at the end of each academic year and register the results. (They should be allowed to take an examination as many times as they want.) In such a system, students do not have to cram so much.

7. Today's diversified examination methods also affect the examination costs students bear. Because the diversification makes examination information more important, students have to bear greater costs by relying on the examination industry (preparatory schools). Further, each senior high school has become unable to provide examination information and is obliged to rely on the examination industry (Amano, 1994).

8. The prisoners' dilemma is a state in which each individual falls into a bad situation because each seeks for his/her own self-interest, though all individuals could achieve better situations through mutual cooperation. This name derives from a game in which two suspects are arrested and charged with a crime. The police do not have sufficient evidence to convict the suspects. The police keep the suspects in separate cells and tell them the consequences that will follow from various actions they might choose. If neither confesses, both will be convicted of a minor offense and sentenced to two months jail. If both confess, both will be sentenced to six months jail. Finally, if one confesses and the other does not, the confessor will be jailed for one month and the other for eight months. These conditions can be described by the table below. Let us call the suspects A and B. The numbers in the table are called payoffs, the first components in the parentheses being A's payoffs and the second B's. The longer one stays in jail, the worse one's welfare, so the payoff of each suspect is expressed by the negative numbers corresponding to the length of stay in jail. When B does not confess, A's payoff will be -2 if A does not confess, and it will be -1 if A confesses. Hence, it is more advantageous for A to confess. Similarly, it is again more advantageous for A to confess when B confesses. Because this game is symmetric with respect to A and B, the same holds when the two suspects' roles are interchanged. Therefore, so far as each suspect seeks for his/her own interest, each will confess. Then, the payoff of each will equal -6. This is less than -2 that would be achievable should they cooperate not to confess.

		B: Don't confess	B: Confess
A	Don't confess	(−2,−2)	(−8,−1)
A	Confess	(−1,−8)	(−6,−6)

Appendix A: Wage Determination in a Perfectly Competitive Labor Market

The purpose of this Appendix is to explain the theory or model of wage determination in a perfectly competitive labor market. We choose the example of a labor market for male college graduate workers who seek jobs offered by many firms. It is assumed here that all these workers are homogeneous (identical) as labor inputs, and all firms and workers know this fact. We choose one firm from the group of firms as a representative and call it firm 1.

Let us consider how firm 1 determines employment of college graduates. (We will omit the adjective "male" in most of the following expressions.) The concepts which are important to discuss this problem are marginal productivity (or marginal product) and marginal value productivity (or marginal value product).

The marginal productivity of labor services of college graduate workers is defined as the increase in total product (or output) in a unit of time (such as a month or a year) obtained by employing an additional unit of labor services of college graduates, or by employing an additional (one more) college graduate. (In the following, we will use the concept of an additional college graduate rather than an additional unit of labor services, because the explanation will be easier.)

Marginal value productivity is defined simply as the marginal productivity times the product price. Thus, marginal value productivity means the increase in the value of total product generated in a time unit by employing an additional college worker.

Fig. A.1 depicts firm 1's marginal value productivity curve as D_1D_1. The horizontal axis of this Figure shows the number of college workers, and the vertical axis money units (yen).

The level of marginal value productivity depends on the number of college graduates firm 1 employs. Economics usually assumes that it is decreasing in the number of employed college graduate workers because the marginal productivity decreases as firm 1 employs more college graduates. In other words, the contribution of an additional worker to the total product decreases as more workers are employed. (This representative firm is assumed to be so small relative to the size of the product market that the product price is constant or not affected by the level of output of this firm. Such a firm is called a price taker in economics.)

The meaning of decreasing marginal productivity can be understood from the fact that when this firm employs too many college graduate workers, it cannot offer productive jobs to additional workers. Corresponding to the assumption of decreasing marginal value productivity, D_1D_1 in Fig. A.1 is decreasing in the number of college graduate workers firm 1 employs.

Suppose that the market wage (rate) for the labor services of college graduates in the above time unit equals w as shown in Fig. A.1. A wage rate is usually defined as the

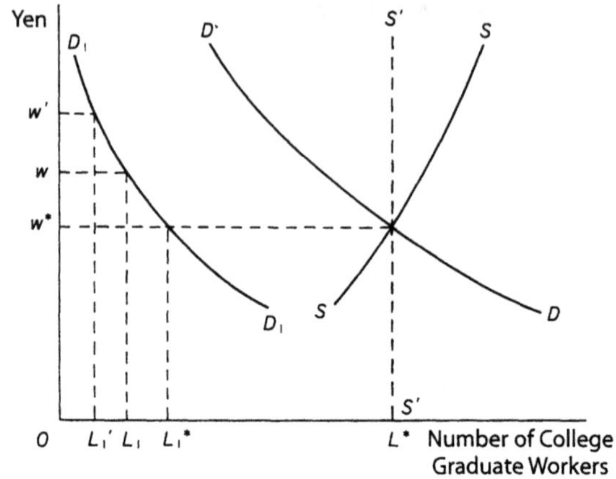

Fig. A.1. Wage Determination in a Perfectly Competitive Labor Market

amount of remuneration per hour. Then, the wage equals the wage rate times the number of work hours. To simplify the explanation, we use here the term "wage" for the amount of remuneration paid to a college graduate worker per unit time.

Facing this wage level, how many college graduates does firm 1 employ? If it employs L_1' which is less than L_1, the marginal value product w' at L_1' will be higher than w or the cost of employing a college graduate worker. In other words, the value generated by employing an additional worker exceeds the cost of employing him. Hence, this firm can increase profits by employing more college graduate workers. (We assume that because there are so many firms in this labor market and because firm 1 is so small relative to the size of the labor market, the market wage does not change even if firm 1 changes its employment policy. In other words, firm 1 is assumed to be a price taker in the labor market as well.)

In contrast, if firm 1 employs more than L_1, the marginal value product will be less than w. Thus, it can increase profits by reducing employment of college graduates. These considerations reveal that when the market wage equals w, firm 1 will employ L_1 college graduate workers. In other words, when the market wage equals w, firm 1's demand for college graduate workers is expressed by L_1.

We note that the level of w is arbitrary in the above argument. In other words, the above argument holds wherever w is located in Fig. A.1. Hence, D_1D_1 represents firm 1's labor demand function for college graduate workers. (A labor demand function is a function which relates different wage levels to a firm's demand for labor.) Put differently, D_1D_1 represents the marginal value productivity when considered as a function of the variable on the horizontal axis or the number of college graduate workers, whereas it represents firm 1's demand for college graduate workers when considered as a function of the variable on the vertical axis or wage.

The above argument shows how to derive firm 1's labor demand function for college graduate workers. In the same fashion, we can derive the labor demand function of each firm in this labor market. The total labor demand for college graduate workers or the labor demand function of this labor market DD can be derived by horizontally adding all these labor demand functions of individual firms. Strictly speaking, this procedure for deriving the total labor demand is valid only when the product price is determined independently of the number of college graduate workers employed in this labor market. We will not enter into detail besides mentioning that this condition is satisfied when the product price is determined in the world market.

Fig. A.1 also depicts the total labor supply curve *SS* of all college graduate workers. It shows how many college graduates want to supply their labor to this market for each wage level. Strictly speaking, the total labor supply is measured by the number of workers times the work hours per worker. Thus, even if the number of college graduate workers in this labor market is fixed, the total labor supply will increase when they intend to work longer. However, in order to simplify the explanation we assume here that the work hours per worker are fixed. *SS* is an increasing function in the wage, since generally more workers supply labor when a wage level is higher. If a fixed number of college graduates supply labor independently of a wage level, the total labor supply curve will become vertical as does $S'S'$ in the Figure.

The equilibrium wage w^* for a college graduate worker is determined at the intersection of the total labor demand curve *DD* and the total labor supply curve *SS* (or $S'S'$). To see this, suppose that the market wage is higher than w^*. Then, the total labor supply exceeds the total labor demand and those who cannot find jobs accept a lower wage. Thus, the market wage decreases. Next suppose that the market wage is lower than w^*. Then, the total labor demand exceeds the total labor supply and the firms which cannot find job applicants offer a higher wage. Thus, the market wage increases.

When and only when the market wage is w^*, the total labor demand is equated with the total labor supply and no force works to adjust the market wage. For this reason w^* is called the equilibrium wage. (A state in which total demand coincides with total supply is called an equilibrium in economics. It should be added, however, that different states are also called equilibria in different situations, so the above is an example of an equilibrium.)

In this equilibrium, L^* workers work in the labor market and each of them earns w^* per unit time. (When the total labor supply curve is $S'S'$, the number of workers who supply labor is initially determined at L^*, so our interest is only in the level of w^*. The market equilibrium wage equals w^* in Fig. A.1 irrespective of whether the total labor supply curve is *SS* or $S'S'$, but this serves only to simplify the Figure.)

In this labor market equilibrium, firm 1 employs $L_1{}^*$ college graduate workers. The marginal value productivity at $L_1{}^*$ is exactly equal to the market wage w^*. The same condition holds for all firms. Because the marginal value productivity can be interpreted as the contribution of a college graduate through production to society or as measuring how useful he is in society, this contribution can be expressed by the market equilibrium wage w^*.

Under what conditions will the equilibrium wage or marginal value productivity be high? First of all, since the marginal value productivity of a college graduate worker equals the marginal productivity times the product price, the equilibrium wage is higher when college graduates have higher productive capability or they can produce more output per unit time. Put differently, higher productive capability implies that D_1D_1 and *DD* are located higher in Fig. A.1 and thus that the equilibrium market wage is higher other things being equal.

Secondly, the further left the supply curve *SS* or $S'S'$ is located in the Figure, the higher the equilibrium wage. This implies that the wage is higher when college graduate workers are scarce. Only in the very special case where *DD* is horizontal is the equilibrium wage constant irrespective of the location of *SS* or *S′S′*.

Thirdly, the higher the product price, the higher the equilibrium wage. By the definition of marginal value productivity, D_1D_1 and *DD* are located higher when the product price is higher. Hence, the equilibrium wage is high by the same logic as in the first case.

Though the above explanation is based on the example of male college graduate workers, the same argument holds for male high-school graduates, female college graduates, and so on. Of course, as different types of workers have different capabilities and different labor supply curves, their wages will be different. But the logic of wage determination is exactly the same.

Against the above model of wage determination one may raise a criticism that reality is not that simple. A variety of complex models are in fact constructed to overcome such criticisms. However, when wages are at issue in economics, we may consider that the argument is based on the above model as far as no special mention is made of the form of labor market.

The above model is frequently used mainly for the following reasons. First, it is quite simple and has high theoretical consistency. Second, it is a well-known model. Third, many more realistic and complex models derive from this model, and thus they reduce to it if details are abstracted away.

Appendix B: Essentials of Regression Analysis

This Appendix will explain the essentials of regression analysis for those readers who do not have knowledge of this statistical method. Explaining details of regression analysis would require much space. In addition, it would not be so easy for beginners to understand the details. Hence, this Appendix aims at an explanation which promotes intuitive understanding. Readers who would like to know more details can consult standard introductory textbooks on econometrics such as Theil (1978) and Johnston (1972).

A regression analysis is often used when one wants to analyze determinants of the level of a variable. Let us first consider a very simple example in which an individual's years of education Y is considered to be determined by his/her parents' income Z_b. The relationship between these two variables may be expressed as

$$Y = a + bZ_b + u, \tag{A.1}$$

where a is a constant, b is the coefficient of Z_b, and u is a stochastic term (random variable).[1]

Eq. A.1 implies first of all that if parents' income increases, the years of education of children tend to increase linearly if b is positive. The variable u is introduced as a stochastic term because Y is not determined solely by Z_b. In other words, it is very common that when Z_b is at a particular value, Y is larger or smaller than $a + bZ_b$. One of the reasons for this is that though there may be other determinants of years of education, they are not introduced into this equation. Another is that human behavior has unpredictable elements unlike some natural phenomena or the motion of machines.

Even when many factors are considered to determine the level of Y, a similar formulation to Eq. A.1 can be used. Suppose for example that Y is determined by parents' income Z_b, father's years of education Z_c, and mother's years of education Z_d. Then, we can assume the following equation:

$$Y = a + bZ_b + cZ_c + dZ_d + u. \tag{A.2}$$

In this kind of equation, Y is called the dependent variable, whereas Z_b, Z_c, and Z_d are called independent variables.

In the following, we will consider the simplest formulation in which there is only one independent variable. (Almost the same statistical properties hold even when there are several independent variables, but knowledge of matrices is necessary to understand it.) In the simplest formulation, let Y be the dependent variable, X the independent variable, α a constant, β the coefficient of X, and u the stochastic term. Then we have the following relation:

$$Y = \alpha + \beta X + u. \tag{A.3}$$

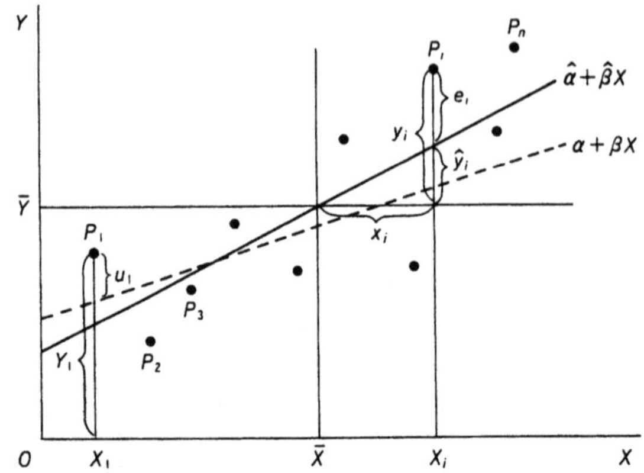

Fig. A.2. Principle of the Method of Least Squares

This is a similar formulation to Eq. A.1. What we especially want to know here is whether X is really a determinant of Y (or Y is really correlated with X) and the values of β and α. In order to know them, we collect data for X and Y to observe some of their realized values.

Fig. A.2 depicts an example of n observation points $P_1, P_2, \ldots, P_n$ for (X, Y). For example, P_1 corresponds to the observation (X_1, Y_1). Eq. A.3 implies that at this observation point the following holds:

$$Y_1 = \alpha + \beta X_1 + u_1, \tag{A.4}$$

where u_1 is the value of the stochastic term which has realized at this observation point. In this Figure, u_1 is positive. (Fig. A.2 shows the "true" equation $\alpha + \beta X$ which is obtained from Eq. A.3 by eliminating the stochastic term.) Similar equations to Eq. A.4 hold for all observation points and we can see, for example, that the realized value of the stochastic term at P_2 is now negative. (It should be noted that the argument about the sign of the realized value of the stochastic term would be possible if we knew the true values of α and β. Because we do not actually know them, it is only a theoretical argument.)

We assume that all u_i are normally distributed with a mean zero and a variance (a measure of dispersion) σ^2. A normal distribution looks very similar to the distribution shown in Fig. A.3. (The function depicted in Fig. A.3 is an example of probability density functions.) Intuitively speaking, with high probabilities u_i takes on values at which the values of the probability density function are large. (That is, u_i takes on values around zero with high probabilities.)

Our knowledge of the relationship between X and Y is limited to information available from the set of n observations. We need to estimate α and β on the basis of information obtainable from this sample. One of the most frequently used estimation methods in regression analyses is called the method of ordinary least squares. In the following we will examine this method and its properties. Let $\hat{\alpha}$ and $\hat{\beta}$ denote the estimates or estimators of α and β calculated by applying this method. (That is, we estimate α and β by applying the method of ordinary least squares to the sample.

What is estimated is usually called an estimate if it is a particular value and an estimator if it is expressed as a function like Eq. A.5 below.)

The method of ordinary least squares fits a line (like $\hat{\alpha} + \hat{\beta}X$ in Fig. A.2) to the n observation points. In doing so, this method minimizes $e_1^2 + e_2^2 + \ldots + e_n^2$, where e_i is the vertical distance between P_i and the fitted line. $\hat{\alpha}$ equals the intercept of this line and $\hat{\beta}$ the slope. A simple calculation can show that they are expressed by the following formulae:

$$\hat{\beta} = \frac{\sum x_i y_i}{\sum x_i^2}, \tag{A.5}$$

$$\hat{\alpha} = \overline{Y} - \hat{\beta}\overline{X}, \tag{A.6}$$

where Σ is an operator for summation from $i = 1$ to $i = n$ (the same holds in the following), $\overline{Y}$ and $\overline{X}$ are the means of the observation values of Y and X respectively, $x_i = X_i - \overline{X}$, and $y_i = Y_i - \overline{Y}$. Eq. A.6 implies that the fitted line passes $(\overline{X}, \overline{Y})$.

In general, $\hat{\alpha}$ and $\hat{\beta}$ obtained in this way are not the same as α and β. While the latter are true (unknown) values, the former are estimated from the sample. If we collected a new sample of n observations, the new estimates of α and β based on the method of ordinary least squares would generally be different from the old ones. This is because u_i would be different for each sample. Using $\hat{\alpha}$, $\hat{\beta}$, and e_i, we have

$$Y_i = \hat{\alpha} + \hat{\beta}X_i + e_i. \tag{A.7}$$

This is called a regression equation.

In most empirical studies, we are interested only in the estimated coefficients of independent variables. Hence, the following discussion will focus mainly on $\hat{\beta}$. In the method of ordinary least squares, σ^2 is estimated by the following formula:

$$\hat{\sigma}^2 = \frac{\sum e_i^2}{n-2}. \tag{A.8}$$

$\hat{\sigma}$ is called the standard error of the regression (or *SER*). From experience we would hope for a percentage of standard error closer to 10% or 15% of the dependent variable mean. Using Eqs. A.5, A.7, etc., we can show that the function

$$t \equiv \frac{\hat{\beta} - \beta}{\sqrt{\hat{\sigma}^2 / \sum x_i^2}} \tag{A.9}$$

follows the t distribution with $n - 2$ degrees of freedom. (In order to gain an intuitive understanding of regression analysis, it is not necessary to understand the concept of degrees of freedom.) Such a function is called a statistic.

Use of this statistic enables us to test a hypothesis that β equals a particular value β_0 ($\beta = \beta_0$). In other words, we can test whether β can be regarded as equal to β_0. The basic idea of this test is the following. If the value of $\hat{\beta}$ estimated from the sample is very different from β_0, i.e., if the value of $\hat{\beta}$ is much larger or smaller than β_0, we reject the initial hypothesis that $\beta = \beta_0$, because β is very unlikely to equal β_0. In contrast, if the value of $\hat{\beta}$ is close to β_0, we do not reject the hypothesis. As mentioned before, even if the hypothesis that $\beta = \beta_0$ is true, it will rarely happen that $\hat{\beta} = \beta_0$, because the value of $\hat{\beta}$ depends on the realized values of n random variables u_i. The fundamental

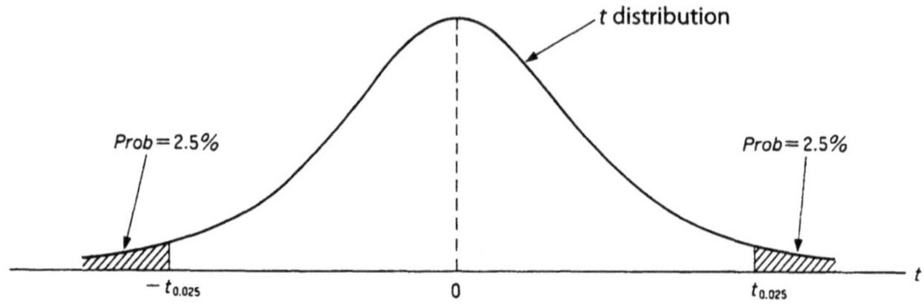

Fig. A.3. t test

idea of this test, however, is that if the hypothesis that $\beta = \beta_0$ is true, the value of $\hat{\beta}$ must be quite close to β_0.

In order to use this idea in actual tests, we need to express whether or not $\hat{\beta}$ is close to β_0 in terms of specific numbers. It is for this purpose that we use Eq. A.9. First, we substitute the hypothesized relation $\beta = \beta_0$ into Eq. A.9 to obtain

$$t = \frac{\hat{\beta} - \beta_0}{\sqrt{\hat{\sigma}^2 / \sum x_i^2}}. \tag{A.10}$$

This statistic follows the t distribution with $n - 2$ degrees of freedom as shown in Fig. A.3.

If the hypothesis that $\beta = \beta_0$ is true, the value of t in Eq. A.10 is likely to be close to zero. If it is far from zero, the probability of this hypothesis being true is very small, though it can be true. Fig. A.3 shows two critical values of t, $t_{0.025}$ and $t_{-0.025}$, by which we judge whether to reject the hypothesis that $\beta = \beta_0$. Here, the probability that t becomes larger than $t_{0.025}$ equals 2.5%, while the probability that it becomes smaller than $t_{-0.025}$ also equals 2.5%. (The shaded areas in Fig. A.3 show the probabilities with which t takes on the corresponding values. The specific values of $t_{0.025}$ and $t_{-0.025}$ depend on the degrees of freedom and can be found in a table in textbooks on econometrics.)

In our present test, we reject the hypothesis that $\beta = \beta_0$ if the value of t computed by Eq. A.10 is larger than $t_{0.025}$ or smaller than $t_{-0.025}$. If the value of t is between these two critical values, we do not reject the hypothesis. In this case, we say that we test the hypothesis at the 5% level of significance. This implies that our judgment about rejection will err with a probability of 5%. Though we can freely choose the level of significance, it is customary to use either 1%, 5%, or 10%.

Many empirical studies test the very special hypothesis that $\beta = 0$. This is the hypothesis that X does not explain Y or that X is not a determinant of Y. If this hypothesis is rejected, X can be regarded as a determinant of Y. This test is nothing but a special case of the above test. Substitution of $\beta_0 = 0$ into Eq. A.10 generates

$$t = \frac{\hat{\beta}}{\sqrt{\hat{\sigma}^2 / \sum x_i^2}}. \tag{A.11}$$

This is what is usually called the t-value. Roughly speaking, when the sample size is larger than 20 to 40, we can reject the hypothesis that $\beta = 0$ at the 10% level of significance if the absolute value of the t-value is larger than 1.7 and at the 5% level of significance if it is larger than 2.0. (To be rigorous, we need to consult a table for the t distribution shown in textbooks, but small differences in the t value do not have important economic implications.) When the hypothesis that $\beta = 0$ is rejected, $\hat{\beta}$ is said to be significant. When the absolute value of the t-value is large, significance is said to be high.

A measure called the coefficient of determination shows the degree to which the fitted line (regression equation) explains the relationship between X and Y. If the variation of Y is expressed as the difference from its mean,

$$y_i = \hat{y}_i + e_i \tag{A.12}$$

as shown in Fig. A.2, where $\hat{y}_i = \hat{\alpha} + \beta X_i - \overline{Y}$. The first term on the right-hand side in Eq. A.12 equals that variation of Y which is explained by the fitted line, while the second equals the residual variation of Y.

The coefficient of determination R^2 is defined as

$$R^2 = \frac{\sum \hat{y}_i^2}{\sum y_i^2}. \tag{A.13}$$

R^2 is the proportion of the total variation in Y explained by the regression of Y on X. Since the part of the variation of Y explained by the fitted (regression) line is no larger than the total variation, $0 \leqq R^2 \leqq 1$. If $R^2 = 1$, the variation of Y is completely explained by the regression line, but such a result would almost never arise in social sciences. In contrast, the regression line has no explanatory power in the case of $R^2 = 0$. The closer R^2 is to 1, the larger the explanatory power of the regression line and thus the more desirable. However, R^2 has an undesirable property such that it increases if more independent variables are introduced.

A measure which has overcome this shortcoming is the coefficient of determination adjusted for degrees of freedom. It is defined as

$$\overline{R}^2 = 1 - \left(1 - R^2\right)\left(\frac{n-1}{n-k-1}\right), \tag{A.14}$$

where k stands for the number of independent variables. It always holds that $R^2 \geqq \bar{R}^2$, and $\bar{R}^2$ can become negative.

When there are several independent variables as in Eq. A.2, we can test a hypothesis that all coefficients are zero. In such a test the following statistic will be used:

$$F = \frac{\sum \hat{y}_i^2 / k}{\sum e_i^2 / (n-k-1)}. \tag{A.15}$$

This statistic follows the F distribution with k and $n - k - 1$ degrees of freedom. Even when none of the estimated coefficients are significant according to the t tests, the hypothesis that all coefficients are simultaneously zero may be rejected on the basis of this F test.

When time series data are used, adjacent stochastic terms (u_i and u_{i+1}) may positively correlate. This is called serial correlation. This arises because variables which are not explicitly introduced into Eq. A.3 but are represented by the stochastic term tend to gradually change over time. It is known that the tests of regression coefficients become inaccurate when there is serial correlation. Thus it becomes important to test whether there is serial correlation.

A frequently used method for this test is based on the following Durbin-Watson statistic:

$$D.W. = \frac{\sum (e_i - e_{i-1})^2}{\sum e_i^2}, \tag{A.16}$$

where the summation operator in the numerator is for $i = 2$ through $i = n$. The values of $D.W.$ which allow us to judge that there is no serial correlation depend on the sample size and the number of independent variables. For details, one needs to consult a table for this test in econometrics textbooks. Roughly speaking, however, we may judge that there is no serial correlation when the value of $D.W.$ is between 1.5 and 2.5. Some people do not place much value on $D.W.$ tests.

We would like to add a note on how to measure and/or express variables. Suppose here that Y in Eq. A.3 stands for the work hours of a married woman and X for her husband's income. There are several different ways to measure and express these two variables. Y can be the work hours either per week, per month, or per year. Further, we may use a hundred hours as the time unit. Similarly, husband's income can be measured either per week, per month, or per year, and the unit of income may be either a thousand yen, ten thousand yen, or something else.

An important property that holds among these alternative methods of measurement and/or expression is that there are proportional relationships among the values of the variables derived from them. It can be easily proved that statistical tests and coefficients of determination are invariant whichever are used. If these statistical concepts were not invariant, they would be useless. Therefore, choices among those measurements and expressions are completely free and can be made according to the researcher's convenience. It should be noted, however, that the values of $\hat{\alpha}$ and $\hat{\beta}$ depend on such a choice.

In relation to the above argument, it can be pointed out that when two variables X_b and X_c have slightly different but almost the same properties, regression results would not differ much whichever was used. Therefore, when several alternative variables (data) exist for a theoretical model, the one that makes the regression analysis (data collection) simplest might be chosen.

Finally, let us go back to Eq. A.2 and add a remark about cases in which there are several independent variables. As stated earlier, what we have seen so far holds even in such cases. But caution is needed when interpreting regression coefficients. Eq. A.2 has parents' income Z_b, father's years of education Z_c, and mother's years of education Z_d as its independent variables. Here, b stands for the increase in the years of children's education due to a one-unit increase in parents' income holding parents' years of education constant.

If parents' income Z_b is used as the only independent variable as in Eq. A.1, an increase in this variable may imply increases in parents' years of education, because rich parents are likely to be highly educated. Put differently, when Z_b is used as the only independent variable, the concept of parents' income includes that of parents' years of education.

In contrast, if parents' years of education are introduced as separate independent variables as in Eq. A.2, *b* shows the effect of parents' income after parents' years of education are controlled for. Thus, *b* does not contain the effects of parents' years of education. These effects are expressed separately by *c* and *d*.

Note

1. A variable *u* is called a random variable if it takes on alternative values with specified probabilities (given by a probability density function such as shown in Fig. A.3). There are countless examples of random variables in daily life. An example is tomorrow's rainfall. We can say for example that it will be less than 10 mm with a probability 60%, between 10 mm and 20 mm with a probability 30%, and more than 20 mm with probability 10%. In this way, a random variable can take on large values or small values. The average of these values is called the mean or expected value. For example, the mean of the random variable shown in Fig. A.3 is zero. The mean of a random variable can be calculated by integrating the product of the random variable and the probability density function in the definition domain.

Appendix C: The Japanese Education System

The main purpose of this Appendix is to provide some information about the Japanese education system that might be useful in understanding the text. But before doing so, first we would like to provide details about the Japanese yen exchange rate, and about prefectures as Japanese geopolitical units because these are used in the text without much explanation.

Knowledge of the yen exchange rate will help readers understand for example just how large the costs of education expressed in terms of yen in the text actually are. Table A.1 is provided to show time-series data for the value of yen per US dollar.

Next some information about Japanese geography is provided. Japan is divided into forty-seven geopolitical units called prefectures in English as shown in Fig. A.4. Each prefecture has at least a few universities and junior colleges, but concentration of institutions in large cities is a prominent characteristic of Japanese higher education. In particular, most leading universities are located in large cities such as Tokyo, Osaka, and Kyoto. Thus many college students live away from their parents. Since the capacity of dormitories is not large, most of these students live in private apartments.

Japanese children enter primary school at the age of six after two or three years of kindergarten education. Primary education continues for six years. After graduation from primary school, they attend junior high school for three years. Primary and junior high-school education is compulsory in Japan. (Though kindergarten education is not compulsory, most children attend.)

After graduation from junior high school, almost all students advance to senior high school. Most take entrance examinations for the senior high schools they want to enter. (Some high schools offer continuous junior and senior high-school education. In such cases no formal entrance examinations are given to "internal" students.) Senior high-school education continues for three years. Japanese secondary educa-

Table A.1. Exchange rate between Yen and US$ (Yen/US$).

1955	1960	1965	1970	1975	1976	1977	1978	1979	1980
360	360	360	358	299	292	257	201	230	217
1981	1982	1983	1984	1985	1986	1987	1988	1989	1990
228	250	236	244	221	160	138	128	142	141
1991	1992	1993	1994	1995					
133	124	107	99	96					

1 Hokkaido	13 Tokyo	25 Shiga	37 Tokushima
2 Aomori	14 Kanagawa	26 Nara	38 Ehime
3 Akita	15 Niigata	27 Wakayama	39 Kochi
4 Iwate	16 Nagano	28 Kyoto	40 Fukuoka
5 Yamagata	17 Yamanashi	29 Osaka	41 Saga
6 Miyagi	18 Toyama	30 Hyogo	42 Nagasaki
7 Fukushima	19 Ishikawa	31 Tottori	43 Oita
8 Gunma	20 Fukui	32 Okayama	44 Kumamoto
9 Tochigi	21 Shizuoka	33 Shimane	45 Miyazaki
10 Ibaragi	22 Aichi	34 Hiroshima	46 Kagoshima
11 Saitama	23 Gifu	35 Yamaguchi	47 Okinawa
12 Chiba	24 Mie	36 Kagawa	

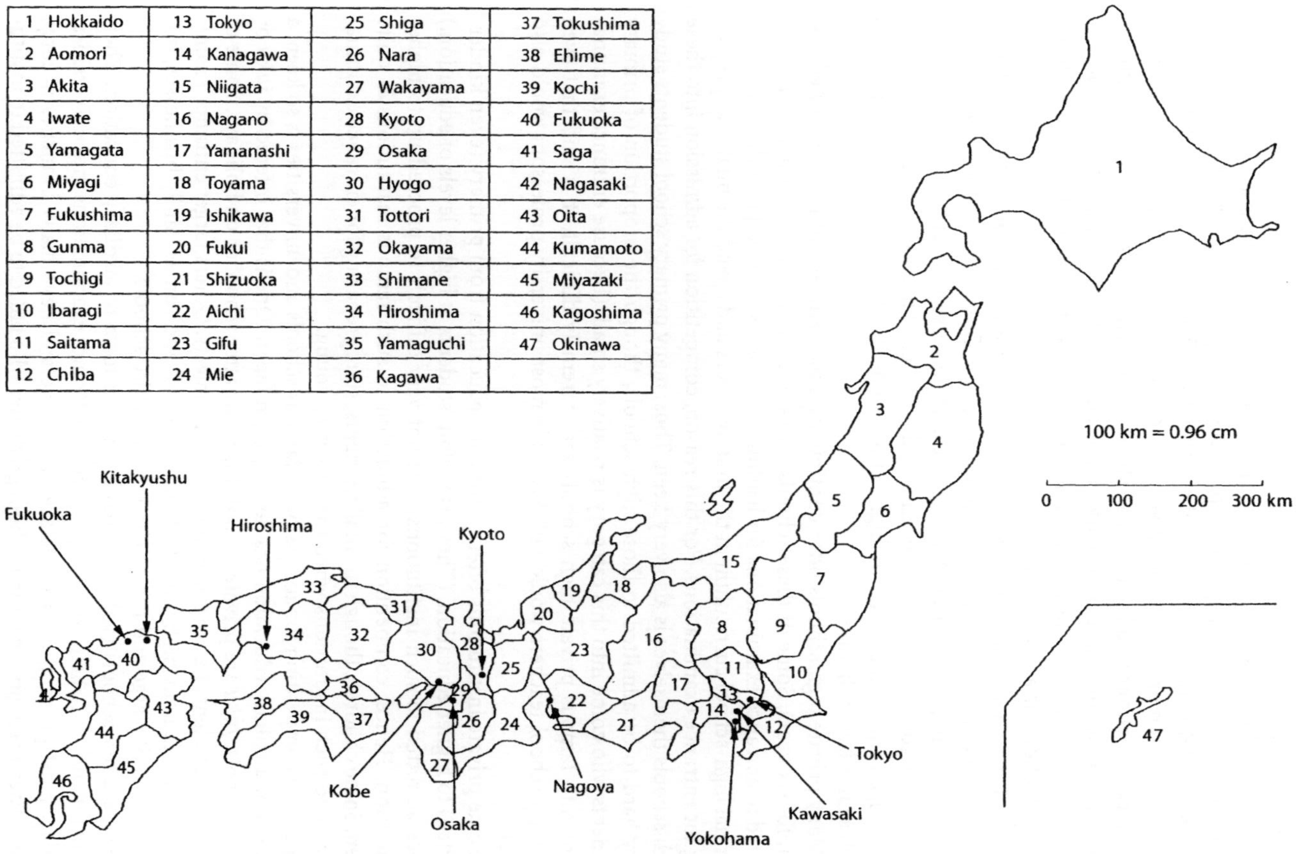

Fig. A.4. Map of Japan: Prefectures and Large Cities

tion consists of junior and senior high-school education. Thus, today almost all Japanese students receive a complete secondary education.

There are several main alternatives to choose from after graduation from senior high school. The first is to advance to university to study for four years. The second is to be enrolled in junior college which provides a two-year education. The third is to go to professional school to study for about two years. There are other types of schools which admit senior high-school graduates. Most of the above institutions give entrance examinations to all applicants. The last main alternative is to start working.

After graduation from university, some advance to graduate school. Graduate schools provide a two-year education for a master's degree and an additional three-year education for a doctorate.

One of the most salient features of Japanese education has been in its very keen competition at the time of entrance into university. One needs to study very hard to pass the entrance examination for a "first-class" university. Because some senior high schools are good at offering education suited to entrance examinations for "first-class" institutions, many junior high-school students work hard to be admitted to such senior high schools.

Many private high schools offer continuous junior and senior high-school education for six years. Some of these schools are especially good at providing instruction suited to entrance examinations for leading universities. It is said that they finish the normal high-school curriculum in the first five years and spend the final year preparing for entrance examinations. For this reason, competition for admission into these high schools themselves is also very keen. Thus, many primary school students study very hard to be admitted to those high schools, though the proportion of primary students who come into this category is relatively small. (Because entrance examinations into famous private high schools are extremely difficult, it is said that even primary school teachers would fail. Probably most university professors would also fail.)

Some private institutions offer continuous education from primary (even kindergarten) to higher education. (They also admit students at higher levels of education.) Once admitted to such institutions, it is not very difficult to proceed up to higher education. Hence, competition for admission to such famous institutions is quite keen. Some children, though in small numbers, start preparing for entrance examinations into such institutions when they are very young.

Because competition for admission to famous schools and universities is so keen, a variety of auxiliary education has developed in Japan. One is that offered by *juku* or cram schools. *Juku* are private schools for study after school or on holidays. Some of them help students better understand school subjects. Others target entrance examinations into famous high schools. Some are small and run as family businesses, but many are quite large and run as chain or franchise schools.

Preparatory schools (*yobiko*) provide another form of auxiliary education. Their main function is to help students prepare for entrance examinations into universities. Today, most preparatory schools are quite large and have many branches in large cities. They teach not only high-school graduates who failed to be admitted to institutions (*ronin*) but also senior high-school students. They regularly undertake several "open" practice examinations which any student can take. They also provide a variety of information about universities' entrance examinations, curriculums, and so on.

References

Aiger, D. J., and Cain, G. G. "Statistical Theories of Discrimination in Labor Markets." *Industrial and Labor Relations Review*, vol.30, 1977, 175–87.

Akerlof, George. "The Economics of Caste and of the Rat Race and Other Woeful Tales." *Quarterly Journal of Economics*, vol.90, 1976, 599–617.

Albrecht, James W. "A Procedure for Testing the Signaling Hypothesis." *Journal of Public Economics*, vol.15, 1981, 123–32.

Alwin, Duane F., and Thornton, Arland. "Family Origins and the Schooling Process: Early versus Late Influence of Parental Characteristics." *American Sociological Review*, vol.49, 1984, 784–802.

Amano, Ikuo. *University: The Age of Change* (Daigaku — Henkaku no Jidai). University of Tokyo Press: Tokyo, 1994.

Amano, Ikuo. *Future of Educational Reforms: In Search of Freedom and Individuality* (Kyoiku Kaikaku no Yukue — Jiyuka to Koseika o Motomete). University of Tokyo Press: Tokyo, 1995.

Amano, Ikuo; Kawakami, Fujiko; Yoshimoto, Keiichi; Yoshida, Aya; and Hashimoto, Kenji. "The Influence of Educational and Socio-economic Conditions on the Career Differentiation of High School Graduates — From a Prefectural Viewpoint." (Shinro Bunkâ no Kitei Yoin to Sono Hendo.) *Tokyo Daigaku Kyoiku Gakubu Kiyo*, vol.23, 1983, 1–43.

Arai, Kazuhiro. "A Study on the Optimal Numbers of Medical Doctors and Dentists." (Ishi Shikaishi no Saitekisu ni kansuru Kosatsu.) *Quarterly Journal of Social Security Research* (Kikan Shakai Hosho Kenkyu), vol.22, 1986, 222–31.

Arai, Kazuhiro. "A Cross-sectional Analysis of the Determinants of Enrollment in Higher Education in Japan." *Hitotsubashi Journal of Economics*, vol.30, 1989, 101–20.

Arai, Kazuhiro. "Japanese Education and Economic Development." In C.H. Lee and I. Yamazawa eds. *The Economic Development of Japan and Korea*. Praeger: New York, 1990a.

Arai, Kazuhiro. "Determinants of Enrollment in Japanese Higher Education." (Daigaku Shingakuritsu no Kettei Yoin.) *Economic Review* (Keizai Kenkyu), vol.41, 1990b, 241–49.

Arai, Kazuhiro. "Wage Profiles: Shape and Variations." *Manchester School of Economic and Social Studies*, vol.65, 1997a, 244–58.

Arai, Kazuhiro. "Cooperation, Job Security, and Wages in a Dual Labor Market Equilibrium." *Journal of Socio-Economics*, vol.26, 1997b, 39–57.

Arrow, Kenneth J. "Uncertainty and the Welfare Economics of Medical Care." *American Economic Review*, vol.53, 1963, 941–73.

Arrow, Kenneth J. "Higher Education as a Filter." *Journal of Public Economics*, vol.2, 1973a, 193–216.

Arrow, Kenneth J. "The Theory of Discrimination." In O. Ashenfelter and A.Rees eds. *Discrimination in Labor Markets*. Princeton University Press: New Jersey, 1973b.

Arrow, Kenneth J., and Levhari, David. "Uniqueness of the Internal Rate of Return with Variable Life of Investment." *Economic Journal*, vol.79, 1969, 560–66.

Ashenfelter, Orley, and Ham, John. "Education, Unemployment, and Earnings." *Journal of Political Economy*, vol.87, 1979, S99–S116.

Ashenfelter, Orley, and Krueger, Alan. "Estimates of the Economic Return to Schooling from a New Sample of Twins." *American Economic Review*, vol.84, 1994, 1157–73.

Ashenfelter, O., and Mooney, J. D. "Graduate Education, Ability, and Earnings." *Review of Economics and Statistics*, vol.50, 1968, 78–86.

Bailey, Duncan, and Schotta, Charles. "Private and Social Rates of Return to Education of Academicians." *American Economic Review*, vol.62, 1972, 19–31.

Bank of Japan. *Financial Institutions in Japan* (Wagakuni no Kinyu Seido). 1986.

Barnett, H. G. "The Nature of the Potlatch." *American Anthropologist*, vol.40, 1938, 349–58.

Bartel, Ann P., and Lichtenberg, Frank R. "The Comparative Advantage of Educated Workers in Implementing New Technology." *Review of Economics and Statistics*, vol.69, 1987, 1–11.

Becker, Gary S. *The Economics of Discrimination*. University of Chicago Press: Chicago, 1957.

Becker, Gary S. *Human Capital: A Theoretical and Empirical Analysis, with Special Reference to Education*, First Edition. Columbia University Press: New York, 1964.

Becker, Gary S. "Human Capital, Effort, and the Sexual Division of Labor." *Journal of Labor Economics*, vol.3, 1985, S33–S58.

Becker, Gary S. *A Treatise on the Family*. Harvard University Press: Cambridge, Massachusetts, 1991.

Becker, Gary S. *Human Capital: A Theoretical and Empirical Analysis, with Special Reference to Education*, Third Edition. University of Chicago Press: New York, 1993.

Becker, Gary S., and Chiswick, Barry. "Education and the Distribution of Earnings." *American Economic Review Papers and Proceedings*, vol.56, 1966, 358–69.

Becker, Gary S., and Lewis, H. Gregg. "On the Interaction between the Quantity and Quality of Children." *Journal of Political Economy*, vol.81, 1973, S279–S288.

Becker, Gary S., and Tomes, Nigel. "Child Endowments and the Quality and Quantity of Children." *Journal of Political Economy*, vol.84, 1976, S143–S162.

Behrman, Jere R. "Intrahousehold Allocation of Nutrients in Rural India: Are Boys Favored? Do Parents Exhibit Inequality Aversion?" *Oxford Economic Papers*, vol.40, 1988, 32–54.

Behrman, Jere R., and Birdsall, Nancy. "Comment on Returns to Education: A Further International Update and Implications." *Journal of Human Resources*, vol.22, 1987, 603–6.

Behrman, Jere R., and Deolalikar, Anil B. "The Intrahousehold Demand for Nutrients in Rural South India: Individual Estimates, Fixed Effects, and Permanent Income." *Journal of Human Resources*, vol.25, 1990, 665–96.

Behrman, Jere R.; Hrubec, Zdenek; Taubman, Paul; and Wales, Terence. *Socioeconomic Success: A Study of the Effects of Genetic Endowments, Family Environment and Schooling*. North-Holland: Amsterdam, 1980.

Behrman, Jere R.; Pollak, Robert A.; and Taubman, Paul. "Parental Preferences and Provision for Progeny." *Journal of Political Economy*, vol.90, 1982, 52–73.

Behrman, Jere R.; Pollak, Robert A.; and Taubman, Paul. "Do Parents Favor Boys?" *International Economic Review*, vol.27, 1986, 33–54.

Behrman, Jere R.; Pollak, Robert A.; and Taubman, Paul. "Family Resources, Family Size, and Access to Financing for College Education." *Journal of Political Economy*, vol.97, 1989, 398–419.

Behrman, J., and Taubman, P. "Intergenerational Earnings Mobility in the United States: Some Estimates and a Test of Becker's Intergenerational Endowments Model." *Review of Economics and Statistics*, vol.67, 1985, 144–51.

Behrman, J., and Taubman, P. "Birth Order, Schooling, and Earnings." *Journal of Labor Economics*, 1986, vol.4, no.3, S121–S145.

Behrman, J., and Wolfe, B. "The Socioeconomic Impact of Schooling in a Developing Country." *Review of Economics and Statistics*, vol.66, 1984, 296–303.

Beller, Andrea H. "Occupational Segregation by Sex: Determinants and Changes." *Journal of Human Resources*, vol.17, 1982, 371–92.

Ben-Porath, Yoram. "The Production of Human Capital and the Life Cycle of Earnings." *Journal of Political Economy*, vol.75, 1967, 352–65.

Benedict, Ruth. *Patterns of Culture*. Houghton Mifflin: Boston, 1970.

Benham, Lee. "Benefits of Women's Education within Marriage." *Journal of Political Economy*, vol.82, 1974, S57–S71.

Bishop, John. "The Effect of Public Policies on the Demand for Higher Education." *Journal of Human Resources*, vol.12, 1977, 285–307.

Blackburn, McKinley L.; Bloom, David E.; and Freeman, Richard B. "The Declining Economic Position of Less-Skilled American Men." In Gary Burtless ed. *A Future of Lousy Jobs? The Changing Structure of U.S. Wages*. Brookings Institution: Washington, D.C., 1990.

Blake, Judith. *Family Size and Achievement*. University of California Press: Berkeley, CA, 1989.

Blaug, Mark. "The Rate of Return on Investment in Education in Great Britain." *Manchester School*, vol.33, 1965, 205–51.

Blaug, Mark. *Economics of Education: A Selected Annotated Bibliography*. Pergamoin Press: Oxford, 1966.

Blaug, Mark. (ed.) *Economics of Education*. Penguin Books: Harmondsworth, 1968.

Blaug, Mark. *An Introduction to the Economics of Education*. Allen Lane The Penguin Press: London, 1970.

Blaug, Mark. "The Empirical Status of Human Capital Theory: A Slightly Jaundiced Survey," *Journal of Economic Literature*, vol.14, 1976, 827–55.

Blinder, Alan S. "On Dogmatism in Human Capital Theory." *Journal of Human Resources*, vol.11, 1976, 8–22.

Bloch, Farrell E., and Smith, Sharon P. "Human Capital and Labor Market Employment." *Journal of Human Resources*, vol.12, 1977, 550–60.

Boissiere, M.; Knight, J. B.; and Sabot, R. H. "Earnings, Schooling, Ability, and Cognitive Skills." *American Economic Review*, vol.75, 1985, 1016–30.

Borjas, George J. "Ethnicity, Neighborhoods, and Human-Capital Externalities." *American Economic Review*, vol.85, 1995, 365–90.

Borjas, George J., and Goldberg, Matthew S. "Biased Screening and Discrimination in the Labor Market." *American Economic Review*, vol.68, 1978, 918–22.

Boullier, Bryan L., and Rosenzweig, Mark R. "Schooling, Search, and Spouse Selection: Testing Economic Theories of Marriage and Household Behavior." *Journal of Political Economy*, vol.92, 1984, 712–32.

Bowles, Samuel, and Gintis, Herbert. "IQ in the US Class Structure." *Social Policy*, 1972, 65–96.

Brinton, Mary C. "The Social-Institutional Bases of Gender Stratification: Japan as an Illustrative Case." *American Journal of Sociology*, vol.94, 1988, 300–34.

Brinton, Mary C. *Women and the Economic Miracle*. University of California Press: Berkeley, 1993.

Brown, Randall S.; Moon, Marilyn; and Zoloth, Barbara. "Incorporating Occupational Attainment in Studies of Male-Female Earnings Differentials." *Journal of Human Resources*, vol.15, 1980, 3–28.

Burdett, Kenneth. "The Testing and Sorting Functions of Higher Education." *Journal of Public Economics*, vol.10, 1978, 117–22.

Burstein, Philip L., and Cromwell, Jerry. "Relative Income and Rates of Return for U.S. Physicians." *Journal of Health Economics*, vol.4, 1985, 63–78.

Butcher, Kristin F., and Case, Anne. "The Effect of Sibling Sex Composition on Women's Education and Earnings." *Quarterly Journal of Economics*, vol.109, 1994, 531–63.

Campbell, R. and Siegel, B. N. "The Demand for Higher Education in the United States." *American Economic Review*, vol.56, 1967, 482–94.

Chiswick, Barry R. "Schooling, Screening, and Income." In Lewis C. Solmon and Paul J. Taubman eds. *Does College Matter*? New York: Academic Press, 1973.

Cho, In-Koo, and Kreps, David. "Signaling Games and Stable Equilibrium." *Quarterly Journal of Economics*, vol.102, 1987, 179–221.

Christensen, Sandra; Melder, John; and Weisbrod, Burton A. "Factors Affecting College Attendance." *Journal of Human Resources*, vol.10, 1975, 174–88.

Cohn, Elchanan. *The Economics of Education.* D.C. Heath: Lexington, Massachusetts, 1972.

Cohn, Elchanan, and Kiker, B. F. "Socioeconomic Background, Schooling, Experience and Monetary Rewards in the United States." *Economica*, vol.53, 1986, 497–503.

Corazzini, Arthur J.; Dugan, Dennis J.; Grabowski, Henry G. "Determinants and Distributional Aspects of Enrollment in U.S. Higher Education." *Journal of Human Resources*, vol.7, 1972, 39–59.

Corcoran, Mary, and Duncan, Greg J. "Work History, Labor Force Attachment, and Earnings Difference between the Races and Sexes." *Journal of Human Resources*, vol.14, 1979, 3–20.

Cox, Donald. "Panel Estimates of the Effects of Career Interruptions on the Earnings of Women." *Economic Inquiry*, vol.22, 1984, 386–404.

Datcher-Loury, Linda. "Family Background and School Achievement Among Low Income Blacks." *Journal of Human Resources*, vol.24, 1989, 528–44.

de Wolff, P., and van Slijpe, A. R. D. "The Relation between Income and Intelligence, Education and Social Background." *European Economic Review*, vol.4, 1973, 235–64.

Deaton, Angus. "Looking for Boy-Girl Discrimination in Household Expenditure Data." *World Bank Economic Review*, vol.3, 1989, 1–15.

Doeringer, Peter B., and Piore, Michael. J. *Internal Labor Markets and Manpower Analysis.* M. E. Sharpe Inc.: New York, 1985.

Dore, Ronald. *Education in Tokugawa Japan.* University of California Press: Berkeley, 1965.

Dranove, David. "Demand Inducement and the Physician/Patient Relationship." *Economic Inquiry*, vol.26, 1988, 281–98.

Duncan, Greg J. "Educational Attainment." In *Five Thousand American Families — Patterns of Economic Progress.* Institute for Social Research: Ann Arbor, Mi, 1974.

Duncan, Greg J. "Earnings Functions and Nonpecuniary Benefits." *Journal of Human Resources*, vol.11, 1976, 462–83.

Eberts, Randall W., and Stone, Joe A. "Male-Female Differences in Promotions: EEO in Public Education." *Journal of Human Resources*, vol.20, 1985, 504–21.

Economic Planning Agency. *Annual Report on Prefectural Accounts.* (Kenmin Keizai Keisan Nempo.)

Economic Planning Agency. *Economic Statistics Abstract.* (Keizai Yoran.)

England, Paula. "The Failure of Human Capital Theory to Explain Occupational Sex Segregation." *Journal of Human Resources*, vol.17, 1982, 358–70.

Evans, Robert G. "Supplier-Induced Demand: Some Empirical Evidence and Implications." In Perlman, Mark ed. *The Economics of Health and Medical Care.* Macmillan: London, 1974.

Farber, Stephen. "The Earnings and Promotion of Women Faculty: Comment." *American Economic Review*, vol.67, 1977, 199–206.

Ferber, Marianne A., and Birnbaum, Bonnie G. "Labor Force Participation Patterns and Earnings of Women Clerical Workers." *Journal of Human Resources*, vol.19, 1981, 416–26.

Ferguson, Brian S., and Crawford, Allan. "Supplier-Induced Demand: A Disequilibrium Test." *Applied Economics*, vol.21, 1989, 597–609.

Figa-Talamanca, Lorenzo. "Private and Social Rates of Return to Education of Academicians: Note." *American Economic Review*, vol.64, 1974, 217–19.

Frank, Robert H. "Why Women Earn Less: The Theory and Estimation of Differential Overqualification." *American Economic Review*, vol.68, 1978, 360–73.

Freeman, Richard B. "Overinvestment in College Training?" *Journal of Human Resources*, vol.10, 1975, 287–311.

Freeman, Richard B. *The Overeducated American*. New York: Academic Press, 1976.

Freeman, Richard B. "The Decline in the Economic Rewards to College Education." *Review of Economics and Statistics*, vol.59, 1977, 18–29.

Freeman, Richard B. "The Facts about the Declining Economic Value of College." *Journal of Human Resources*, vol.15, 1980, 124–42.

Freeman, Richard B. "Demand for Education." In Orley Ashenfelter and Richard Layard eds. *Handbook of Labor Economics*. North Holland: Amsterdam, 1986.

Fuchs, Victor R. "The Supply of Surgeons and the Demand for Operations." *Journal of Human Resources*, vol.13, 1978, 35–56.

Fujino, Shozaburo. *Higher Education and the Market Mechanism* (Daigaku Kyoiku to Shijo Kiko). Iwanami Shoten: Tokyo, 1986.

Fuller, Winship C.; Manski, Charles F.; and Wise, David A. "New Evidence on the Economic Determinants of Postsecondary Schooling Choices." *Journal of Human Resources*, vol.17, 1982, 477–95.

Galper, H., and Dunn, R. M. Jr. "A Short-run Demand Function for Higher Education in the United States." *Journal of Political Economy*, vol.77, 1969, 765–77.

Goldin, Claudia, and Polachek, Solomon. "Residual Differences by Sex: Perspectives on the Gender Gap in Earnings." *American Economic Review Papers and Proceedings*, vol.77, 1987, 143–51.

Greenhalgh, Susan. "Sexual Stratification in East Asia: The Other Side of 'Growth with Equity' in East Asia." *Population and Development Review*, vol.11, 1985, 265–314.

Griliches, Zvi. "Notes on the Role of Education in Production Functions and Growth Accounting." In W. Lee Hansen ed. *Education, Income, and Human Capital*. National Bureau of Economic Research: New York, 1970.

Griliches, Zvi. "Estimating the Returns to Schooling: Some Econometric Problems." *Econometrica*, vol.45, 1977, 1–22.

Griliches, Zvi, and Mason, William M. "Education, Income, and Ability." *Journal of Political Economy*, vol.80, 1972, S74–S103.

Groshen, Erica L. "The Structure of the Female/Male Wage Differential: Is It Who You Are, What You Do, or Where You Work?" *Journal of Human Resources*, vol.26, 1991, 457–72.

Gullason, Edward G. "The Consumption Value of Schooling: An Empirical Estimate of One Aspect." *Journal of Human Resources*, vol.24, 1989, 287–98.

Handa, M. L., and Skolnik, M. L. "Empirical Analysis of the Demand for Education in Canada." In Sylvia Ostry ed. *Canadian Higher Education in the Seventies*. Information Canada: Ottawa, 1972.

Handa, M. L., and Skolnik, M. L. "Unemployment, Expected Returns, and the Demand for University Education in Ontario: Some Empirical Results." *Higher Education*, vol.4, 1975, 27–43.

Hansen, W. L. "Total and Private Rates of Return to Investment in Schooling." *Journal of Political Economy*, vol.81, 1963, 128–41.

Hansen, W. L.; Weisbrod, B. A.; and Scanlon, W. J. "Schooling and Earnings of Low Achievers." *American Economic Review*, vol.60, 1970, 409–18.

Hanushek, Eric A. "The Trade-off between Child Quantity and Quality." *Journal of Political Economy*, vol.100, 1992, 84–117.

Hause, John C. "Earnings Profiles: Ability and Schooling." *Journal of Political Economy*, vol.80, 1972, S108–S138.

Hause, John C. "Ability and Schooling as Determinants of Lifetime Earnings, or If You're So Smart, Why Aren't You Rich?" In F. T. Juster ed. *Education, Income and Human Behavior*. McGraw-Hill: New York, 1975,

Hauser, Robert M. "Trends in College Entry among Whites, Blacks, and Hispanics." In Charles T. Clotfelter and Michael Rothschild eds. *Studies of Supply and Demand in Higher Education*. The University of Chicago Press: Chicago, 1993.

Haveman, Robert, and Wolfe, Barbara. "Education and Economic Well-Being: The Role of Nonmarket Effects." *Journal of Human Resources*, vol.19, 1984, 377–407.

Heckman, James J., and Hotz, V. Joseph. "An Investigation of the Labor Market Earnings of Panamanian Males: Evaluating the Sources of Inequality." *Journal of Human Resources*, vol.21, 1986, 507–42.

Heckman, J. J., and Polachek, S. "Empirical Evidence on the Function Form of the Earnings-Schooling Relationship." *Journal of the American Statistical Association*, vol.69, 1974, 350–54.

Higuchi, Yoshio. "Intergenerational Income Transfer through Education." (Kyoiku o tsujita Sedaikan Shotoku Iten.) *JCER Economic Journal* (Nihon Keizai Kenkyu), no.22, 1992, 137–65.

Hill, Russel, and Stafford, Frank P. "Allocation of Time to Preschool Children and Educational Opportunity." *Journal of Human Resources*, vol.9, 1974, 323–41.

Hill, Russel, and Stafford, Frank P. "Intergenerational Wealth Transfers and the Educational Decisions of Male Youth: An Alternative Interpretation." *Quarterly Journal of Economics*, vol.97, 1978, 515–20.

Hines, Fred; Tweeten, Luther; and Redfern, Martin. "Social and Private Rates of Return to Investment in Schooling, by Race-Sex Groups and Regions." *Journal of Human Resources*, vol.5, 1970, 318–40.

Horowitz, Stanley A., and Sherman, Allan. "A Direct Measure of the Relationship between Human Capital and Productivity." *Journal of Human Resources*, vol.15, 1980, 67–76.

Huffman, Wallace E. "Allocative Efficiency: The Role of Human Capital." *Quarterly Journal of Economics*, vol.91, 1977, 59–79.

Jain, B. "Returns to Education: Further Analysis of Cross Country Data." *Economics of Education Review*, vol.10, 1991, 353–58.

Johnson, George, and Stafford, Frank. "The Earnings and Promotion of Women Faculty." *American Economic Review*, vol.64, 1974, 888–903.

Johnston, J. *Econometric Methods*, second edition. McGraw-Hill: New York, 1972.

Jones, Ethel B., and Jackson, John D. "College Grades and Labor Market Rewards." *Journal of Human Resources*, vol.25, 1990, 253–66.

Jovanovic, Boyan. "Job Matching and the Theory of Turnover." *Journal of Political Economy*, vol.87, 1979, 972–90.

Kagan, Jerome S., and Moss, H. A. "Parental Correlates of Child IQ and Height." *Child Development*, vol.30, 1959, 325–32.

Kane, Thomas J. "College Entry by Blacks since 1970: The Role of College Costs, Family Background, and the Returns to Education." *Journal of Political Economy*, vol.102, 1994, 878–911.

Kaneko, Motohisa. "A Time-Series Analysis of the Enrollment Rate in Higher Education." (Koto Kyoiku Shingakuritsu no Jikeiretsu Bunseki.) *Daigaku Ronshu*, vol.16, 1986, 43–63.

Kaneko, Motohisa. "Re-increasing Demand for College Graduate Labor." (Futatabi Zodaisuru Daisotsu Rodoryoku Juyo.) *Education and Information*. (Kyoiku to Joho), 1989.

Katz, Lawrence F., and Revenga, Ana L. "Changes in the Structure of Wages: The United States vs. Japan." *Journal of the Japanese and International Economics*, vol.3, 1989, 522–53.

Kikuchi, Joji. "Why Is the Rate of University Enrollment Stagnant in Japan?" (Wagakuni no Koto Kyoiku Shingakuritsu wa Naze Teitai Shiteiruka.) *IDE*, 1981, 72–80.

Kikuchi, Joji. "The Economics of Education Demand." (Kyoiku Juyo no Keizaigaku.) In Ichikawa, Kikuchi, and Yano eds. *The Economics of Education* (Kyoiku no Keizaigaku). Daiichi Hoki: Tokyo, 1982, 15–38.

King, Allan G. "Is Occupational Segregation the Cause of the Flatter Experience-Earnings Profiles of Women?" *Journal of Human Resources*, vol.12, 1977, 541–49.

Kitamura, Kazuyuki. *The Age of University Selection* (Daigaku Tota no Jidai). Chuo Koron sha: Tokyo, 1990.

Kodde, David A., and Ritzen, Jozef M. "Integrating Consumption and Investment Motives in a Neoclassical Model of Demand for Education." *Kyklos*, vol.37, 1984, 598–608.

Kodde, David A., and Ritzen, Jozef M. "Direct and Indirect Effects of Parental Education Level on the Demand for Higher Education." *Journal of Human Resources*, vol.23, 1988, 356–71.

Kohn, Meir G.; Manski, Charles F.; and Mundel, David S. "An Empirical Investigation of Factors Which Influence College-Going Behavior." *Annals of Economic and Social Measurement*, vol.5, 1976, 391–419.

Kosugi, Reiko. "Labor Markets of Graduates from Professional Schools." (Senshu Gakko Sotsugyousha no Rodo Shijo.) *Monthly Journal of the Japan Institute of Labour* (Nihon Rodo Kenkyu Zasshi), no.405, 1993, 34–43.

Kroch, Eugene A., and Sjoblom, Kriss. "Schooling as Human Capital or a Signal: Some Evidence." *Journal of Human Resources*, vol.29, 1994, 156–80.

Lang, Kevin, and Kropp, David. "Human Capital versus Sorting: The Effects of Compulsory Attendance Laws." *Quarterly Journal of Economics*, vol.101, 1986, 609–24.

Layard, R., and Psacharopoulos, G. "The Screening Hypothesis and the Return to Education." *Journal of Political Economy*, 1974, vol.82, 985–98.

Lazear, Edward P. "Education: Consumption or Production?" *Journal of Political Economy*, vol.85, 1977a, 569–98.

Lazear, Edward P. "Academic Achievement and Job Performance: Note." *American Economic Review*, vol.67, 1977b, 252–54.

Lazear, Edward P., and Rosen, Sherwin. "Male-Female Wage Differentials in Job Ladders." *Journal of Labor Economics*, vol.8, 1990, S106–S123.

Lehr, D., and Newton, J. "Time-series and Cross-sectional Investigations of the Demand for Higher Education." *Economic Inquiry*, vol.16, 1978, 411–22.

Leibowitz, Arleen. "Home Investment in Children." In T. W. Schultz ed. *Economics of the Family*. University of Chicago Press: Chicago, 1974a.

Leibowitz, Arleen. "Education and Home Production." *American Economic Review*, vol.64, 1974b, 243–50.

Leibowitz, Arleen. "Education and the Allocation of Women's Time." In F. T. Juster ed. *Education, Income, and Human Behavior*. McGraw-Hill: New York, 1975.

Leibowitz, Arleen. "Years and Intensity of Schooling Investment." *American Economic Review*, vol.66, 1976, 321–34.

Leibowitz, Arleen. "Parental Inputs and Children's Achievement." *Journal of Human Resources*, vol.12, 1977, 242–51.

Levin, Henry M. "Book Review: The Overeducated American by Richard B. Freeman." *Harvard Educational Review*, vol.47, 1977, 226–31.

Lewis, Gregory B. "Gender and Promotions: Promotion Chances of White Men and Women in Federal White-Collar Employment." *Journal of Human Resources*, vol.21, 1986, 406–19.

Light, Audrey, and Ureta, Manuelita. "Panel Estimates of Male and Female Job Turnover Behavior: Can Female Nonquitters Be Identified?" *Journal of Labor Economics*, vol.10, 1992, 156–81.

Light, Audrey, and Ureta, Manuelita. "Early-Career Work Experience and Gender Wage Differentials." *Journal of Labor Economics*, vol.13, 1995, 121–54.

Lillard, L.; Smith, J.; and Welch, F. "What Do We Really Know about Wages?" *Journal of Political Economy*, vol.94, 1986, 489–506.

Lillard, Lee A., and Willis, Robert J. "Intergenerational Educational Mobility: Effects of Family and State in Malaysia." *Journal of Human Resources*, vol.29, 1994, 1126–66.

Liu, Pak-Wai, and Wong, Yue-Chim. "Educational Screening by Certificates: An Empirical Test." *Economic Inquiry*, vol.20, 1982, 72–83.

Lucas, Robert E. "Hedonic Wage Equations and Psychic Wages in the Returns to Schooling." *American Economic Review*, vol.67, 1977a, 549–58.

Lucas, Robert E. "Is There a Human Capital Approach to Income Inequality?" *Journal of Human Resources*, vol.12, 1977b, 387–95.

MacDonald, Glenn M. "Person-Specific Information in the Labor Market." *Journal of Political Economy*, vol.88, 1980, 578–97.

Maglen, L. R. "Challenging the Human Capital Orthodoxy: The Education-Productivity Link Re-examined." *Economic Record*, vol.66, 1990, 287–94.

Mailath, George J. "Incentive Compatibility in Signaling Games with a Continuum of Types." *Econometrica*, vol.55, 1349–66.

Malkiel, Burton G., and Malkiel, Judith A. "Male-Female Pay Differentials in Professional Employment." *American Economic Review*, vol.63, 1973, 693–705.

Mare, Robert D. "Social Background and School Continuation Decisions." *Journal of the American Statistical Association*, vol.75, 1980, 295–305.

Mashiko, Machiya. "Mythology of the Potlatch: Logic of Death and Reincarnation among the Tlingit." (Potlatch no Shinwa-gaku.) *Japanese Journal of Ethnology* (Minzokugaku Kenkyu), vol.47, 1982, 221–44.

Mathios, Alan D. "Education, Variation in Earnings, and Nonmonetary Compensation." *Journal of Human Resources*, vol.24, 1989, 456–68.

Mattila, J. P. "Determinants of Male School Enrollment: A Time-Series Analysis." *Review of Economics and Statistics*, vol.64, 1982, 242–51.

Maurizi, Alex. "Rates of Return to Dentistry and the Decision to Enter Dental School." *Journal of Human Resources*, vol.10, 1975, 521–8.

McDowell, John M. "Obsolescence of Knowledge and Career Publication Profiles: Some Evidence of Differences among Fields in Costs of Interrupted Careers." *American Economic Review*, vol.72, 1982, 752–68.

McMahon, Walter W., and Geske, Terry G. eds. *Financing Education*. University of Illinois Press: Urbana, Illinois, 1982.

McPherson, Michael S., and Schapiro, Morton Owen. "Does Student Aid Affect College Enrollment? New Evidence on a Persistent Controversy." *American Economic Review*, vol.81, 1991, 309–18.

Mennemeyer, Stephen T. "Really Great Returns to Medical Education?" *Journal of Human Resources*, vol.13, 1978, 75–90.

Michael, R. T. "Measuring Non-Monetary Benefits of Education: A Survey," In W. W. McMahon and T. G. Geske eds. *Financing Education*. University of Illinois Press: Urbana, 1982.

Micklewright, John. "Choice at Sixteen." *Economica*, vol.56, 1989, 25–39.

Miller, Paul W., and Volker, Paul A. "The Screening Hypothesis: An Application of the Wiles Test." *Economic Inquiry*, vol.22, January 1984, 121–27.

Mincer, Jacob. "The Distribution of Labor Incomes: A Survey With Special Reference to the Human Capital Approach." *Journal of Economic Literature*, vol.3, 1970, 1–26.

Mincer, Jacob. *Schooling, Experience, and Earnings*. Columbia University Press: New York and London, 1974.

Mincer, Jacob, and Ofek, Hiam. "Interrupted Work Careers: Depreciation and Restoration of Human Capital." *Journal of Human Resources*, vol.17, 1982, 3–24.

Mincer, Jacob, and Polachek, Solomon. "Family Investments in Human Capital: Earnings of Women." *Journal of Political Economy*, vol.82, 1974, S76–S108.

Ministry of Education. *Basic School Survey* (Gakko Kihon Chosa Hokoku.)

Ministry of Education. *International Comparisons of Education Indicators* (Kyoiku Shihyo no Kokusai Hikaku).
Ministry of Education. *Survey of Student Life* (Gakusei Seikatsu Chosa).
Ministry of Education. *Survey of the Financial Situations of Private Schools* (Shiritsu Gakko no Zaimu Jokyo ni kansuru Chosa Hokoku).
Ministry of Education. *Abstract of Education Statistics* (Monbu Tokei Yoran).
Ministry of Labor. *Basic Survey of Wage Structures* (Chingin Kozo Kihon Tokei Chosa.).
Ministry of Labor. *Monthly Labor Statistics Abstract* (Maitsuki Kinro Tokei Yoran).
Ministry of Labor. *Annual Report on Labor Markets* (Rodo Shijo Nempo).
Ministry of Public Welfare. *Survey of Physicians, Dentists, and Pharmacists* (Ishi, Shikaishi, Yakuzaishi Chosa).
Ministry of Public Welfare. *A Consideration of the Number of Dentists* (Shikaishi Su o Kangaeru). Nihon Iji Shimpo sha: Tokyo, 1985.
Ministry of Public Welfare. *Final Opinion of the Committee for Examination of the Future Demand for and Supply of Dentists* (Shorai no Shikaishi Jukyu ni kansuru Kento Iinkai Saishu Iken). 1986a.
Ministry of Public Welfare. *A Consideration of the Number of Physicians* (Ishi Su o Kangaeru). Nihon Iji Shimpo sha: Tokyo, 1986b.
Murnane, Richard J.; Maynard, Rebecca A.; and Ohls, James C. "Home Resources and Children's Achievement." *Review of Economics and Statistics*, vol.63, 1981, 369–77.
Murphy, Kevin, and Welch, Finis. "Empirical Age-Earnings Profiles." *Journal of Labor Economics*, vol.8, 1990, 202–29.
Nakamura, Atsushi. "Aspects of Wage Indicators." (Chingin Shihyo no Sho Sokumen.) In Kanamori *et al.* eds., *Dictionary of the Japanese Economy* (Nihon Keizai Jiten). Nihon Keizai Shimbun sha: Tokyo, 1981.
Nakata, Yoshi-fumi, and Mosk, Carl. "The Demand for College Education in Postwar Japan." *Journal of Human Resources*, vol.22, 1987, 377–404.
National Personnel Authority. *Facts about Wages in the Private Sector* (Minkan Kyuyo no Jittai).
Nelson, Richard R., and Phelps, Edmund S. "Investment in Humans, Technological Diffusion, and Economic Growth." *American Economic Review*, vol.56, 1966, 69–75.
Nickell, Stephen. "Education and Lifetime Patterns of Unemployment." *Journal of Political Economy*, vol.87, 1979, S117–S131.
Nishimura, Shuzo. *An Economic Analysis of Medical* Care (Iryo no Keizai Bunseki). Toyo Keizai Shimpo sha: Tokyo, 1987.
Ogura, Masatatsu, and Wakai, Katsutoshi. "An Econometric Model of the Japanese Market of Higher Education under Quantitative Restriction: Why Do We Still Have Intense Competition for College Entrance?" (Koto Kyoiku Shijo no Ryoteki Kisei ni kansuru Keiryo Keizaigaku Model.) *JCER Economic Journal* (Nihon Keizai Kenkyu), no.21, 1991, 14–33.
Olson, Lawrence; White, Halbert; and Shefrin, H. M. "Optimal Investment in Schooling When Incomes Are Risky." *Journal of Political Economy*, vol.87, 1979, 522–39.
Onuki, Yoshio. "Totem Poles: Their Social and Historical Significance." (Totem Poles: Sono Shakaiteki Rekishiteki Igi ni tsuite.) *Japanese Journal of Ethnology* (Minzokugaku Kenkyu), vol.41, 1977, 317–29.
Osawa, Machiko. *Economic Changes and Female Labor* (Keizai Henka to Joshi Rodo). Nihon Hyoron sha: Tokyo, 1993.
Osterman, Paul ed. *Internal Labor Markets.* MIT Press: Cambridge, Mass., 1984.
Paglin, Morton, and Rufolo, Anthony M. "Heterogeneous Human Capital, Occupational Choice, and Male-Female Earnings Differences." *Journal of Labor Economics*, vol.8, 1990, 123–44.
Parish, William L., and Willis, Robert J. "Daughters, Education, and Family Budgets: Taiwan Experiences." *Journal of Human Resources*, vol.28, 1993, 863–98.

Parsons, Donald O. "Intergenerational Wealth Transfers and the Educational Decisions of Male Youth." *Quarterly Journal of Economics*, vol.89, 1975, 603–17.

Parsons, Donald O. "Intergenerational Wealth Transfers and the Educational Decisions of Male Youth: The Mother's Home Time Hypothesis." *Quarterly Journal of Economics*, vol.92, 1978, 521–4.

Passin, Herbert. *Society and Education in Japan*. Teachers College Press, Columbia University; New York, 1965.

Phelps, Edmund. "The Statistical Theory of Racism and Sexism." *American Economic Review*, vol.62, 1972, 659–61.

Pissarides, Christopher A. "Staying-on at School in England and Wales." *Economica*, vol.48, 1981, 345–63.

Polachek, Solomon William. "Potential Biases in Measuring Male-Female Discrimination." *Journal of Human Resources*, vol.10, 1975, 205–29.

Polachek, Solomon William. "Occupational Segregation: An Alternative Hypothesis." *Journal of Contemporary Business*, vol.5, 1976, 1–12.

Polachek, Solomon William. "Sex Differences in College Major." *Industrial and Labor Relations Review*, vol.31, 1978, 498–508.

Polachek, Solomon William. "Occupational Segregation Among Women: Theory, Evidence, and Prognoisis." In Cynthia B. Lloyd, Emily Andrews, and Curtis Gilroy eds. *Women in the Labor Market*. Columbia University Press: New York, 1979.

Polachek, Solomon William. "Occupational Self-Selection: A Human Capital Approach to Sex Differences in Occupational Structure." *Review of Economics and Statistics*, vol.62, 1981, 60–69.

Psacharopoulos, George. *Returns to Education: An International Comparison*, Elsevier Scientific Publishing Company: Amsterdam, 1973.

Psacharopoulos, G. "Returns to Education: A Further International Update and Implication." *Journal of Human Resources*, vol.20, 1985, 583–604.

Psacharopoulos, G. "Time Trends in the Returns to Education." *Economics of Education Review*, vol.8, 1989, 225–31.

Radner, R., and Miller, L. S. "Demand and Supply in U.S. Higher Education: A Progress Report." *American Economic Review*, vol.60, 1970, 326–34.

Ragan, James F., and Smith, Sharon P. "The Impact of Differences in Turnover Rates on Male/Female Pay Differences." *Journal of Human Resources*, vol.16, 1981, 343–65.

Ram, Rati. "Role of Education in Production: A Slightly New Approach." *Quarterly Journal of Economics*, vol.94, 1980, 365–73.

Rice, Patricia G. "The Demand for Post-compulsory Education in the UK and the Effects of Educational Maintenance Allowances." *Economica*, vol.54, 1987, 465–75.

Riley, John G. "Competitive Signaling." *Journal of Economic Theory*, vol.10, 1975, 174–86.

Riley, John G. "Information, Screening and Human Capital." *American Economic Review*, vol.66, 1976, 254–60.

Riley, John G. "Testing the Educational Screening Hypothesis." *Journal of Political Economy*, 1979a, vol.87, S227–S252.

Riley, John G. "Informational Equilibrium." *Econometrica*, vol.47, 1979b, 331–59.

Rogers, D. C. "Private Rates of Return to Education in the United States: A Case Study." *Yale Economic Essays*, vol.9, 1969, 89–137.

Rosen, Sherwin. "Human Capital: A Survey of Empirical Research." In Ronald G. Ehrenberg ed. *Research in Labor Economics*, vol.1, JAI Press: Greenwich CT, 1977, 3–39.

Rosenzweig, Mark R., and Schultz, T. Paul. "Market Opportunities, Genetic Endowments, and Intrafamily Resource Distribution: Child Survival in Rural India." *American Economic Review*, vol.72, 1982, 803–15.

Rosenzweig, Mark R., and Wolpin, Kenneth I. "Are There Increasing Returns to the Intergenerational Production of Human Capital? Maternal Schooling and Child Intellectual Achievement." *Journal of Human Resources*, vol.24, 1994, 670–93.

Rubinger, Richard. *Private Academies in Tokugawa Japan*. Princeton University Press: Princeton, 1982.

Rumberger, Russell. "The Economic Decline of College Graduates: Fact or Fallacy?" *Journal of Human Resources*, vol.15, 1980, 99–112.

Sandell, Steven H., and Shapiro, David. "Work Expectations, Human Capital Accumulation, and the Wages of Young Women." *Journal of Human Resources*, vol.15, 1980, 335–53.

Satterthwaite, M. A. "Consumer Information, Equilibrium Industry Price and the Number of Sellers." *Bell Journal of Economics*, vol.10, 1979, 483–502.

Schultz, T. Paul. "School Expenditures and Enrollments, 1960–80: The Effects of Income, Prices, and Population Growth." In D. G. Johnson and R. D. Lee eds. *Population Growth and Economic Development*. University of Wisconsin Press: Madison, 1985.

Schultz, T. Paul. "Education Investments and Returns." In H. Chenery and T. N. Srinivasan eds. *Handbook of Development Economics*, vol.I. North-Holland: Amsterdam, 1988.

Schultz, T. Paul. "Investments in the Schooling and Health of Women and Men." *Journal of Human Resources*, vol.28, 1993, 694–734.

Schultz, Theodore W. *The Economic Value of Education*. Columbia University Press: New York, 1963.

Schultz, Theodore W. *Investment in Human Capital*. The Free Press: New York, 1971.

Schultz, Theodore W. "The Value of the Ability to Deal with Disequilibria." *Journal of Economic Literature*, vol.13, 1975, 827–46.

Schumann, Paul L.; Ahlburg, Dennis A.; and Mahoney, Christine Brown. "The Effects of Human Capital and Job Characteristics on Pay." *Journal of Human Resources*, vol.29, 1994, 481–503.

Scully, Gerald W. "Mullahs, Muslims, and Marital Sorting." *Journal of Political Economy*, vol.87, 1979, 1139–43.

Sekiguchi, Isao. *The Lifetime Employment System* (Shushin Koyosei). Bunshindo: Tokyo, 1996.

Shigeno, Yukiko, and Matsuura, Katsumi. "Choice between Private and Public Schools." (Shiritu Gakko to Koritsu Gakko no Sentaku.) Institute for Post and Telecommunication Policy Discussion Paper Series, no.1995-2, 1995.

Shimada, Haruo, and Higuchi, Yoshio. "An Analysis of Trends in Female Labor Force Participation in Japan." *Journal of Labor Economics*, vol.3, 1985, S355–S374.

Shirai, Taishiro. *Personnel Management in Modern Japan* (Gendai Nihon no Romu Kanri). Toyo Keizai Shimpo sha: Tokyo, 1982.

Spence, Michael. "Job Market Signaling." *Quarterly Journal of Economics*, vol.87, 1973, 354–74.

Spence, Michael. *Market Signaling: Informational Transfer in Hiring and Related Screening Processes*. Harvard University Press: Cambridge, Massachusetts, 1974a.

Spence, Michael. "Competitive and Optimal Responses to Signals: Analysis of Efficiency and Distribution." *Journal of Economic Theory*, vol.7, 1974b, 296–332.

Spence, Michael. "Signaling, Screening, and Information." In Sherwin Rosen ed. *Studies in Labor Markets*. The University of Chicago Press: Chicago, 1981.

Stafford, Frank. "Women's Work, Sibling Competition, and Children's School Performance." *American Economic Review*, vol.77, 1987, 972–80.

Statistics Bureau. *Population Census of Japan* (Kokusei Chosa.) 1980.

Statistics Bureau. *National Survey of Prices* (Zenkoku Bukka Tokei Chosa). 1982.

Statistics Bureau. *Employment Status Survey* (Shugyo Kozo Kihon Chosa). 1982.

Statistics Bureau. *Labor Force Survey* (Rodoryoku Chosa).

Steelman, Lala Carr, and Powell, Brian. "Sponsoring the Next Generation: Parental Willingness to Pay for Higher Education." *American Journal of Sociology*, vol.96, 1991, 1505–29.

Stiglitz, Joseph E. "The Theory of 'Screening', Education, and the Distribution of Income." *American Economic Review*, vol.65, 1975, pp.283–300.

Suzuki, Yoshio (ed.) *Finance and Banks in Japan* (Nihon no Kinyu to Ginko). Toyo Keizai Shimpo sha: Tokyo, 1989.

Tanaka, Yasushi. "A Time-Series Analysis of the Demand for Higher Education in Postwar Japan." (Sengo Nihon no Daigaku Kyoiku Juyo no Jikeiretsu Bunseki.) *Keizai-Keiei Ronso*, 1994, 73–95.

Tannen, Michael. "The Investment Motive for Attending College." *Industrial and Labor Relations Review*, vol.31, 1978, 489–97.

Taubman, Paul. "On Heritability," *Economica*, vol.48, 1981, 417–20.

Taubman, P. J., and Wales, T. J. "Higher Education, Mental Ability, and Screening." *Journal of Political Economy*, vol.81, 1973, 28–55.

Theil, H. *Introduction to Econometrics*. Prentice-Hall: Englewood Cliffs, New Jersey, 1978.

Thomas, Duncan. "Intra-Household Resource Allocation: An Inferential Approach." *Journal of Human Resources*, vol.25, 1990, 635–64.

Thurow, Lester C. "Education and Economic Equality." *Public Interest*, 1972, 66–81.

Thurow, Lester C. *Generating Inequality*. Basic Books: New York, 1975.

Tokita, Tadahiko (ed.) *The Japanese Medical Economy* (Nihon no Iryo Keizai). Toyo Keizai Shimposha: Tokyo, 1995.

Tomaske, John A. "Private and Social Rates of Return to Education of Academicians: Note." *American Economic Review*, vol.64, 1974, 220–4.

Tomes, Nigel. "The Family, Inheritance, and the Intergenerational Transmission of Inequality." *Journal of Political Economy*, vol.89, 1981, 928–58.

Veblen, Thorstein. *The Theory of the Leisure Class*. George Allen & Unwin: London, 1899.

Vella, Francis. "Gender Roles and Human Capital Investment: The Relationship between Traditional Attitudes and Female Labour Market Performance." *Economica*, vol.61, 1994, 191–211.

Wallace, T. D., and Ihnen, L. A. "Full Time Schooling in Life-Cycle Models of Human Capital Accumulation." *Journal of Political Economy*, vol.83, 1975, 135–56.

Wakisaka, Akira. *Company-Type Women* (Kaishagata Josei), Dobunkan: Tokyo, 1990.

Weisbrod, B. A. "Education and Investment in Human Capital." *Journal of Political Economy*. vol.70, 1962, 106–23.

Weiss, Andrew. "A Sorting-cum-Learning Model of Education." *Journal of Political Economy*, vol.91, 1983, 420–42.

Weiss, Yoram. "The Risk Element in Occupational and Educational Choices." *Journal of Political Economy*, vol.80, 1972, 1203–13.

Welch, F. "Education in Production." *Journal of Political Economy*, vol.78, 1970, 35–59.

Whitfield, Keith, and Wilson, R. A. "Staying on in Full-time Education: The Educational Participation Rate of 16-year-olds." *Economica*, vol.58, 1991, 391–404.

Willis, Robert J. "A New Approach to the Economic Theory of Fertility Behavior." *Journal of Political Economy*, vol.81, 1973, S14–S64.

Willis, Robert J. "Wage Determinants: A Survey and Reinterpretation of Human Capital Earnings Functions." In Orley Ashenfelter and Richard Layard eds. *Handbook of Labor Economics*. North Holland: Amsterdam, 1986.

Willis, Robert J., and Rosen, Sherwin. "Education and Self-Selection." *Journal of Political Economy*, vol.87, 1979, S7–S36.

Wise, David A. "Academic Performance and Job Performance." *American Economic Review*, vol.65, 1975, 350–66.

Wolfe, John R. "The Impact of Family Resources on Childhood IQ." *Journal of Human Resources*, vol.17, 1982, 213–35.

Wolpin, Kenneth I. "Education and Screening." *American Economic Review*, vol.67, 1977, 949–58.
Wozniak, Gregory D. "Human Capital, Information, and the Early Adoption of New Technology." *Journal of Human Resources*, vol.22, 1987, 101–12.
Yamamoto, Shin-ichi. "An Analysis of the Factors Determining the Percentage of Applicants for Admission to Universities." (Daigaku Shingaku Kiboritsu Kitei Yoin no Bunseki.) *Journal of Educational Sociology* (Kyoiku Shakaigaku Kenkyu), vol.39, 1979, 93–103.
Yano, Shinwa. "The Economics of Women's Education." (Joshi Kyoiku no Keizaigaku.) In Ichikawa, Kikuchi, and Yano eds. *The Economics of Education* (Kyoiku no Keizaigaku). Daiichi Hoki: Tokyo, 1982, 68–80.
Yano, Shinwa. "The Determinants of Individual Demand for Higher Education." (Daigaku Shingaku Juyo Kansu no Keisoku to Kyoiku Seisaku.) *Journal of Educational Sociology* (Kyoiku Shakaigaku Kenkyu), vol.39, 1984, 216–28.
Yano, Shinwa. *The End of the Examination Age* (Shiken Jidai no Shuen). Yushindo: Tokyo, 1991.

Author Index

Subject Index